# A HISTORICAL
# ATLAS OF TEXAS

# A HISTORICAL ATLAS OF TEXAS

By William C. Pool

Maps by Edward Triggs
and Lance Wren

THE ENCINO PRESS AUSTIN

©1975 : The Encino Press
510 Baylor : Austin, Texas
ISBN 0-88426-033-X

# PREFACE

LOOKING BACK over more than four decades, I find that my interest in maps goes back to the time when I learned to read and write. In those days, the mid-years of Harding and Coolidge's "normalcy," one of the books in our farm home was a small, faded volume titled *A First Book in American History*, written by Edward Eggleston, published by D. Appleton and Company, and used by my mother and her sisters when they attended the one-room Center Point school in the Bosque River valley. I read it daily and was impressed by the relief maps of the James River section of Virginia, the battles of the American Revolution, and the Mississippi delta at the time of the battle of New Orleans. In my young mind, Eggleston ranked with Hans Christian Anderson. It wasn't many years later when I discovered Rand, McNally and Company's *Pocket Map and Shippers Guide of Indian and Oklahoma Territories* and their *Pocket Map and Shippers Guide of Texas* (1904) in my grandfather's high-topped desk. I pored over these little volumes for hours at a time. This great interest in the maps of our land increased as the school years passed and sharpened during the years of World War II when, as a pilot in the old Army Air Corps, I had to transfer the detailed information written on the aeronautical charts to the visual recognition of rivers, lakes, elevations, towns, railroads, roads, and urban areas on the ground.

I was glad, therefore, when William Wittliff, after reading John W. Morris and Edwin C. Reynold's *Historical Atlas of Oklahoma*, asked me if I wouldn't be interested in working on a similar publication for Texas. The fact that no one has published such a book in the past is no great tribute to professional historians in Texas and the Southwest. The need is quite apparent to all who have taught the history of the state on either the secondary-school or the college-and-university level. While my graduate students at Southwest Texas State University have expressed their interest in more adequate maps, I, like my colleagues, was slow to respond to the need.

Using a technique pioneered by the late Walter P. Webb, I have tried to recognize the relationship between an environment and the civilization resting upon it by beginning with the geology and topography, and building upon this foundation "the superstructure of the flora, fauna, and anthropology, arriving at last at the modern civilization growing out of this foundation." It has been a demanding but enjoyable task. As I traced the advance of the western frontier from the coastal plains and the Red River valley of pre-Revolutionary Texas, I was reminded, as I tried to locate each new area of settlement, that I have never been to a locale within the boundaries of the state that I did not like. Perhaps this is why I have chosen to remain at home—I like the land and the people.

Many of the basic maps essential to the project were furnished by the staffs of the Texas State Library, the Texas Highway Department, the General Land Office of Texas, and the library of Southwest Texas State University. I am indebted to the employees of all of these institutions. While archival and secondary materials have been cited at the proper point within the text, I wish to give special recognition to Walter P. Webb and H. Bailey Carroll's *The Handbook of Texas* (2 vols., Austin, 1952), to *The Texas Almanac* (all issues since 1950, but especially to the excellent issue for the years 1964-1965), to the old WPA project entitled

*Texas, A Guide to the Lone Star State* (New York, 1940), and to Rupert N. Richardson's *Texas, the Lone Star State* (Englewood Cliffs, 1958). These four sources were consulted so frequently in the preparation of individual maps that a note of this fact in the text would amount to an endless repetition—my debt to them, however, is limitless. The archeological map and the notes for its description were prepared by state archeologist Curtis Tunnell of Austin.

Two summers ago a group of graduate students in Texas history gave wise counsel and did much of the spadework for the early stages of the project; therefore, I acknowledge my debt to Elton Churchill, Henry B. Masur, Doris Holmes Pybus, Kay Calloway, George A. Grantham, Frank Sales, Keith Uekert, Cara Wernli, Robert Downtain, Carolyn Andrews, Monroe Barta, Betty Bishop, Willie H. Cervenka, Chester Ellis, Donald Farmer, Kate Hawksley, Allen Heil, Kent Mc-Dougall, Robert T. Neill, John D. Hurst, Linda Schmidt, Melvin E. Strey, and Jerry Wilson. In more recent days Jolene Maddox, Steve Sansom, Toni Miller, and Larry Hamann took care of many of the office details and brightened the general scene in Evans Academic Center. At home, as always, my wife, Sarah Jeannette Pool, set the stage for uninterrupted work, offered encouragement and advice, did much of the editorial work on the first drafts, and found time to type the finished manuscript. Finally, the free time for the completion of the job came from a Faculty Development Leave awarded by the administration and my faculty colleagues at Southwest Texas State University; I shall be eternally grateful for the opportunity afforded by this grant.

WILLIAM C. POOL

*San Marcos, Texas*

# CONTENTS

# INTRODUCTION

 TEXAS, an important part of the greater Spanish-American Southwest, has a land area second only to that of Alaska. The United States Census report for 1960 listed 262,840 square miles or 168,217,600 acres as the Texas land area exclusive of inland waters and the submerged tideland area along the coast of the Gulf of Mexico. The boundaries of the state extend from latitude 25°31'W at the easternmost bend of the Sabine River in Newton County to longitude 106°38'W at the intersection of the Rio Grande and the 32° parallel, north latitude, northwest of El Paso. As a result, the longest straight line distance, northwest to southeast, is 801 miles (Dallam County to Cameron County) while the greatest east-west distance measures 773 miles from the Sabine River in Newton County to a point on the Rio Grande above El Paso.

An examination of a relief map of the United States reveals that Texas is made up of at least three physical divisions: (1) the Atlantic Gulf Coastal Plain, (2) the Great Plains of Central North America, and (3) the Rocky Mountain system. These three physiographic systems join within the present boundaries of Texas to give variety, contrast, and diversity to the topography, climate, and natural resources of the state. Also, it is of interest to the historian, as the late Walter P. Webb points out in *The Great Plains*, that Texas was settled by Anglo-American pioneers who "were the outriders of the American frontier." Their settlements, 1821-1836, made Texas the center of three contesting and conflicting civilizations—that of the Mexicans, that of the Americans, and that of the Plains Indian. All of these factors—the three physical divisions plus the three separate civilizations—combine to give depth and meaning to the history of Texas.

This unique situation is further complicated by virtue of the fact that the 98° meridian divides Texas into two additional contrasting physical regions—that of the Great Plains (known to the 19th century pioneer as the Great American Desert) and that of the eastern woodlands. It was here, therefore, that Southerners from Tennessee, Kentucky, Mississippi, Alabama, and the other states of the Old South, came into contact with the desert conditions, forcefully imposed upon them by the very nature of the land and the climate of the plains region. As a result, their ways of life and living changed; institutions were either broken and remade or else greatly altered as Texas and Texans found themselves torn between the old way of life brought across the Sabine from the antebellum South and the modifications rendered essential by being an integral part of the American West—by either living on the desert proper or on its rimland. Only in the woodlands of deep East Texas have the descendants of the pioneers been spared these adaptations.

# A HISTORICAL
# ATLAS OF TEXAS

# THE GEOLOGY OF TEXAS

 CONDITIONED by the diverse natural elements resulting from the extensive boundaries of the state, the geological foundations upon which Texas rests vary in age from the earliest to the recent. In brief, the formations of the geologic series, listed in order of chronology, include: (1) the pre-Cambrian formations of the Llano Uplift, structurally a great dome the top of which has been removed by erosion; (2) the early Paleozoic formations encircling the pre-Cambrian formations of the Llano Uplift and featuring sands, limestones, and dolomite; (3) the later Paleozoic formations that also dip away from the uplift; (4) the Permian formations which outcrop over a wide belt northwest of the Llano region and extend over much of the North Central Plains; (5) the Triassic formations that appear at the base of the Llano Estacado; (6) the formations of the lower and upper Cretaceous ages surrounding those of the Llano region and extending over extensive areas in Central and North Central Texas; (7) the early and late Tertiary formations found further to the east and southeast; and (8) the formations of the Pleistocene age (the latest found in Texas) which are found adjacent to the Gulf Coast.

The geological history of Texas through millions of years has been characterized by forces that brought on the disappearance of an extensive shallow sea that covered West and Northwest Texas in early geological ages and a corresponding eroding away of the great mountain chain that once ran from north to south through present Central Texas. Thus it may be said that a great uplift of land and the waters of the ages have combined to produce the present physiography of Texas. In brief, these principal geologic structures include the following areas:

(1) The West Texas Permian Basin covers a large area of West Texas and an area of eastern New Mexico. The formations of this region are exposed over a wide area of Central and North Central Texas and extend under the High Plains with the soils and rocks of later ages deposited above it. In portions of Trans-Pecos Texas and eastern New Mexico it is again found at the surface. The basin of this former sea dips downward from the location of McCulloch, Brown, and Stephens counties to a low point in Midland County and then rises to its ancient western shoreline in New Mexico. This formation has produced some of the greatest petroleum reservoirs of the state.

(2) The Gulf Coastal Plains with the subordinate East Texas and Rio Grande embayments slant generally to the southeast to form catchment basins for great quantities of underground water of considerable economic importance. This region, with its salt domes, has some of the most significant oil, gas, and sulphur deposits of Texas.

(3) The mountain ranges of Trans-Pecos Texas that form the western edge of the Permian Basin cross the far western regions of Texas in a north-south direction.

(4) The Amarillo-Wichita-Muenster sub-surface mountain formations of Northwest Texas lie deep beneath the surface in the Northwest Texas region south of the Red River but are exposed in the Wichita Mountains of southwestern Oklahoma.

(5) A zone of complex geological structures between the Permian basin on the north and west and the Gulf Coastal Plains on the southeast gives character to the physiography of Central and West Central Texas. Included in this region are the Bend Arch, the Central Basin structures, and the roots of the great mountain

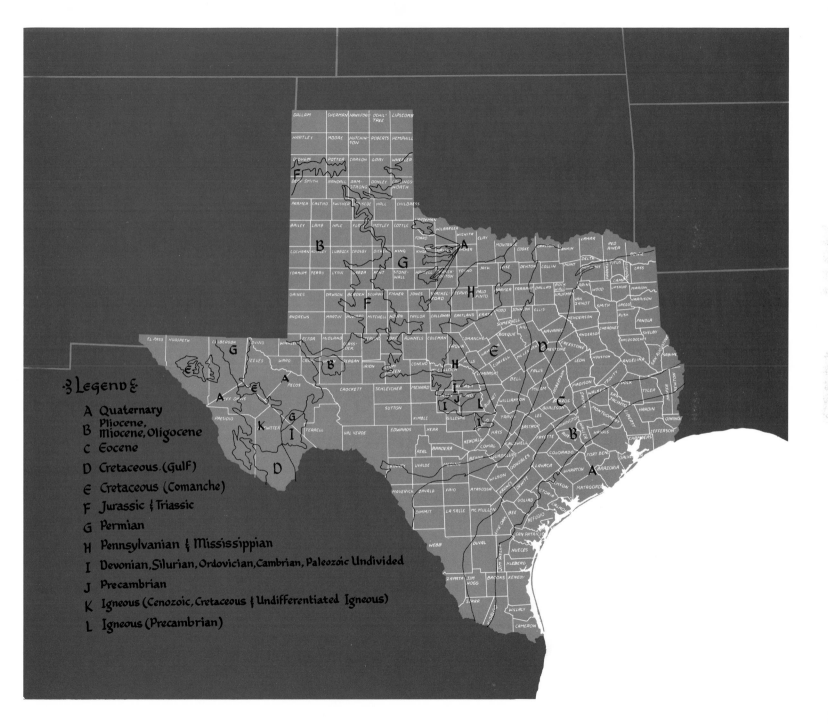

Legend

A Quaternary
B Pliocene, Miocene, Oligocene
C Eocene
D Cretaceous (Gulf)
E Cretaceous (Comanche)
F Jurassic & Triassic
G Permian
H Pennsylvanian & Mississippian
I Devonian, Silurian, Ordovician, Cambrian, Paleozoic Undivided
J Precambrian
K Igneous (Cenozoic, Cretaceous & Undifferentiated Igneous)
L Igneous (Precambrian)

range that once bordered the eastern edge of the Permian Sea.

In addition to the above, E. H. Sellards points to the Sabine uplift, the Tyler basin, the Houston salt dome, the Rio Grande embayment, and the Balcones and Mexia-Luling faults as other fundamental structures of Texas geology.

Significant contributions to a knowledge of the geology of Texas have been made by Randolph B. Marcy, who explored the Red River region in 1852; by Ferdinand Roemer, the German natural historian who traveled across Texas in 1845-1846; by Major William H. Emory, who surveyed the Mexican boundary in 1854; by G. C. Shumard, J. W. Glenn, and Samuel B. Buckley, three surveyors of the area between 1857 and 1875; by the significant reports of Dr. Robert T. Hill, 1884-

1935; by the survey of Edwin T. Dumble, 1888-1894; and by the studies of E. H. Sellards and others during the first three decades of the twentieth century.

William H. Emory, *Report on the United States and Mexican Boundary Survey* (2 vols., Washington, 1857-1859).

Robert T. Hill, Geography and Geology of the Black and Grand Prairie, Texas, *Twenty-first Annual Report of the United States Geological Survey*, VII (Washington, 1901).

Robert T. Hill, *Physical Geography of the Texas Region*, Folio 3 of the Topographical Atlas of the United States (Washington, 1900).

Ferdinand Roemer, *Texas* (Oswald Mueller, tr.), (San Antonio, 1935).

E. H. Sellards, *Handbook of Texas*, I, 680-682.

E. H. Sellards, W. S. Adkins, and B. F. Plummer, Geologic Map of Texas, Part 5 of vol. I of *The Geology of Texas* (Austin, 1933).

# THE NATURAL REGIONS OF TEXAS

 BASED on the geology of Texas, the natural regions of the state include the following areas:

(1) The Gulf Coastal Plains, a large area of relatively level land, extends inland from the Gulf of Mexico to the Balcones Fault, a geological fault running from Del Rio on the Rio Grande east and northeast to Austin and thence to the Waco region. The several subregions of the Coastal Plains include (a) the Coastal Prairies, that part of the plains bordering the tidewater, (b) the Pine Belt, a section of piney woods lying above the Coastal Prairies and extending some 100 miles westward from the Sabine River boundary, (c) the Post Oak Belt, a crescent-shaped region extending from

eastern Lamar and western Red River counties on the north to a point southeast of San Antonio, (d) the Blackland Prairies, a relatively level area of land extending from the Paris and Clarksville area south to a point southeast of San Antonio, and (e) the Rio Grande Plain or Embayment, an extension of the Coastal Plain adjacent to the Rio Grande.

(2) The North Central Plains, an area of Texas located between the Blackland Prairies on the east and the Cap Rock Escarpment on the west, can be subdivided into (a) the Eastern and Western Cross Timbers, running from the Red River southward to southern Hill County and from the Red River in Montague County southward to Burnet County, (b) the Grand

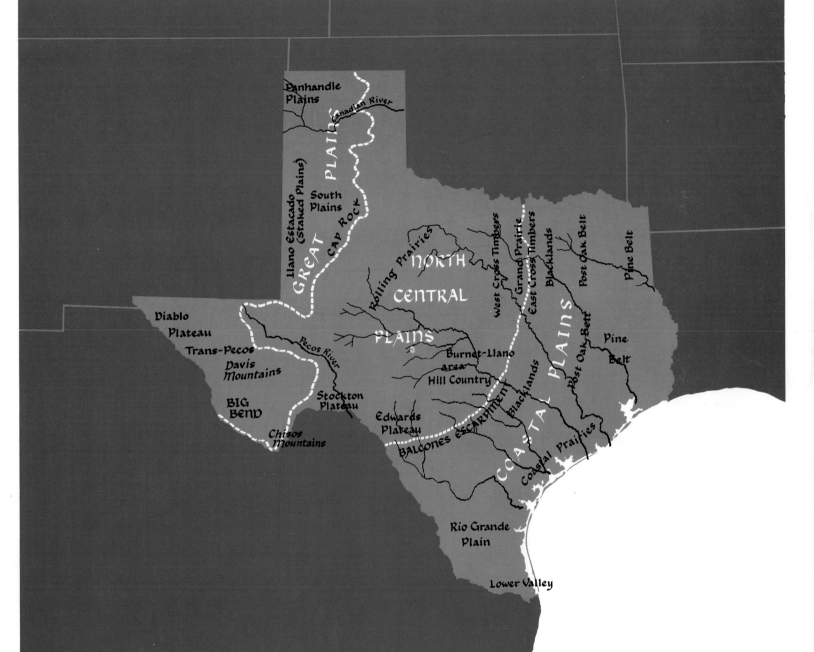

Prairie, an area of limestone soils extending south from near the Red River and including land just west of Fort Worth and Waco to a southern point in the Georgetown-Burnet area, (c) the Burnet-Llano Region, also known as the Central Basin and the central mineral region, and (d) the West Texas Rolling Plains, a wide area located between the Western Cross Timbers on the east and the Cap Rock Escarpment on the west (this region features the distinctive Callahan Divide between the watershed of the Brazos and the Colorado river drainage basins.)

(3) The High Plains, an extension of the Great Plains region of the United States, can be subdivided into the Llano Estacado or Staked Plains, a level area of land lying above the west of the Cap Rock Escarp-

ment, and the Edwards Plateau (also known as the Texas Hill Country), a region of rolling hills between the Great Plains to the west and the Coastal Plains to the southeast.

(4) Trans-Pecos Texas, a vast region of far West Texas, lies between the Pecos River on the east and El Paso on the west. This region, comprised of a high plateau which is actually a part of the Rocky Mountain system, can be sub-divided into (a) the Stockton Plateau, (b) the Big Bend, the rugged region encompassed by the southward bend of the Rio Grande, (c) the Davis Mountain area, (d) the Diablo Plateau, and (e) the upper Rio Grande valley.

Elmer H. Johnson, *The Natural Regions of Texas* (Austin, 1931).

# THE SOILS OF TEXAS

 THE SOILS OF TEXAS, featuring more than 500 varieties, range from loose deep sands to heavy dark clays; from soils made by ancient geological formations to the alluvial deposits of modern times. The map on the opposite page is based on M. K. Thornton and W. T. Carter's "The Soils of Texas" found in the *Southwestern Historical Quarterly*, LXI (July, 1957). In summary, Thornton calls attention to the following soil belts:

A. The East Texas Timber Country (including the Eastern Cross Timbers) comprises an area of 26 million acres including upland soils that feature a light-colored sandy loam and sands. Included within the scope of this region are the Bowie, Norfolk, Ruston, Kirwin, Nacogdoches, Boswell, Lufkin, and Lakeland

series. The vegetation in this region comprises the loblolly and shortleaf pine and various species of oaks. The East Texas bottom land soils, including the dark-colored and acid sandy loams and clays, are significant because of the hardwoods found here.

B. The Gulf Coast Prairie includes a total area of 8 million acres that feature dark-colored, limy, crumbly clays of the Lake Charles, Beaumont, Harris, Hockley, and Edna series. This region is marked by tall bunch grasses and is used for cotton, corn, and pasture lands.

C. The Blackland Prairie of Texas includes some 11 million acres of land extending from the Red River on the north to a point east of Austin on the south. This region comprises the dark-colored, crumbly clays (the Houston, Hunt, Bell, Austin, and Lewisville

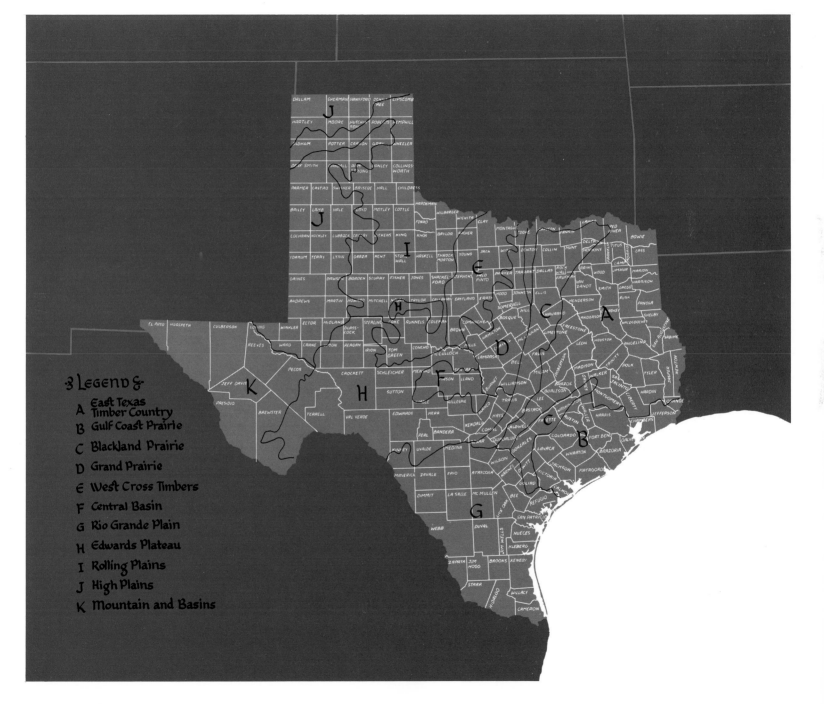

Legend

A  East Texas Timber Country
B  Gulf Coast Prairie
C  Blackland Prairie
D  Grand Prairie
E  West Cross Timbers
F  Central Basin
G  Rio Grande Plain
H  Edwards Plateau
I  Rolling Plains
J  High Plains
K  Mountain and Basins

series) that give rise to tall prairie grasses that mark the region.

D. The Grand Prairie region of Texas, located between the Blackland Prairie and the Western Cross Timbers, contains some 7 million acres which include the San Saba, Denton, Crawford, and Tarrant series. This picturesque section of Texas features tall prairie grasses and mottes of live oak and Spanish oak along the ridges.

E. The Western Cross Timbers, a forested belt running from the Red River on the north to the northern rimlands of the Edwards Plateau on the south, includes approximately 7 million acres of land comprising the Windhorst, Nimrod, Stephenville, Darnell, and May series. This significant soil belt extends over a region of Texas that includes the Wilson, Crockett, and Irving series of acid loams and clays. As a result the uplands are characterized by tall prairie grasses and the several varieties of Texas white oak while the bottom lands along the streams are covered with elm and several species of Texas hardwoods. The range lands of this region feature the growth of peaches, watermelon, cantaloupe, peanuts, and grain sorghums.

F. The Central Basin region of Texas includes about 2 million acres of red and stony sandy loam soils of the Tishomingo, Pontotac, and Pedernales series. Used extensively as range land and for the growth of small grains, the soils of the Central Basin support a growth of mesquite, live oak, and post oak trees as well as a variety of grasses.

G. The Rio Grande Plain, a region totaling 22½ million acres, comprises sandy loam soils of the Victoria, Monteola, Hidalgo, Willacy, Duval, Nueces, and Webb series. Grasses and thorny shrubs grow in abundance in this South Texas region; and the fertile land is used for pasture, citrus fruit, commercial vegetables, cotton, and grain sorghums.

H. The Edwards Plateau comprises 22½ million acres of limestone clays of the Tarrant, Valera, and Ector series. This region of cedar, live oak, shin oak, and mesquite trees is used mostly as a range for cattle, sheep, and goats.

I. The Rolling Plains, an area of 24½ million acres, is composed of dark brown and red clay and loam soils of the Abilene, Miles, Foard, Valera and Tillman series. Featuring short and bunch grasses, this region is utilized primarily in ranching and in the growth of cotton and small grains.

J. The High Plains of West Texas, an area of 21 million acres, is composed of brown and red sandy and clay loam soils of the Amarillo, Mansker, Patten, and Brownfield series. This fertile region is utilized in ranching and in the growth of wheat, cotton, and grain sorghums.

K. Comprising 17 million acres, the Mountain and Basin region of West Texas is composed of light-colored sands and clays of the Reeves, Reagan, Brewster, and Ector series. These soils support short grasses and desert shrubs; irrigation has been a great aid in restricted localities.

C. A. Bonner, "Factors Influencing Texas Agriculture," *Types of Farming in Texas*, Bulletin 964, Texas A and M College, College Station, Texas.

W. T. Carter and M. K. Thornton, "A Brief Description of the Soils of Texas," *Southwestern Historical Quarterly*, LXI.

WRITING of the area of the American West beyond the 98° meridian, Walter P. Webb explains "there has been in this region a constant and persistent search for water . . . this search for water has been the continuous and persistent movement that has gone on in the Great Plains country. . . . In their efforts to provide a sufficiency of water where there was not one, men have resorted to every expedient from prayer to dynamite." Since the western section of Texas lies beyond the 98° meridian, the state obviously has a water problem that all through its history has continued to plague the land and the people.

A recent issue of the *Texas Almanac* reports "rainfall [in Texas] is not evenly distributed and varies greatly from year to year. Average annual rainfall along the Louisiana border is in excess of 55 inches; in Texas' western extremity it is less than 9 inches." Walter P. Webb, in his *More Water for Texas*, points out that the average annual precipitation (rain, sleet, hail, and snow) is 27.32 inches unevenly distributed "from less than 10 inches in West Texas to over 50 inches in East Texas," and (dividing the state into ten precipitation bands) he also calls attention to the fact that sixty percent of the state receives less than the 30 inches of precipitation adequate for agriculture. Therefore, the line of thirty inches of rainfall is of major importance. This line runs southward from Clay County on the Red River through points a little to the west of Fort Worth and Austin and to the east of San Antonio to curve toward the Coastal Bend at Corpus Christi Bay. According to Webb, it is this line that separates East Texas from West Texas—to the east the average annual precipitation varies from a surplus to amounts that are usually adequate for agriculture; to the west, the annual amount of moisture is critical in a wide belt of West Central Texas and deficient west of the Cap Rock and the Edwards Plateau.

Even in normal years, there are periods when moisture in the form of rain and related types of precipitation is inadequate for normal agriculture. As a result periods of drouth have been an oft-repeated theme in Texas history. A bulletin of the Texas Water Commission reveals that eleven major drouths have occurred in Texas during the seventy-year period of available records. With the prolonged drouth of the 1950's subdivided into three (because a drouth is defined as a period where the precipitation is 15 percent below normal), in order of severity the major Texas drouths are 1954-1956, 1916-1918, 1909-1912, 1901, 1953, 1933-1934, 1950-1952, 1924-1925, 1891-1893, 1937-1939, and 1896-1899. It is safe to say that there will be more dry years in the future.

Falling on the soils of Texas as outlined by the following map, the average annual precipitation, or lack of it, has been the major influence in the evolution of Texas plant life in the several well-defined vegetational regions.

*The Report of the U.S. Study Commission—Texas,* A Report to the President and to the Congress by the U.S. Study Commission on the Neches, Trinity, Brazos, Colorado, Guadalupe, San Antonio, Nueces, and San Jacinto rivers (1962).
Walter P. Webb, *More Water for Texas* (Austin, 1954); *The Great Plains* (Boston and New York, 1931).

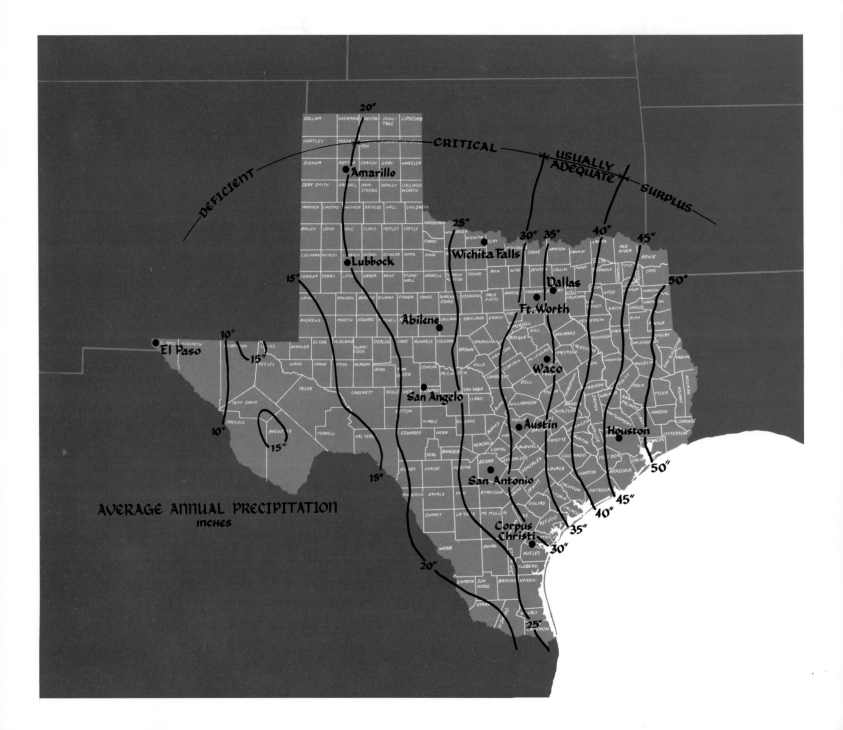

AVERAGE ANNUAL PRECIPITATION
INCHES

# TEXAS PLANT LIFE

THE DIVERSE SOILS of Texas, the varying rainfall, and other topographical and climatical features combine to cause a noticeable contrast in trees, shrubs, grasses, wild flowers, and other forms of native plant life. While this is neither the time nor the place for a detailed summary of the fauna and flora of Texas, the major characteristics of the regions depicted on the map follow:

1. The East Texas forest region extends from the Red River valley on the north to the region bordering Galveston Bay on the south. This region—an area characterized by heavy rains and numerous rivers, creeks, and bayous—is characterized by a dense growth of pine (longleaf, shortleaf, loblolly, and slash) and a variety of hardwoods such as oak, elm, hickory, magnolia, sweet and black gum, and others. Almost all of the commercial production of timber comes from this East Texas region.

2. The secondary forests and woodlands form a region immediately west of the primary forest belt. This secondary forest region, often referred to as the Post Oak Belt, extends from the Red River on the north to DeWitt, Lavaca, Wharton, and Fort Bend counties on the south. In addition to a variety of oaks, this region features a growth of elm, pecan, walnut, and other water-demanding trees.

3. The Blackland Prairie region extends from the vicinity of the Red River on the north to Bexar County and the San Antonio River basin on the south. Now fertile farmland, many years ago this region was largely an immense tract of native grassland. The streams of the region are bordered by a variety of oaks as well as elm, bois d'arc, pecan, and ash.

3a. The Eastern Cross Timbers, a narrow belt of timber separating the Blackland and Grand Prairie regions, extends south from the Red River valley to a point in present Hill and McLennan counties. This region features a plant life similar to that of the Western Cross Timbers and the Blackland Prairie region.

4. The Grand Prairie and the Western Cross Timbers, considered as a single region, extends from the southern rim of the Red River valley on the north to the Colorado River valley on the south. Post oak, blackjack oak, elm, pecan, cottonwood, and ash border the rivers and creeks of this region. The slopes of the flat-topped hills feature a growth of Spanish oak, shin oak, live oak, and mountain juniper (cedar). In the mid-years of the last century the Grand Prairie (and to a lesser extent the Western Cross Timbers) was covered with a sea of native Texas grasses.

5. The Mesquite Woodlands and Grasslands, a large area extending south from the eastern Panhandle and the Red River valley to the Concho River country, comprises the rolling plains of Northwest Texas.

6. The High Plains, a vast treeless region known to the Spanish as the *llano estacado*, extends from the borders of the Panhandle southward to Andrews and Martin counties and features (where undisturbed by the plow) a growth of buffalo and grama grasses.

7. The Pecos Valley and the Trans-Pecos Plains, a region of light rainfall, features a growth of short grasses and such desert shrubs as lechuguilla, ocotillo, yucca, cenizo, and other forms of plant life characteristic of the western deserts of North America.

8. The Trans-Pecos Mountains and Plains, a region extending over the arid section of far West Texas, features a wide variety of desert plants and shrubs.

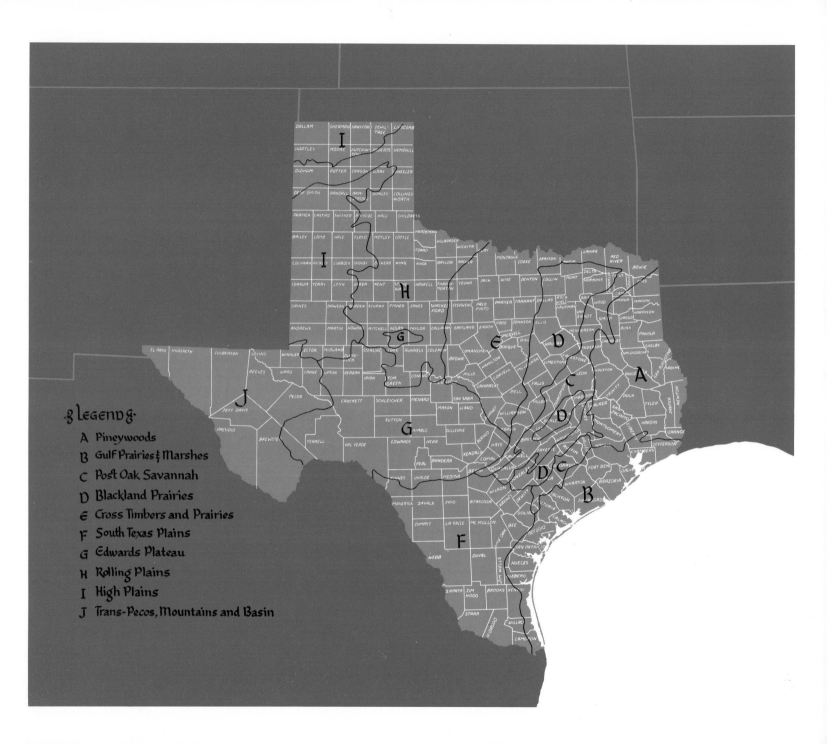

Legend

A Pineywoods
B Gulf Prairies & Marshes
C Post Oak Savannah
D Blackland Prairies
E Cross Timbers and Prairies
F South Texas Plains
G Edwards Plateau
H Rolling Plains
I High Plains
J Trans-Pecos, Mountains and Basin

Native grasses, pine, and juniper appear on the mountain slopes.

9. The Edwards Plateau, a vast area of rolling hills extending from the Rio Grande northward to the Concho-Colorado country, features a grass cover to the west and a wooded area to the east which comprises such trees as cypress, mountain juniper (cedar), Spanish oak, live oak, shin oak, and hundreds of other shrubs that flourish in the limestone soils.

10. The Cedar Brakes, actually a sub-division of the Edwards Plateau, includes an area extending from the Balcones Fault on the east to the Llano-Burnet country on the northwest. Sometimes called the true "Hill Country of Texas," the region supports a plant life similar to that of the Edwards Plateau with cedar as the predominant tree.

11. The Rio Grande Plain Timbers and Brush, the late J. Frank Dobie's beloved "brush country," forms the southern tip of Texas. In this region the principal trees are mesquite, live oak, post oak, and a large variety of thorn-covered shrubs characteristic of the Spanish border lands.

12. The Coastal Prairie, a region adjacent to the Gulf and extending from the Guadalupe basin on the southwest to the headwaters of the Sabine River, represents a plant life region consisting principally of marsh and salt grasses near the tidewater and coarse bunch grasses further inland. Oak, elm, pine, and other hardwoods are scattered along the watercourses that traverse the region.

The major native grasses of Texas include big and little bluestem, Indian grass, Texas wintergrass, blue grama, buffalo grass, and wheat grass in the eastern areas of the state. The West Texas grasses include black, blue, and side-oats gramas, curly mesquite, bush muhly, and tobosa. The Edwards Plateau region is covered (except where overgrazed) with little and pinhole bluestem, buffalo, curly mesquite, fall witchgrass, and others. In a wide belt along the Grand Prairie and Western Cross Timbers many of the above varieties overlap.

Benjamin C. Thorp, *Texas Range Grasses* (Austin, 1952).
Robert A. Vines, *Trees, Shrubs, and Woody Vines of the Southwest* (Austin, 1960).
Eula Whitehouse, *Wild Flowers of Texas* (Dallas, 1948).

# ARCHEOLOGY

 1. *Panhandle-Plains Area*: Archeological sites in this part of the state include mammoth and bison kill sites, campsites around the shores of the intermittent lakes (playas), flint quarries, campsites in stratified stream terraces, rock art locations, small rockshelters, and ruins of stone slab houses on bluffs overlooking the Canadian River and its tributaries. The oldest known sites are those where early Americans killed and butchered mammoths and large bison between 8,000 and 12,000 years ago (Miami and Plainview sites). Other early sites have been found near playa lakes at Lubbock and Midland (Scharbauer Site). Indians have quarried and used the colorful Alibates Flint (Metamorphosed dolomite)

13

from the Alibates quarries for many thousands of years. Sandstone cliffs along the eastern escarpment of the plains form small rockshelters where Indians lived and left paintings and carvings on the smooth bluffs in more recent times. Just before the arrival of Europeans, agricultural Indians settled along the Canadian River across the north panhandle, built multiple-roomed apartment houses of stone and carried on trade with the Pueblos to the west and the Woodland villages to the east. The following Panhandle Plains sites are represented on the map: (a) Wolf Creek Ruins, (b) Lipscomb Bison Quarry, (c) Miami Mammoth Kill, (d) Antelope Creek Ruins, (e) Alibates Flint Quarries, (f) Saddleback Mesa Ruins, (g) Sunday Canyon Site, (h) Plainview Bison Kill, (i) Lubbock Lake Site, (j) Garza Site, (k) Scharbauer Site, (l) Blue Mountain Rockshelter, and (m) Robert Lee Reservoir Sites.

2. *North Central Area*: Archeological sites found here include layers of occupation debris in stratified stream terraces, small rockshelters in limestone cliffs bordering the valleys, and extensive village sites. The stream terraces contain the earliest evidence of man which has been found in the area at the present time. Supposed hearths at the Lewisville site have been radiocarbon dated at older than 30,000 years. Although many of the rockshelters have been looted by relic hunters, several have been carefully excavated and have furnished excellent information about the Indians who used them in relatively recent times. Village sites in the Forney Reservoir area often have a large conical pit of unknown function in the habitation area. The historic Wichita Indians built their villages along the broad terraces of the Red River, grew their crops of corn, and hunted the remnants of the great bison herds. The following North Central Area sites are shown on the map: (a) Spanish Fort Village, (b) Halsell Reservoir Sites, (c) Harrell Site, (d) Lewisville Site, (e) Thompson Lake Site, (f) Forney Reservoir Sites, (g) Bardwell Reservoir Sites, (h) Navarro Mills Reservoir Sites, (i) Kyle Rockshelter, (j) Blum Rockshelter, and (k) Proctor Reservoir Sites.

3. *Eastern Woodlands Area*: The older woodland campsites are usually found on the uplands and have been heavily eroded in recent decades because of clearing and cultivation of the hills. Some early campsites are also found buried in the high river terraces. For the last 2,000 years the woodlands have been inhabited by groups of agriculturalists such as the historic Caddoes. Almost every valley has traces of villages composed of groups of houses made of poles covered with thatch and clay daub. The dependable food supply composed of corn, squash, beans, and other crops produced a relatively dense population and large thriving communities. Indian artisans produced large quantities of fine pottery vessels. Some villages became ceremonial centers and large temple mounds and burial mounds of earth were constructed in central plazas. Widespread trade contacts are indicated by the presence of fancy artifacts made from copper, marine shells, and exotic types of stone. In recent years many mounds have been destroyed and many burial grounds looted by collectors digging for attractive pottery vessels. The following Eastern Woodlands area sites are shown on the map: (a) Sanders Mounds, (b) Sam Coffman Mounds, (c) Hatchell Mound, (d) Knights Bluff Site, (e) Keith Mound, (f) Pearson Site, (g) Gilbert Site, (h) Harroun Mounds, (i) Whelan Mound, (j) Yarborough Site, (k) Malakoff Site, (l) George C. Davis Mounds, (m and n) Toledo Bend Reservoir Sites, (o) Jonas Short Mound, (p) Sawmill Site, (q) Livingston Reservoir Sites, and (r) Honea Reservoir Sites.

4. *Trans-Pecos Area*: This arid region is dominated by the Guadalupe, Davis, Chisos, and other rugged

GRADY MIDDLE SCHOOL LIBRARY

mountain ranges. There are high plateaus with desert vegetation and some deep canyons along the major rivers.

The most common types of archeological sites in the Trans-Pecos area are rockshelters, sotol pits, and small open campsites. These abundant sites represent at least 12,000 years of nomadic habitation in the region. Rock art (pictographs and petroglyphs) is common in and near the rockshelters and caves used by the Indians—Miers Springs and Hueco Tanks are excellent examples. The sotol pits are donut shaped rings of burned rock around a pit oven used for baking sotol and other desert plants. The open campsites scattered over the plateaus were usually only occupied for brief periods by nomadic hunters and gatherers. In more recent times Indian agriculturalists occupied the Rio Grande valley between El Paso and the canyons of the Big Bend area. These people lived in pit house villages and raised corn, gourds, squash, beans, and cotton in their irrigated gardens. These groups still lived in the area when the Spanish arrived. The sites shown on the map include (a) Hot Wells Ruins, (b) Ceremonial Cave, (c) Hueco Tanks Sites, (d) Shelby-Brooks Shelter, (e) Carved Rock Shelter, (f) Redford Sites, (g) Bee Cave, (h) Reagan Canyon Sites, and (i) Miers Springs Sites.

5. *Edwards Plateau Area*: At the western edge of the plateau, in the canyons of the Pecos, Rio Grande, and Devils rivers, there are numerous large rockshelters in the limestone cliffs. These shelters contain dry deposits which accumulated during 12,000 years of occupation. Mummies, baskets, mats, sandals, and other perishable artifacts are commonly preserved— although most sites have been extensively vandalized. On the walls of the shelters are some of the finest polychrome murals (representing thousands of years of Indian art) found anywhere in the Western Hemisphere. Some stratified silt terraces adjacent to the

rivers have produced up to 35 feet of cultural strata.

The Central Texas hill country was also occupied over thousands of years by nomadic Indians. Here there are numerous small rockshelters, few of which are dry. The hilltops and valleys are dotted with burned rock middens (massive accumulations of hearthstones) which represent thousands of years of food preparation. Rock art is less common in Central Texas and the stratified stream terraces are not so deeply occupied as those to the west although they represent many thousands of years of accumulation. The Edwards Plateau sites shown on the map include (a) Paint Rock Site, (b) Grimes-Houy Site, (c) Stillhouse Hollow Reservoir Sites, (d) Fall Creek Sites, (e) Lake Buchanan Sites, (f) Lehmann Rockshelter, (g) Levi Rockshelter, (h) Smith Rockshelter, (i) Oblate Rockshelter, (j) Granberg Site, (k) Kincaid Rockshelter, (l) Montell Rockshelter, (m) Devil's Mouth Site, (n) Fate Bell Shelter, (o) Centipede Shelter, and (p) Eagle Cave.

6. *Coastal Area*: The predominant type of site found in the coastal area is the shell midden. These mounds of shell were accumulated over thousands of years at favorite Indian camping areas around the bays and bayous. Marine and freshwater mollusks were utilized. Bone, shell, ceramic, and stone tools are found in the middens. Many of the shell heaps have been destroyed by being used as a road-surfacing material. Although the Indians were primarily hunters and gatherers, they made a variety of types of pottery, some of which were decorated with asphaltum found on the beaches. Other types of sites found in the coastal area include shallow stream terrace sites, small open camps, midden covered knolls (Morhiss Site), and burial grounds. The map includes the following sites: (a) Addicks Basin Sites, (b) Cedar Bayou Sites, (c) Wallisville Reservoir Sites, (d) Caplen Site, (e) Morhiss Site, (f) Bee County Localities,

(g) Live Oak Point and Kent Crane Sites, (h) Ingleside Cove Sites, and (i) Oso Creek Sites.

7. *Southwest Area*: This area is very poorly known archeologically. A surface survey of part of Dimmitt County recorded extensive campsites, most heavily eroded, along the stream valleys. Investigations in the Falcon Reservoir area produced evidence of open campsites and some stratified river terraces with buried cultural debris. In historic times this region was occupied by nomadic groups of Coahuiltecan Indians who subsisted on cactus tunas, small game, and any other available edible substances. When additional explorations are carried out in Southwest Texas,

it will probably be found to contain numerous and varied archeological sites. The following sites are shown on the map: (a,b,c) Dimmitt County Sites and (d,e) Falcon Reservoir Sites.

Scholars who have made significant contributions to Texas archeology include T. N. Campbell, W. C. Holden, Jack T. Hughes, A. T. Jackson, Edward B. Jelks, J. Charles Kelley, Alex D. Krieger, J. E. Pearce, E. B. Sayles, E. H. Sellards, and Dee Ann Suhm Storey.

Curtis Tunnell to William C. Pool, April 3, 1968.

# THE INDIANS OF TEXAS

IN DESCRIBING the transition from the prehistoric past to the historic era, W. W. Newcomb, Jr., points out that "In this day of increasing conformity and standardization, the sprawling state of Texas remains the meeting ground and melting pot of the Old South, the Spanish Southwest, and the Midwest. So it was in Indian times, but magnified many times over. The various tribes and nations of Texas Indians were not fashioned from the same cloth; . . . ." Some of these tribes were indigenous to Texas, some were forced into the area by the pressure of hostile tribes to the north, and some were forced into the region of East Texas by the pressure from the advancing American frontier to the east.

During the earliest decades of European exploration, the largest group of Indians living in Texas was of the Caddo tribes of East and Northeast Texas.

This large family of related tribes can be subdivided into (1) the Hasinai Confederacy, separate tribes living in the southeastern section of the Texas Pine Belt and extending over into Louisiana; (2) the Caddo proper group of Northeast Texas and nearby sections of Arkansas, Oklahoma, and Louisiana; and (3) the Wichita group of the middle Red River valley and North Central Texas. The Caddo tribes occupy a significant place among Texas Indians. They achieved a level of cultural development unsurpassed by other Indians of the state; in brief, they were successful agriculturalists who dwelt in permanent abodes.

Along the Gulf Coast, the Attacapas, the Deadoses, and the Arkokisas ranged the Coastal Prairies from the Sabine River to Galveston Island. To the south, Karankawas ranged from the island side of Galveston Bay to the vicinity of Corpus Christi Bay. Between the Gulf Coast and the Rio Grande and north to San Antonio, the several sub-divisions of the Coahuiltecan tribes lived; they tried to eke out a bare physical survival in a land where ordinary agricultural methods would not work.

To the north and northwest of the Karankawa and Coahuiltecan lands, the tribes of the Central Texas area included Tamique, Xaraname, and possibly others. To the north of these, and wedged between the Caddo tribes and the Lipan Apaches to the west, were the Tonkawa tribes of the territory of the Edwards Plateau and Brazos River. During the early historic period, the Tonkawas apparently comprised a number of scattered bands, but after their numbers were reduced during the Spanish Colonial period, the survivors united in one tribe.

During the decades of the mission era in the history of Texas, the West Texas region, from San Antonio to the arid, rugged reaches of Trans-Pecos Texas, constituted the home range of the warlike Lipan Apache tribes, the eastern sub-division of a numerous, widespread, and powerful assembly of tribes extending westward over the lands of New Mexico and Arizona. To the north, on the South and High Plains of Texas, lived the famed Comanche tribes and their associates, the Kiowa Apache and Kiowa tribes. The most stubborn and fearsome adversaries faced by the Texas frontiersmen, these so-called "wild" Indians of the west raided both Spanish, Mexican, and American frontier settlements from the earliest time of settlement until after they were placed on reservations.

In conclusion, it should be pointed out that during the nineteenth century, the woodlands of East Texas furnished a refuge for Indian tribes forced westward because of frontier expansion in the territory of the United States east of the Mississippi River. The more significant of these tribes to enter Texas were the Cherokees (for a brief and unhappy experience in Northeast Texas); the Choctaw and Chickasaw from Mississippi and Georgia, who settled along the Sabine and Neches rivers; the Alabama-Coushatta from Alabama, who settled along the Trinity and Sabine rivers and remained in Texas; the Kickapoo and Potawatomi from Illinois who entered Texas and settled on the headwaters of the Sabine and Trinity rivers; the Delaware and Shawnee, two tribes migrating from Missouri to the Red River valley of Texas; the Quapaw, who moved from their original home along the Arkansas and White rivers to Sulphur Creek; and the Creek, who moved from Alabama and Georgia to establish themselves in Northeast Texas.

W. W. Newcomb, Jr., *The Indians of Texas* (Austin, 1961).

Mary Atkinson, *The Texas Indians* (San Antonio, 1935).

Roy Bedichek, *Karankawa Country* (Garden City, N.Y., 1950).

Walter P. Webb, *The Great Plains* (Boston and New York, 1931, 1936).

Frederick Webb Hodge, *Handbook of American Indians North of Mexico* (Washington, 1907).

Rupert N. Richardson, *The Comanche Barrier to South Plains Settlement* (Glendale, Calif., 1933).

Ernest Wallace and E. A. Hoebel, *The Comanches, Lords of the South Plains* (Norman, 1952).

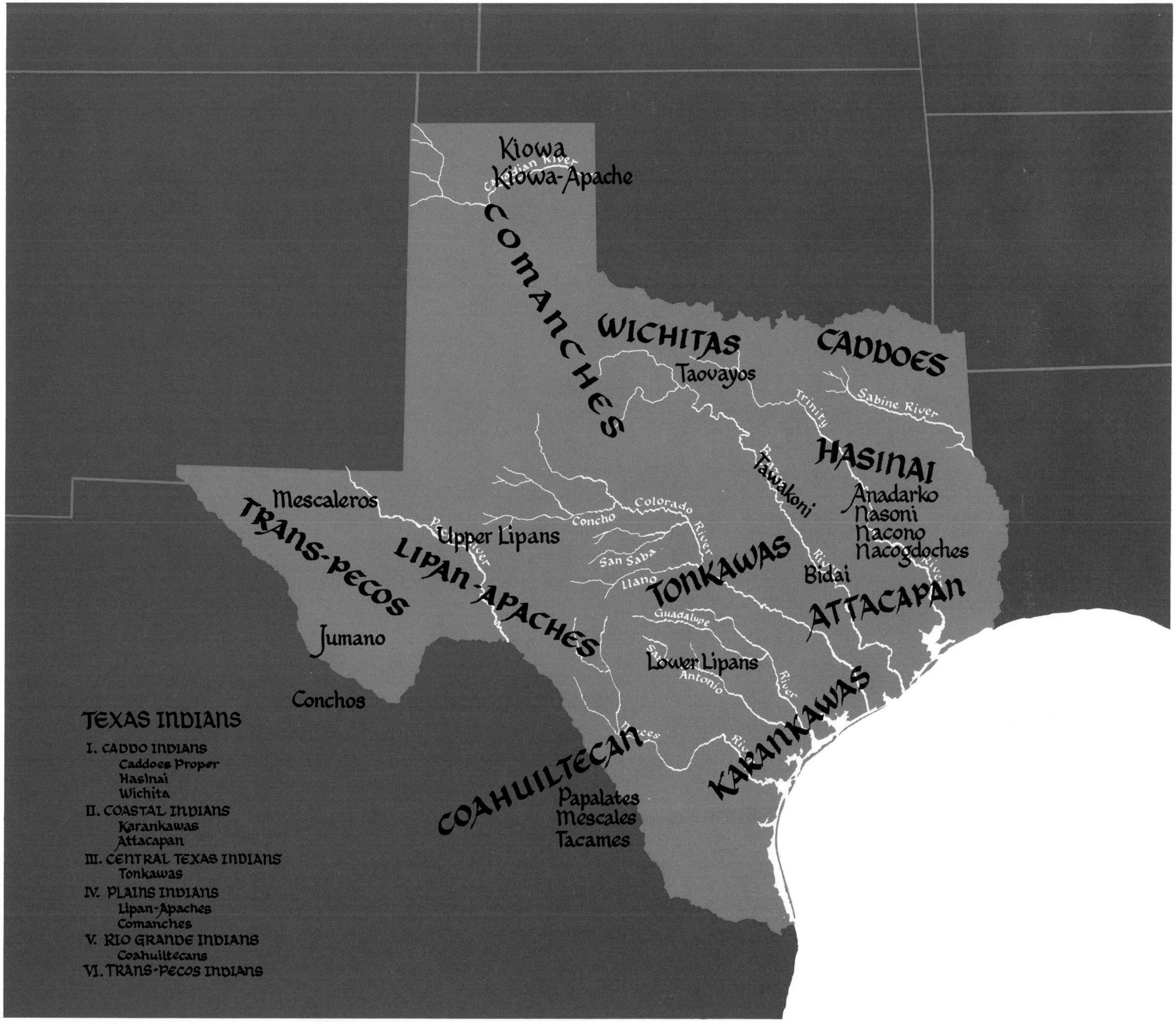

Kiowa
Kiowa-Apache

COMANCHES

WICHITAS

CADDOES

Taovayos

Trinity

Sabine River

HASINAI

Mescaleros

Colorado River

Tawakoni

Anadarko
Nasoni
Nacono
Nacogdoches

TRANS-PECOS

Upper Lipans

LIPAN-APACHES

Concho

San Saba

Llano

TONKAWAS

Bidai

ATTACAPAN

Jumano

Guadalupe

Conchos

Lower Lipans

Antonio

KARANKAWAS

TEXAS INDIANS

I. CADDO INDIANS
    Caddoes Proper
    Hasinai
    Wichita
II. COASTAL INDIANS
    Karankawas
    Attacapan
III. CENTRAL TEXAS INDIANS
    Tonkawas
IV. PLAINS INDIANS
    Lipan-Apaches
    Comanches
V. RIO GRANDE INDIANS
    Coahuiltecans
VI. TRANS-PECOS INDIANS

COAHUILTECAN

Nueces

Papalates
Mescales
Tacames

THE DAWN of the European period of Texas history began when a tropical storm forced Alvar Núñez Cabeza de Vaca and his companions ashore on Galveston Island. Cabeza de Vaca had sailed from Cuba in 1528 as secretary-treasurer of the ill-fated expedition of Pánfilo de Narváez. After reversals in Florida, Narváez ordered the construction of crude boats in which the land party (his ships had returned to Spain leaving about half of the expedition stranded) hoped to sail to the Panuco settlement in New Spain. The boat carrying Cabeza de Vaca was wrecked by a storm and the survivors reached shore at a place called Malhado by the Spaniards. While there is a difference of opinion among scholars concerning the location of Malhado, the Texas coast in the vicinity of Galveston Island was probably the site of landfall. Earlier, in 1519, Alonzo Álvarez de Piñeda had mapped the Texas coast.

In a short time most of the survivors of the Narváez expedition died of disease, exposure, starvation, or at the hands of the Indians of the Texas coast. After fleeing the island, Cabeza de Vaca and three companions escaped after a six-year residence with the Indian tribes and journeyed westward across the Hill Country and Edwards Plateau region of southwest Texas to El Paso. From this point the courageous Spaniards moved west across Chihuahua and Sonora to Culiacán on the Pacific coast of Mexico. Because of a difference of opinion among historians, two possible routes are shown on the map.

Inspired by the wondrous stories of Cabeza de Vaca and Fray Marcos, Francisco Vásquez de Coronado was appointed to lead an expedition northward to the seven cities of Cibola. The Coronado expedition—gathered at Compostela in January, 1540—included some 1000 men, 1500 horses and mules, and cattle and sheep. The advance guard of the expedition moved northward in April, 1540. The route led north along the west coast of Mexico through Sinaloa and Sonora to enter the present United States at a point in southeastern Arizona. Continuing northward to the Zuñi Indian village of Hawikuh (which was taken by storm), Coronado explored the region to the north and east.

Coronado spent the winter of 1540-1541 at Tiguex, a village on the Rio Grande, and the following spring he moved east and north—guided by an Indian known as El Turco—in search of Quivira. His route led across the vast level plains of the *llano estacado* of New Mexico and Texas. At a spot near the Palo Duro and Tule canyons, he determined that the main army should return to Tiguex while he took a small group further into the interior in search of Quivira. Apparently Coronado and thirty-six of his men continued northward across the Canadian River and into the Great Plains region bordering the Arkansas River. After giving up the search, he returned to Tiguex, where the Spaniards spent the winter of 1541-1542. In the spring of 1542, the Coronado expedition returned to Mexico by the route that they had followed northward two years before.

In one of the most interesting interpretations of southwestern history in recent years, Mr. J. W. Williams of Wichita Falls, Texas, takes issue with the traditional explanations of the Coronado route. Using the narratives of the expedition for a description of the topography, fauna, and flora combined with his own calculations relative to rate and time of travel,

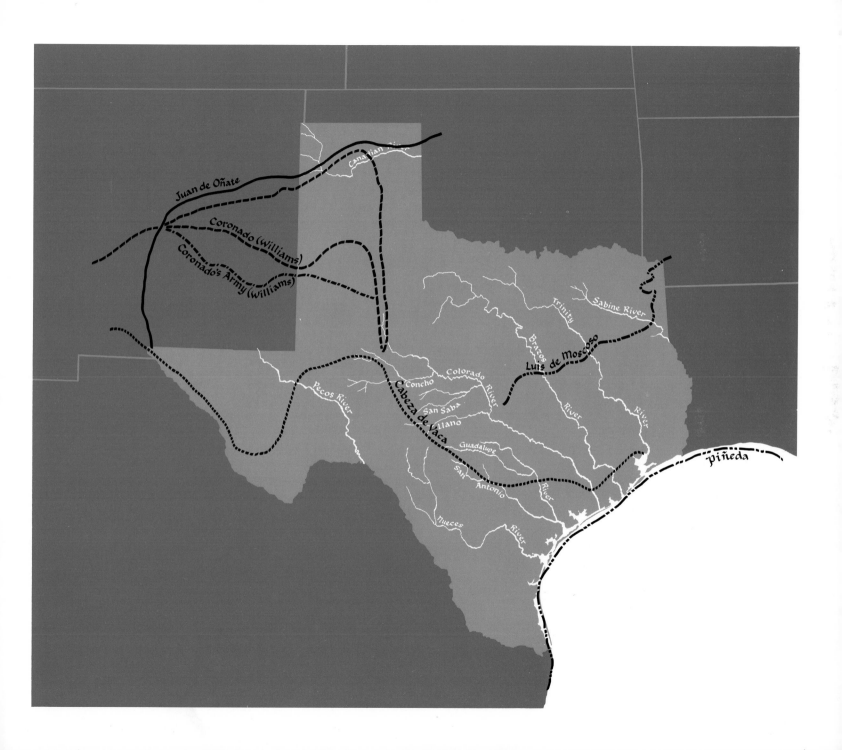

Williams concludes that the army of Coronado traveled generally southeast from Tiguex by way of the Cap Rock and Brazos rivers, then south by way of present Snyder to a point on the North Concho River northwest of present San Angelo. Williams marks the Coronado return to Tiguex by way of the Brazos River, Lubbock, and Portales, New Mexico.

Luis de Moscoso, in command of the remnants of the Hernando de Soto expedition (which had wandered extensively over the southeastern section of the present United States, 1540-1542), crossed into Texas in the summer of 1542 by way of the Red River near present Texarkana. While historians argue about the exact route of the Moscoso expedition, it is probable that he led his men westward to the eastern edge of the buffalo plains and then southward to the region between the Trinity and Brazos rivers. From this vague location, Moscoso retraced his steps to the Mississippi River. From here he led his men to Mexico by way of the Mississippi River and the Gulf of Mexico.

The late Professor Walter P. Webb points out that while the Spaniards were very successful in exploring the regions to the east and west of the Great Plains, from 1535 to 1706 "no Spanish force made its way entirely across the Great Plains." The Spaniards probably could have gone into the Plains before the dawn of the eighteenth century, but the expedition of De Soto and Coronado had revealed nothing to arouse their desires. As a result, the north central section of New Spain was neglected for a century and a half.

H. H. Bancroft, *History of the North Mexican States and Texas* (2 vols., San Francisco, 1884).

Fanny Bandelier (ed.), *The Journey of Alvar Núñez Cabeza de Vaca* (New York, 1905).

James Newton Baskett, "A Study of the Route of Cabeza de Vaca," *Quarterly of the Texas State Historical Association,* X.

Harbert Davenport and Joseph K. Wells, "The First Europeans in Texas," *Southwestern Historical Quarterly,* XXII.

David Donoghue, "The Route of the Coronado Expedition in Texas," *Southwestern Historical Quarterly,* XXXIII.

George P. Hammond and Agapito Rey, *Narratives of the Coronado Expedition* (Albuquerque, 1940).

J. W. Williams, "Coronado: From the Rio Grande to the Concho," *Southwestern Historical Quarterly,* LXIII.

George P. Winship, *The Journey of Coronado, 1540-1542* (New York, 1904).

# FRANCE IN TEXAS

THE CLAIM of France to Texas was based on the explorations of Rène Robert Cavelier, Sieur de la Salle and the establishment of Fort St. Louis in 1685. After extensive explorations in the Illinois and Great Lakes regions and southward to the mouth of the Mississippi River, La Salle sailed from France in the summer of 1684 to establish a colony at the mouth of the Mississippi River. Missing the delta of the Mississippi, the four ships of the La Salle expedition continued along the Texas coast to Matagorda Bay. The French pioneers explored the land bordering on the bay and followed the Lavaca River inland. Fort St. Louis was constructed in July, 1685, near the Lavaca River in the southern part of

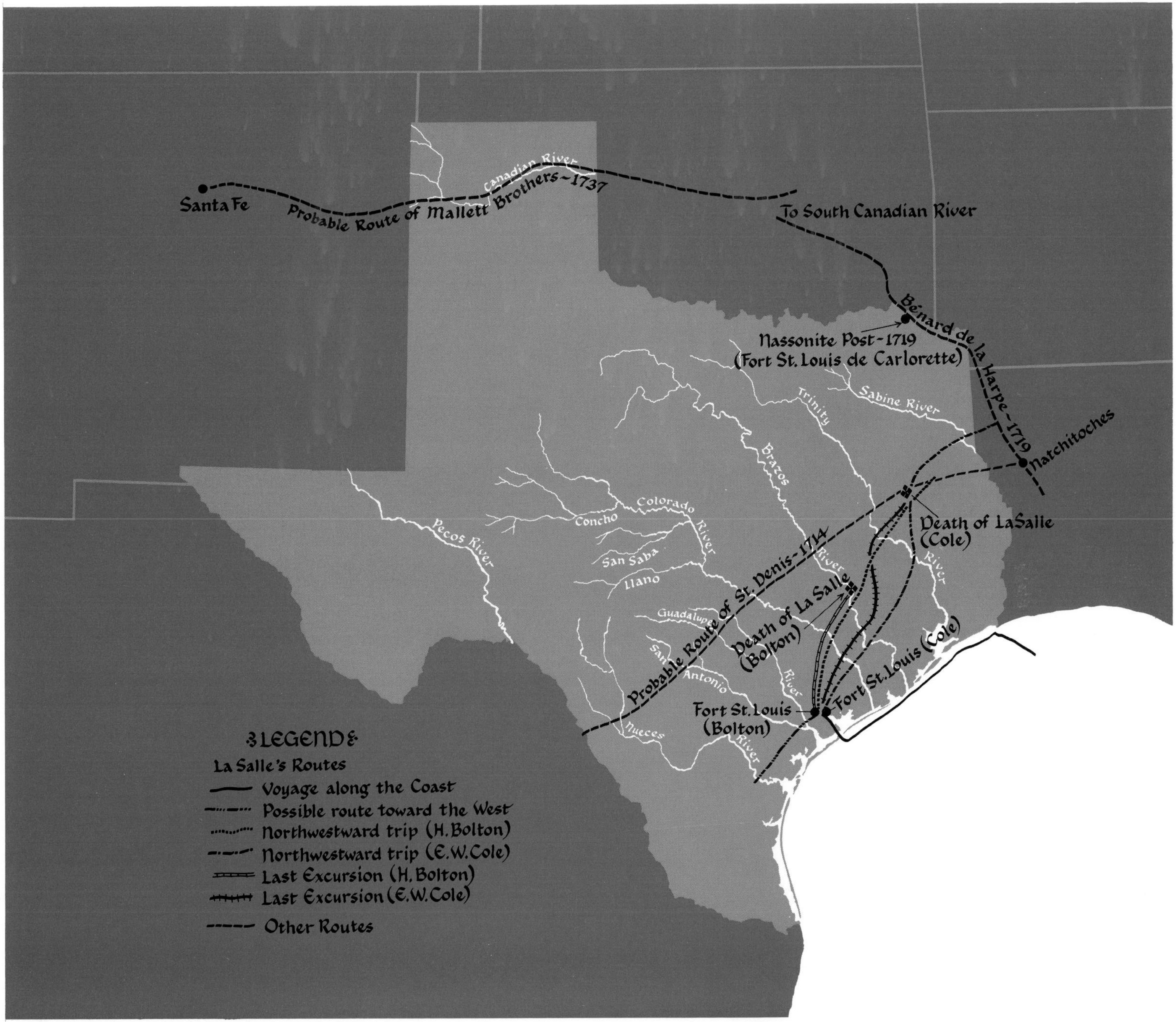

Santa Fe

Probable Route of Mallett Brothers~1737

Canadian River

To South Canadian River

Bénard de la Harpe~1719

Nassonite Post~1719
(Fort St. Louis de Carlorette)

Natchitoches

Trinity

Sabine River

Brazos

Colorado River

Concho

San Saba

Llano

Pecos River

River

River

Death of LaSalle
(Cole)

Probable Route of St. Denis~1714

Guadalupe

Death of La Salle
(Bolton)

San Antonio

River

Fort St. Louis (Cole)

Nueces

Fort St. Louis
(Bolton)

River

3LEGEND&
La Salle's Routes

———— Voyage along the Coast
—·—·— Possible route toward the West
········· Northwestward trip (H.Bolton)
—·—·— Northwestward trip (E.W.Cole)
++++++ Last Excursion (H.Bolton)
++++++ Last Excursion (E.W.Cole)
- - - - Other Routes

present Jackson County. La Salle subsequently led his men on three extended expeditions inland—one to the vicinity of the Rio Grande, one eastward to the Hasinai lands along the Neches and Trinity rivers, and a final journey into the east Texas region; it was on this third expedition (the second attempt to reach the Mississippi) that La Salle was killed by his disgruntled companions on March 20, 1687. The exact location of La Salle's death is a matter of interpretation; Herbert Eugene Bolton places the site on the Brazos River near present Navasota, E. W. Cole's study points to a site on Larrison Creek in present Cherokee County, C. E. Castañeda places the scene of the murder on the banks of the Navasota River rather than the Brazos, and Francis Parkman locates the scene of La Salle's untimely end on a tributary of the Trinity River. The few unfortunate colonists left at Fort St. Louis were attacked and killed by the Indians of the Texas coastal region in 1689; Alonzo de León finally located the ruins of Fort St. Louis.

Following their unsuccessful venture near Matagorda Bay, the French made no concerted effort to occupy Texas. In 1714 Louis Juchereau de St. Denis, a French trader along the Red River in northern Louisiana, journeyed westward from Natchitoches, Louisiana, to cross Texas in an effort to establish an overland trade route with the Spanish settlements in Mexico. St. Denis arrived at San Juan Bautista on the Rio Grande on July 18, 1714, causing general alarm among the Spanish residents and authorities. On his return trip across Texas in 1716, he was accompanied by a Spanish expedition commanded by Domingo Ramón. In August, 1718, Bénard de la Harpe established a trading post (Fort St. Louis de Charlotte) in the Caddo Indian lands of present Red River County. Several years later, La Harpe attempted to establish a trading post on the Texas coast (Galveston Bay) but hostile Indians forced him to withdraw. In 1739 Pierre and Paul Mallet traveled from the Missouri Country across the Great Plains to Santa Fe, New Mexico. On their return trip, the Mallet brothers followed the Canadian River valley across the Panhandle of Texas and present Oklahoma to the French trading post on the Arkansas River. While the Mallet expedition had no direct result on the course of Texas history, it is significant that this journey ended the French efforts to establish a vague claim to the land west of the Sabine River.

Herbert E. Bolton, "Location of La Salle's Colony on the Gulf of Mexico," *Mississippi Valley Historical Review*, XI; also *Southwestern Historical Quarterly*, XXVII.

Robert Carlton Clark, "Louis Juchereau de St. Denis and the Re-establishment of the Tejas Missions," *Southwestern Historical Quarterly*, VI.

E. W. Cole, "La Salle in Texas," *Southwestern Historical Quarterly*, XLIX.

Isaac Joslin Cox, "The Louisiana-Texas Frontier," *Southwestern Historical Quarterly*, X.

Henri Joutel, *Journal of La Salle's Last Voyage* (Henry Reed Stiles, ed.), (Albany, 1906).

Ralph A. Smith, (tr.), "Account of Bénard de la Harpe: Discovery Made by Him of Several Nations Situated in the West," *Southwestern Historical Quarterly*, LXII.

# THE NORTHERN FRONTIER OF MEXICO, 1519-1700

THE EUROPEAN APPROACH to Texas properly begins with the expedition of Hernán Cortés in 1519. Following in the footsteps of Hernández de Córdoba and Juan de Grijalva, Cortés departed from Cuba with eleven ships, sixteen horses, fourteen cannon, 119 workers, 200 Indian servants, and 400 soldiers. Touching the coast at Cozumel and continuing on to a point near present Vera Cruz, Cortés led his men over the mountains into the valley of Mexico and Tenoxtitlán, the center of the Aztec civilization. The native Indian civilization was subdued and destroyed, 1520-1521, and the Spanish conquistador found himself the master of all Mexico.

Expansion to the west and to the north followed almost immediately. The province of Nueva Galicia, the lands northwest of Mexico, resulted largely from the work of Nuño de Guzmán, probably the most unsavory of the conquistadors. After a brief career at the eastern outpost of Panuco (on the Panuco River near present Tampico), Guzmán moved into the Tarascan lands to the west, where he applied the torch to the homes (and to some of the people) of present Michoacán and Jalisco. Burning the native villages, building crosses, and organizing *encomiendas,* he completed his conquest and renamed the territory Nueva Galicia. Guadalajara, Arabic for "rocky river," was founded in 1531 in the Antemarac River valley near the Rio Grande de Santiago. Morelia, first known as Valladolid, was founded in 1541 by Viceroy Antonio de Mendoza; in 1582 Valladolid became the capital of Michoacán. Compostela and Culiacán were maintained as military outposts to the northwest. It will be remembered that the venerable Cabeza de Vaca reached Compostela in 1536 near the end of his wanderings; in 1539 and 1540 the expedition of Fray Marcos de Niza and Coronado followed the route from Compostela to Culiacán on the first stage of their journeys to the north.

Beyond the northern borders of Nueva Galicia, lying astride the mountains and hills of the Sierra Madre Occidental, the province of Nueva Viscaya was established by young Francisco de Ibarra, the nephew of Don Diego Ibarra, who had made a fortune in the Zacatecas silver mine. In 1548 in a wind-swept mountain gorge soon to be the new town of Zacatecas, four men—Juan de Tolasa, Cristóbal de Oñate, Diego de Ibarra, and Treviño de Banuelos—discovered rich deposits of silver and launched the first mining rush in the history of New Spain.

In 1561 Francisco de Ibarra was commissioned as governor and captain general to rule the northern regions not yet subject to Spanish dominion. Young Ibarra named the territory Nueva Viscaya and the never-ending search for gold and silver continued. Durango, established by Alonzo Pacheco in 1563, became the capital of Nueva Viscaya. To the north of the central plateau, the rimlands of Nueva Viscaya include the arid plains and mountains of the great northern desert. South of the Rio Grande a vast area in the present state of Chihuahua is drained by Rio Conchos, a stream rising on the eastern slopes of the Sierra Madre range and flowing north to empty into

To upper Rio Grande

The road to the Rio Grande~
Used by Espéjo, Rodriguez
and others.

Pecos River

Rio Casas Grandes

Rio Sta. Maria

Rio Conchos

La Junta
de los Rios

Rio Grande

Del Rio

Chihuahua

Rio Pedro

San Juan Bautista

Rio Florido

Rio Salado

Laredo

Rio Yaqui

San Ygnacio

Santa Barbara

Rio del Fuerte

NUEVA VISCAYA

Monclova

Mier

Camargo

Reynosa

Brownsville

Cerralvo

Rio San Juan

Matamoros

Rio Culiacan

Culiacan

Saltillo

Monterrey

NUEVA GALICIA

Durango

Rio Purificación

NUEVO
LEON

Rio de mezquit

Zacatecas

San Luis Potosi

Tampico

Rio Panuco

Compostela

Rio de Santiago

Aguascalientes

Rio

Rio Moctezuma

Guadalajara

Rio Lerma

Queretaro

Morelia

Mexico

the Rio Grande south of the big bend of the river. It was from Santa Bárbara and vicinity that the Spanish priests and soldiers—Fray Agustín Rodríquez, Antonio de Espejo, Fray Bernardino Beltrán, and Juan de Oñate—began their expeditions to the Rio Grande and New Mexico in the 1580's and 1590's. A mission settlement was founded at La Junta de los Rios (near present Presidio) in 1683-84.

Far to the east the Spanish frontiersmen established the province of Nuevo León. In 1584 Luis de Carvajal, the provincial governor, established the settlement at Monterrey. To the northeast, Cerralvo, first called the villa de León was established a few months later. Saltillo was founded in 1586 near a Franciscan mission that had been built in 1582 and Monclova was established by Carvajal in 1590. In seven decades the northward march of the Spanish mission and military frontier had moved to the southern border of present Texas. Over forty years were to pass, however, before José de Escandón colonized the valley of the lower Rio Grande.

H. H. Bancroft, *History of the North Mexican States and Texas* (2 vols., San Francisco, 1889).

Carlos Castañeda, *Our Catholic Heritage in Texas*, I-III (Austin, 1936-1938).

Paul Horgan, *Great River, The Rio Grande in North American History* (2 vols., New York and Toronto, 1954).

# 17th & 18th CENTURY SPANISH EXPLORATIONS

 IT IS SIGNIFICANT that the efforts of Spain to explore the American Southwest did not end with the journeys of Cabeza de Vaca, Coronado, and De Soto. During the two centuries that followed, many valiant Spanish soldiers and scholars traversed the large area east and north of the Rio Grande in search of both information and new trails. During the 1600's and 1700's the history of Texas is closely associated with the settlements along the upper Rio Grande in New Mexico. Perhaps it should also be pointed out that while the efforts of the earlier conquistadores were associated with adventure and treasure seeking, those of the later period (in addition to the above) were related to the establishment of settlements and were directed toward locating roads between the settlements of the mission frontier. While it is impossible to examine the contributions of all of these men, the successful work of Juan Oñate, Antonio Margil, Pedro Vial, Alonzo de León, Marquis de Aguayo, Juan Domínguez de Mendoza, Athanase de Mézières, and Martín de Alarcón should be traced on a map.

Following in the footsteps of Friar Agustín Rodríguez, Friar Bernardo Beltrán, Antonio de Espejo, and Gaspar Costaño de Sosa (all pioneers of the long trail from the small Mexican village of Santa Barbara to El Paso del Norte), Juan de Oñate, with 400 men (183 families) journeyed from the waters of the Rio

Conchos directly to El Paso del Norte and then into New Mexico to establish the upper Rio Grande settlements in the spring of 1598.

A century passed before the Spanish penetrated the boundaries of present Texas. With the exception of the Mendoza-López expedition down the Rio Grande and on to the confluence of the Concho rivers in 1683, the first to move north of the Rio Grande was Alonzo de León, who made five attempts to explore and colonize Texas between 1686 and 1690. It was in the year 1689 that De León, on his fourth expedition, crossed the Rio Grande and found the ruins of Fort St. Louis. The following year (1690), he founded the East Texas mission of San Francisco de los Tejas. After Louis Juchereau de St. Denis made his unobserved journey across Texas from Natchitoches, Louisiana, to the Spanish outpost and mission of San Juan Bautista on the Rio Grande in the year 1714, the interest of the Spanish in the Texas region intensified considerably. San Antonio de Bexar traces its origins to the establishment of the mission San Antonio Valero on May 1, 1718. The *villa* de Bexar was established a few days later. This significant colonization effort was led by Martín de Alarcón and Fray Antonio de Olivares. Following in the footsteps of St. Denis and Diego Ramón, Alarcón continued his journey to East Texas and Louisiana along El Camino Real.

Two years after the establishment of San Antonio de Bexar, an expedition under the leadership of the Marquis de Aguayo (in response to the French invasion of 1719) crossed the Rio Grande on March 20, 1721, and continued across Texas by way of San Antonio, the San Marcos River, the Colorado near present Austin, the Little River east of present Belton, and Brazos River near present Waco. From here Aguayo continued on to reestablish the East Texas missions. The Aguayo expedition, in addition to the increase of mission activity in East Texas, established a definite Spanish claim to Texas. In addition, along with the others before, Aguayo helped establish El Camino Real.

After the journey of the Marquis de Rubí in 1766-67, Athanase de Mézières, a French merchant, trader, and planter employed by Spain, made several expeditions into Texas, 1771-1779, and recorded his experiences in classic reports to his superiors. A few years later, Pedro Vial (1786) was commissioned to explore a direct route from San Antonio to Santa Fe. As a result of his subsequent wandering, Vial became one of the first Europeans to see the lands bordering the Llano, Colorado, Brazos, and Red rivers of far West Texas. On his return in 1788, Vial generally followed the Red River valley from present New Mexico to a point near present Sherman and Denison. From here he followed the waters of the Sabine to Natchitoches. The following year he made a second journey from San Antonio to Santa Fe.

By the middle and late decades of the eighteenth century the Spanish frontier in Texas consisted of far-flung mission settlements, each with a two-fold purpose—(1) to convert the Indian and (2) to extend, civilize, and hold the northern frontier. Considered as a temporary and transitory agency rather than a permanent institution, the Texas missions were established by the Franciscan order, and nearly all of the missionaries were sent out by the College of Santa Cruz de Querétaro, established at Querétaro in 1683, or the College of Nuestra Señora de Guadalupe de Zacatecas, founded at Zacatecas in 1707.

The center of Spanish mission efforts in Texas was San Antonio. It was here that the missionaries experienced their greatest success. The mission San Antonio de Valero, established by Alarcón and Father Olivares in 1718, was joined by the removal of the East Texas missions to the San Antonio area in 1731—the new establishments were commonly called Con-

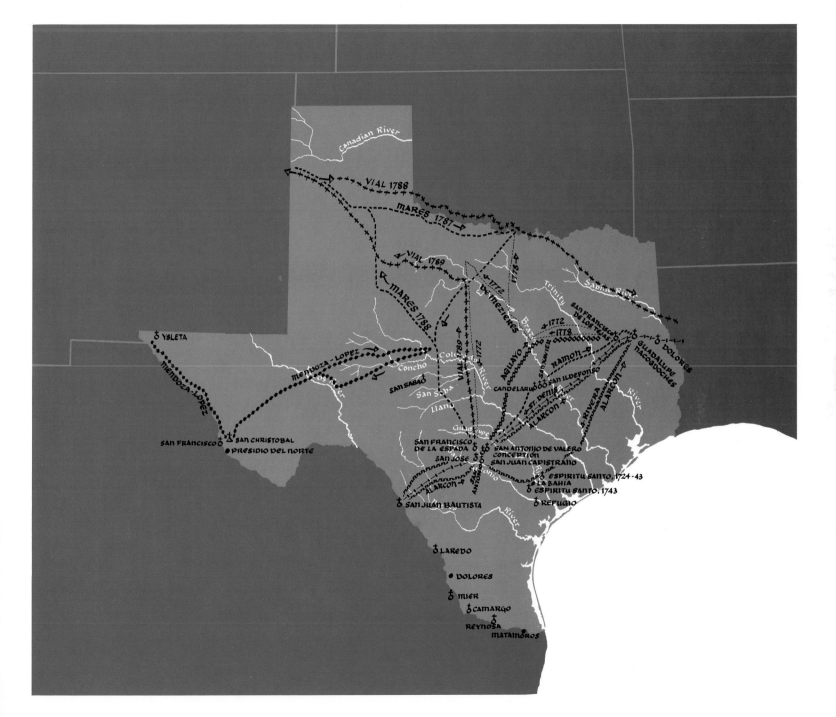

cepción, San Juan, and Espada. It was there that the villa of San Fernando de Bexar was given a measure of self-government—the only mission settlement in Texas to receive such a reward.

While the map on the preceding page locates both the more significant early and later missions, it also represents two areas of expansionist activity during the mid-century years. Concern about the deserted strip of land stretching from Tampico on the South to Corpus Christi and Matagorda bays on the north prompted Spanish officials to grant a colonization contract to José de Escandón in 1746. Two years later, Escandón moved into the lands bordering the Rio Grande with 750 soldiers and 2500 civilians. As a part of the plan, the La Bahía presidio and mission were transferred from the Guadalupe River to the San Antonio River. Escandón then proceeded to establish civil settlements at Dolores (1750) and Laredo (1755). On the south bank of the Rio Grande, he established settlements at Revilla, Mier, Comargo, and Reynosa; all of these communities were founded between 1749 and 1755. In the years immediately following, José Antonio de la Garza, José Vásquez de Borrego, Tomás Sánchez, and Blas María de la Garza Falcón pioneered the cattle industry between the Nueces and the Rio Grande. Spain's second effort at expansion resulted in the establishment of the ill-fated San Saba mission and the presidio of San Luis de los Amarillos near present Menard, Texas, in the spring of 1757.

The third quarter of the eighteenth century was also notable because of the explorations of Athanase de Mézières, Pedro Vial, and José Mares—all three of these significant journeys appear on the map. De Mézières devoted his attention to the pacification of the tribes of central and northern Texas; Vial and Mares pioneered the search for a practical road to Santa Fe. As the century came to an end, Zebulon M. Pike and the filibusters were just around the corner.

H. E. Bolton (ed.), *Spanish Exploration in the Southwest, 1542-1706* (New York, 1925).

H. E. Bolton, *Texas in the Middle Eighteenth Century* (Berkeley, 1915).

Carlos E. Castañeda, *Our Catholic Heritage in Texas* (Austin, 1936, 1942, 1950).

Odie B. Faulk, *A Successful Failure* (Austin, 1965).

C. W. Hackett (ed.), *Historical Documents Relating to New Mexico, Nueva Vizcaya, and Approaches Thereto to 1773* (2 vols., Washington, D. C., 1923-1926).

Map of Texas and Adjacent Territories in the Eighteenth Century Archives, University of Texas Library, Austin, Texas.

# TEXAS & THE UNITED STATES, 1803-1820

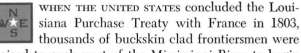 WHEN THE UNITED STATES concluded the Louisiana Purchase Treaty with France in 1803, thousands of buckskin clad frontiersmen were poised to push west of the Mississippi River to begin the conquest of a new land; a rapid conquest of the fertile farm lands, the sea of grass, the towering mountains with their glittering pockets of precious metals and the diversified peltry of the forest followed. The trans-Mississippi West was explored by Lewis and Clark, Zebulon M. Pike, Stephen H. Long, and hun-

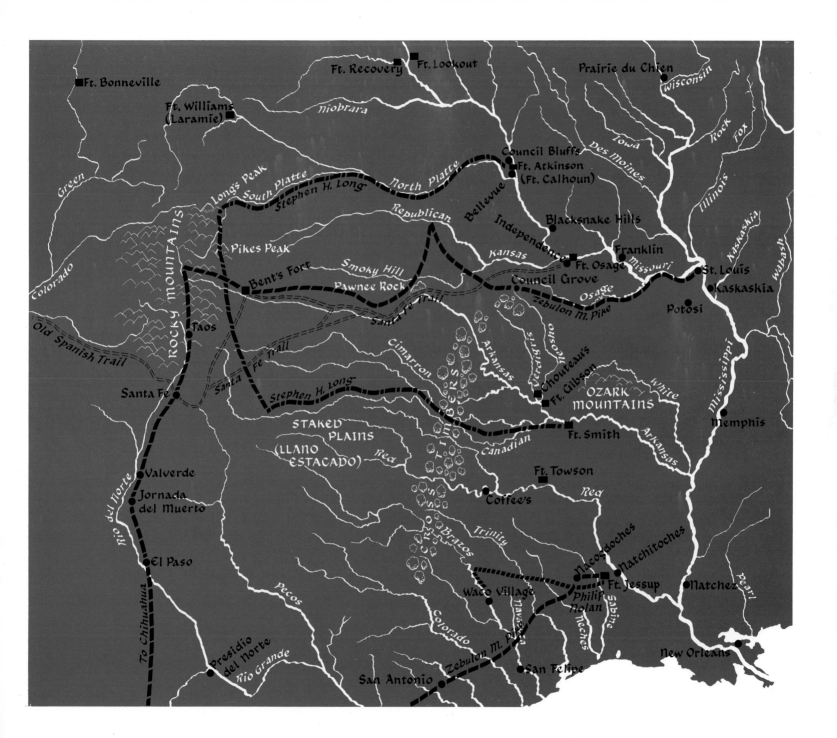

dreds of hunters and trappers in search of a fortune in fur.

In the southwest the vanguard of settlement was led by Philip Nolan, who, in 1800, entered Texas for the fourth time "in search of wild horses," built Fort Nolan on Nolan's Creek in the northwestern corner of present Hill County, and was killed in a battle with Spanish soldiers somewhere near present Waco on March 4, 1801. In 1807 Zebulon M. Pike and his men marched across Texas on their return to the United States from Mexico following their ill-fated attempt to explore the headwaters of the Arkansas and Red rivers. Over a decade later (in 1820), Major Stephen H. Long, after missing the source of the Red River, followed the Canadian River across the present Panhandle of Texas on his return to Fort Smith, Arkansas. Both Pike and Long agreed that the region west of the 95° meridian was an arid waste unsuited to habitation; thus, these two explorers contributed to the origin of the myth of a barren wasteland known to the generation to come as the Great American Desert. The legend of a barren wasteland grew as other explorers returned from the west and by the late 1820's every literate American firmly believed the region between the 95° meridian and the Rocky Mountains to be an extensive, unusable desert.

After more than a decade of a boundary dispute with Spain concerning the western limits of the Louisiana Purchase, the question was settled by the Florida Purchase Treaty of 1819 and the subsequent Adams-Oñis survey. According to the Adams-Oñis line, the western boundary of the United States began at the mouth of the Sabine River and followed that stream to the 32° parallel, then went due north to the Red River, along the south bank of the Red to the 100° meridian, north along the 100° meridian to the Arkan-

sas River, along the Arkansas to its source, then due north to the 42° parallel, and along the 42° parallel west to the Pacific—thus the United States gave up all claim to Texas and the Spanish Southwest.

The Adams-Oñis boundary survey separated American and Spanish territory from 1819-20 to the close of the Mexican War in 1848. Long before 1819, however, the American frontiersmen pressed against the Sabine River barrier. As Ray L. Billington expresses it in *Westward Expansion*, "The westward advance of the Anglo-American frontier was accomplished only by absorbing or pushing aside prior occupants of the continent. . . . Now, in the nineteenth century, the same fate waited the Spanish Americans whose ranches, mission stations, pueblos, and presidios dotted the trans-Mississippi West from Texas to California. Before the American frontiersmen could reach the shores of the Pacific, the Spanish barrier must be overrun."

This process commenced when the first American squatters quietly moved beyond the Sabine to establish their log cabin homes in Spanish Texas. Dr. James Long, Augustus W. Magee, and Bernardo Gutiérrez de Lara helped pave the way during the Mexican War of Independence; and when Moses Austin conceived the idea of an American colony on Spanish soil, eventual conquest became inevitable. Next, we will take a closer look at the Anglo-American approach to Texas, especially to the expeditions of the so-called filibusters and to the initial efforts of Moses and Stephen F. Austin.

Ray L. Billington, *Westward Expansion, A History of the American Frontier* (New York, 1950).
Walter P. Webb, *The Great Plains* (Boston and New York, 1936).

# THE AMERICAN APPROACH TO TEXAS, 1800-1822

THE MORE DIRECT ASPECT of the American approach to the Spanish lands beyond the Sabine includes the unfortunate expeditions of Philip Nolan, the filibustering expeditions of Bernardo de Gutiérrez and Augustus W. Magee, the journeys of Dr. James Long, and the first trips to Texas by Moses and Stephen F. Austin.

Philip Nolan was a young Irishman who moved out to Kentucky in 1788 and took up residence in the home of General James Wilkinson. In subsequent years, Nolan spent much of his time at or near Nacogdoches. After several trips to the Spanish frontier in Texas, Nolan set out for Texas in December, 1800; he entered the region west of Nacogdoches and built a small fort on Nolan's River in present Hill County. He was killed, probably near the present location of Waco, on March 4, 1801, in a skirmish with a Spanish force sent out to arrest him.

The Gutiérrez-Magee expedition of 1812-1813 was a by-product of Mexico's war of independence against Spain. José Bernardo Gutiérrez de Lara, an envoy representing the Mexican rebels, arrived in Washington in December, 1811. After a series of conferences in the nation's capital, Gutiérrez journeyed to New Orleans, where he enlisted the services of a number of adventurers. An invading army was organized under the command of Lieutenant Augustus W. Magee. The Gutiérrez-Magee expedition entered Texas (130 men strong) in August, 1812; the small army captured Nacogdoches on August 12, marched to Trinidad in September, and then to La Bahía in early November.

After the death of Magee at La Bahía, Samuel Kemper succeeded to command. Kemper followed Governor Manuel María Salcedo's loyalist army to San Antonio, where the Spanish were defeated in the battle of Rosalis. Gutiérrez's cruel execution of the loyalist leaders in early 1813 caused many Americans to abandon the enterprise. The fragmented army that remained was defeated by a Spanish army in August, 1813, in the battle of the Medina River.

The Dr. James Long expedition was sponsored by the citizens of Natchez, Mississippi, who were upset over the Adams-Oñis boundary settlement of 1819. Long and some three hundred men crossed the Sabine in June, 1819. Nacogdoches was captured and the "independence" of Texas was declared. After attempts to secure aid from Jean Lafitte failed, the American adventurers were driven out of Texas by Spanish troops in late October, 1819. Long escaped capture and fled to Natchitoches. The following year, he attempted to reorganize his forces at Point Bolivar. In September, 1821, Long and fifty-two men captured La Bahía; a few days later, the Americans surrendered to the Spaniards.

In the autumn of 1820 Moses Austin followed the Old San Antonio Road into Texas; the following year, Stephen F. Austin followed in his father's footsteps. After a conference with Spanish authorities at San Antonio, the younger Austin explored the Texas Gulf Coastal prairies from the San Antonio River to the Brazos River, and, of course, chose this region as the site for the Austin Colony.

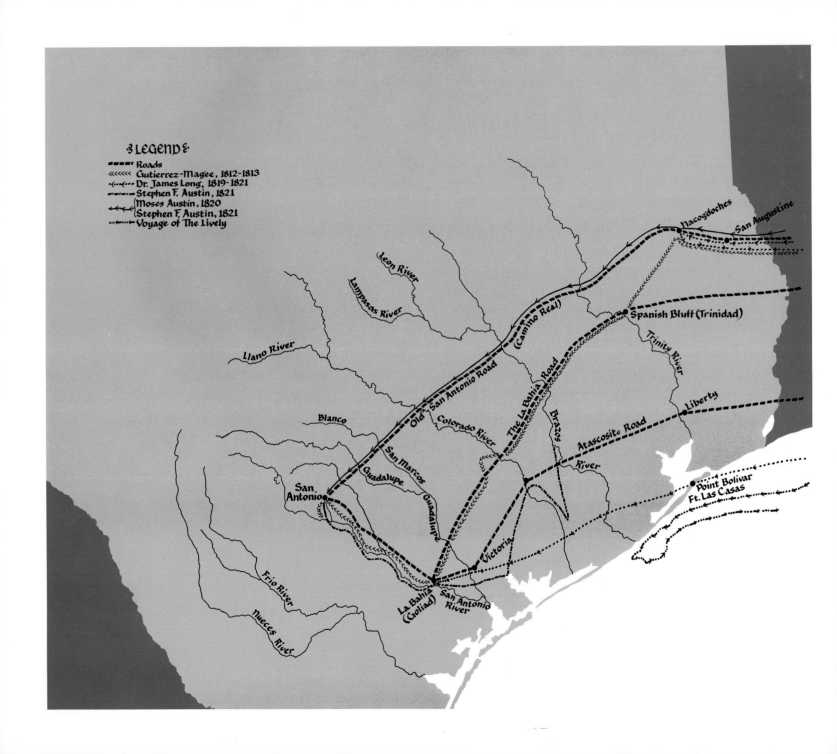

**LEGEND**

- - - - Roads
<<<<< Gutierrez-Magee, 1812-1813
-·-·-·- Dr. James Long, 1819-1821
- - - - Stephen F. Austin, 1821
———— Moses Austin, 1820
←←←← Stephen F. Austin, 1821
·····→ Voyage of The Lively

Leon River
Lampasas River
Llano River
Blanco
Nueces River
Frio River
San Antonio
Guadalupe
San Marcos
Guadalupe
Colorado River
Old San Antonio Road
(Camino Real)
The La Bahia Road
Brazos River
Atascosito Road
Liberty
Spanish Bluff (Trinidad)
Trinity River
Nacogdoches
San Augustine
Victoria
La Bahia (Goliad)
San Antonio River
Point Bolivar
Ft. Las Casas

The glamorous activities of the filibustering expedition have caught the eye of both the historian and his reader. In the meanwhile, however, an equally important advance (if not more important) of American settlers was quietly taking place in the canebrakes bordering the Red River and in the forests of deep Northeast Texas.

# THE NORTHEAST TEXAS FRONTIER, 1810-1820

 THE FIRST AMERICAN SETTLERS to enter Spanish Texas came to the fertile valley of the Red River and the Pine Belt of deep East Texas. In the extreme north, hunters and traders from Tennessee and Kentucky moved west through what was then the Territory of Arkansas to establish crude family dwellings along the Red River in what is now southeastern Oklahoma. It was inevitable that a few of these people would cross to the south bank of the Red and establish homes in Spanish Texas.

Pecan Point, a well-known landmark for many decades before the War of 1812, became a focus of settlement along the southern bank of the Red River when several fugitives from justice took up residence there in 1811. In the summer of 1815, George and Alex Wetmore built a trading post near the ancient buffalo crossing of the Red, and a few months later William Mabbitt set up a rival trading house. Permanent Anglo-American settlement began in 1816 when Walter Pool and Charles Burkham settled at Pecan Point. In September, 1816, they were joined by the Claiborne Wright family. By 1818 five Indian traders and twelve families were living at this center of settlement.

Jonesborough, a second settlement, was located near the junction of Lower Pine Creek and the Red River. The community was named for Henry Jones, who hunted along the river as early as 1815. Other settlers moving into the Jonesborough community between 1815 and 1817 included Adam Lawrence, Caleb Greenwood, William Hensley, William Cooper, and John Ragsdale. Other pioneer families in the Pecan Point-Jonesborough area included those of Andrew Robinson, Jonathan Anderson, Henry Stout, William Scrutchfield, William Rabb, and Joseph English.

In 1820 Miller County was created by the legislature of the Territory of Arkansas; the lands south of the Red River were included within the boundaries of the new county. In addition to the frontier settlements along the Red River, it is well known that thousands of other American backwoodsmen crossed the Sabine River into Spanish Texas long before 1820-1821. Eugene C. Barker points out that these squatters were located in five well-defined groups: (1) around Nacogdoches, (2) in the vicinity of present San Augustine (Ayish Bayou), (3) in the territory known as the

• Ft. Towson (1824)
• Jonesborough Settlement
• Miller County Courthouse
• Pecan Point Settlement
TRAMMEL'S
TRACE

Boundary of Miller County, Arkansas

Municipality of TENAHA

Nacogdoches •
Ayish Bayou •
Sabinetown •

municipality of Tenaha, (4) near Sabinetown, and (5) on the lower Trinity and San Jacinto rivers. All of these pioneer settlers were without title to their lands (because of their illegal entry) and, as a result, information concerning them is fragmentary and difficult to find. It is of significance, however, that American names began to appear in the census reports, now a part of the Nacogdoches Archives, as early as the 1790's.

Eugene C. Barker, *The Life of Stephen F. Austin: Founder of Texas* (Nashville, 1925).
Rex Strickland, "Miller County, Arkansas Territory: The Frontier That Men Forgot," *Chronicles of Oklahoma*, XVIII (1940).

# EMPRESARIO GRANTS, 1821-1834

IN 1821 Mexico won her independence from Spain and by the Imperial Colonization Law of January 3, 1823, confirmed a Spanish grant of January 27, 1821, to Moses Austin by transferring the provisions of the earlier grant to Stephen F. Austin. In opening the door of the frontier to foreigners, the law invited immigrants of Roman Catholic faith to settle in Mexico and provided for the employment of immigration agents, known as empresarios, to settle families on the vacant lands of Texas. The empresario system was continued by the National Colonization Law of 1824 and the State Colonization Law of March 25, 1825, and the major empresarios (and some of the minor) are listed on the following map. Beginning on the Red River in northeast Texas and moving south and west (counter-clockwise) the primary empresario grants were as follows:

1. Arthur G. Wavell, a native of Scotland and a soldier of fortune, became interested in Texas land because of his friendship with Stephen F. Austin and Benjamin R. Milam. On March 9, 1826, the state legislature awarded Wavell a grant to settle 400-500 families in the border zone along the Red River and Louisiana boundary. Wavell, however, was completely unsuccessful in his attempt to develop the lands of his grant.

2. Dr. John Cameron, another native of Scotland, received an empresario contract to settle 100 families along the Colorado River and another grant for a colony immediately south of the Red River. Cameron is typical of the land speculator type that descended on the government of Coahuila and Texas during the late 1820's and early 1830's. It should be obvious that Cameron had no chance to fulfill his contracts.

3. J. L. Woodbury and Company received a grant covering the lands west of the Colorado River in the heart of the Texas Hill Country and Edwards Plateau. It was completely unreasonable to expect colonization to succeed so far west; therefore, Woodbury and his associates made no attempt to settle families in this region.

4. The Department of Bexar retained complete jurisdiction over a large strip of the Texas Hill Country west of San Antonio as well as the San Antonio River valley between San Antonio and the ten league coastal zone.

5. The McMullen and McGloin Colony was founded in 1828 by John McMullen and James McGloin. San Patricio and the adjacent territory was their leading settlement. The McMullen and McGloin contract was suspended by the Law of April 6, 1830, and renewed in 1834—too late for any effective action.

6. James Power and James Hewetson were granted special permission on September 29, 1826, to establish a colony within the ten league coastal zone between Corpus Christi Bay and San Antonio Bay. These two energetic empresarios brought 350 Irish settlers to Texas during the years that followed.

7. Martín de León, a native of Mexico, was granted permission to establish a colony along the lower Guadalupe River. Beginning his colony in 1825 as an adjunct to his cattle ranch, De León established a settlement in the vicinity of present Victoria, Texas.

8. Green C. DeWitt, a native of Kentucky, was one of the first Americans to become interested in a Texas colonization enterprise. He was awarded a grant by the state legislature in April, 1825, to settle 400 families along the Guadalupe River between the De León grant and the Old San Antonio Road. With the assistance of James Kerr and Byrd Lockhart, DeWitt established the settlement of Gonzales at the junction of Kerr's Creek and the Guadalupe. By 1830 the DeWitt colony was fairly well settled.

9. Benjamin R. Milam was awarded an empresario contract to the lands immediately west of the Old San Antonio Road and south of the Colorado River. Because of his many other interests, Milam did not develop his colony.

10. Stephen F. Austin was awarded four grants in all, covering in general the lands between the Brazos and Colorado rivers from the Texas Gulf Coast to the Western Cross Timbers. These extensive grants will be covered in more detail on the map that immediately follows.

11. Sterling C. Robertson and the Nashville Company received a grant to the land northwest of the Old San Antonio Road and between the Navasota River on the east and the Brazos-Colorado watershed on the west, and extending northwest to the Old Comanche Trail in the Western Cross Timbers. Robertson lost his rights under the restrictive terms of the Law of April 6, 1830, and the Robertson grant was transferred to Stephen F. Austin and Samuel M. Williams.

12. In extreme East Texas, the woodland region was granted to Vicente Filisola, David G. Burnet, Joseph Vehlein (a German merchant in Mexico City), and Lorenzo de Zavala. None of these empresarios was successful and in the early 1830's they transferred their colonization rights to the Galveston Bay and Texas Land Company.

In the years between 1830 and 1832, Dr. John Charles Beales and others (under the name of the Rio Grande and Texas Land Company) received contracts from the Coahuila and Texas government for the establishment of a colony or colonies in far West Texas. Beales's one attempt, the settlement at Dolores in the arid region of Southwest Texas, resulted in failure.

H. H. Bancroft, *The North Mexican States and Texas* (2 vols., San Francisco, 1882-1890).

David Vigness, *The Revolutionary Decades* (Austin, 1965).

Louis J. Wortham, *A History of Texas* (5 vols., Fort Worth, 1924).

Vito Alessio Robles, *Coahuila y Texas* (2 vols., Mexico, 1945-46).

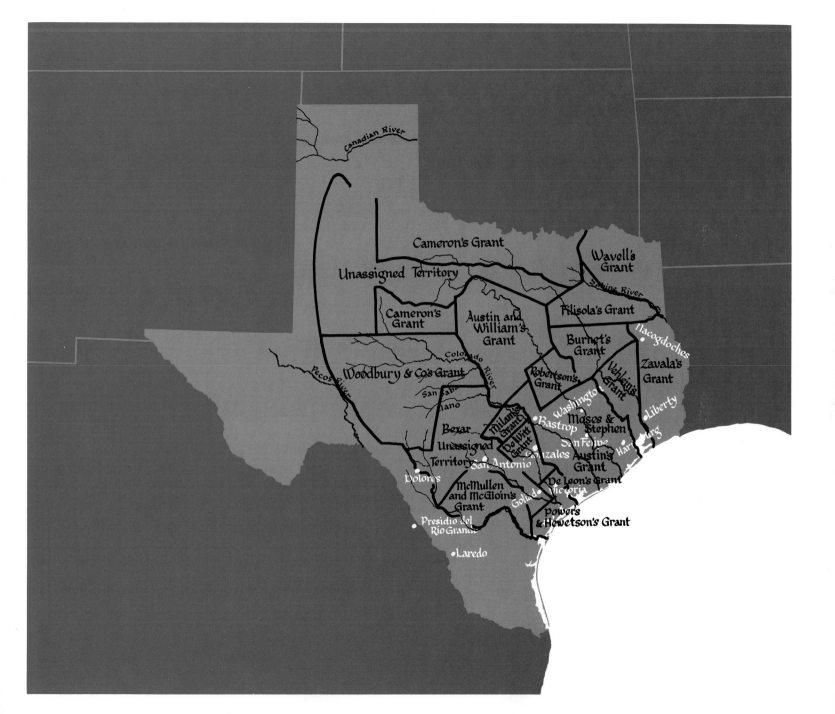

# THE STEPHEN F. AUSTIN COLONY,
## 1822-1836

OF ALL the Anglo-American colonies in Mexican Texas, that of Stephen F. Austin was far and away the most significant. In spite of the several grants awarded to Austin, the heartland of his colony—and the heartland of the Anglo-American Texas—was that portion of the present state bounded by the San Jacinto River on the east, the Old San Antonio Road on the north and west, and the Lavaca River on the southwest. It was in this region that more than 8000 Americans settled prior to the Texas Revolution. With the possible exception of the Green DeWitt Colony and the Martín de León Colony, the Austin Colony stands alone as the only successful American colonization experiment in Texas, and, strange as it may seem, it was this area that offered the most resistance to separation from Mexico during the months just prior to the outbreak of the Texas Revolution.

San Felipe de Austin, located at the Atascosita crossing of the Brazos River, was established in July, 1823, as the headquarters of the colony by Baron de Bastrop and others. From the date of its founding until its destruction by Sam Houston's army in April, 1836, San Felipe was the most important settlement in Anglo-American Texas. In his *Evolution of a State*, Noah Smithwick recalls that "The town was still in its swaddling clothes when the writer made his advent there in 1827. Twenty-five or perhaps thirty log cabins strung along the west bank of the Brazos River was all there was of it, while the whole human population of all ages and colors could not have exceeded 200."

Smithwick, in what he calls "a pen picture of the old town," points to the leading residents of San Felipe in 1827 as Stephen F. Austin, Seth and Ira Ingram, Hosea N. League, David G. Burnet, William Pettus, Jonathan Peyton, Walter White, Godwin B. Cotten, Gail Borden, Thomas J. Pilgrim, and others. Other towns in the Austin Colony included Brazoria, established in 1828 as a river port by John Austin; Richmond, founded in 1822 by Randal and Henry Jones; Columbia, surveyed in 1826 by Josiah H. Bell; Washington-on-the-Brazos, established in 1822-23 when Andrew Robinson began operating a ferry across the river, was actually laid out as a townsite by John Hall, John W. Kinney, and Asa Hoxey in 1830; Bastrop, a settlement in the "upper colony," was established as Mina in 1829 by William (Uncle Billy) Barton, Reuben Hornsby, and Josiah Wilbarger; and Velasco, located four miles from the mouth of the Brazos, dates from the voyage of the *Lively* in 1821. As the years passed, other communities were founded near the coast at Harrisburg, Lynch's Ferry (Lynchburg), Stafford's Prairie House, New Kentucky, and New Washington. Further inland settlements were founded at Bolivar, Columbus, Beason's Ferry, Burnham's Crossing (La Grange), and at a score of rural agricultural locations.

In the spring of 1834, Colonel Juan N. Almonte reported on the Austin Colony as a part of the Department of the Brazos: "The following are the municipalities and towns of the Department, with the population:—San Felipe, 2,500; Columbia, 2,100; Matagorda,

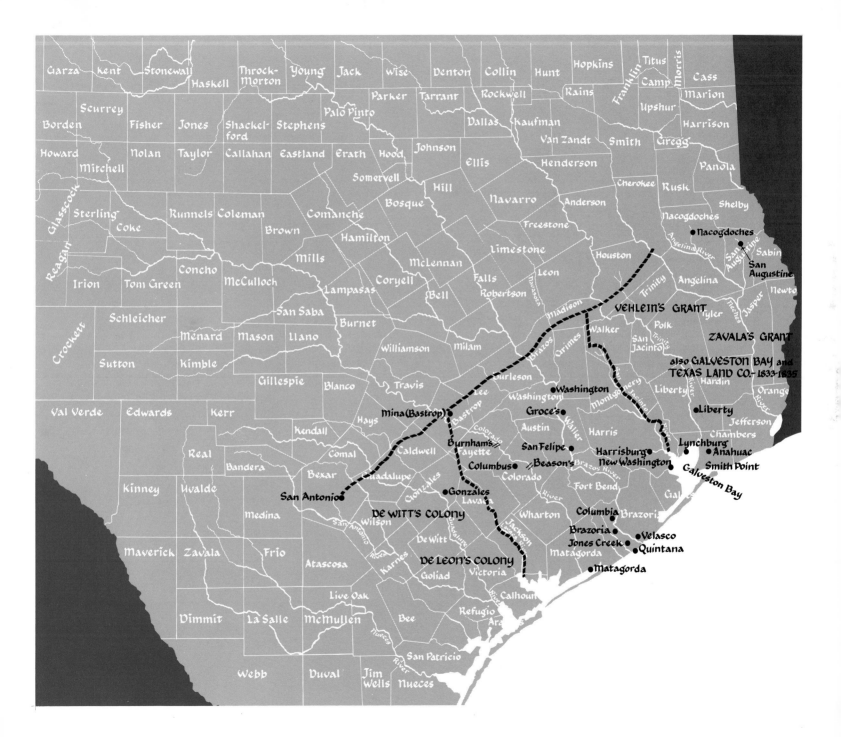

1,400; Gonzales, 900; Mina, 1,100: total 8000. Towns: Brazoria, Harrisburg, Velasco, Bolivar. . . . The most prosperous colonies of this Department are those of Austin and DeWitt."

Stephen F. Austin's Map of Texas, 1829, Archives, Texas State Library.

Eugene C. Barker, *The Life of Stephen F. Austin, Founder of Texas* (Nashville, 1925); *Readings in Texas History* (Dallas, 1929).

Ernest Wallace and David M. Vigness, *Documents of Texas History* (Lubbock, 1960).

# SAN FELIPE DE AUSTIN

 SAN FELIPE DE AUSTIN, located at the old Atascosita crossing on the Brazos River, was chosen as the "capital" of the Austin Colony by Stephen F. Austin and Baron de Bastrop. The townsite was surveyed in July, 1823, on a high prairie overlooking the south bank of the Brazos. In July, 1824, the "Plan de la Villa de Austin" was drawn up, probably by Baron de Bastrop. This annotated drawing reveals the rectangular survey characteristic of all Spanish-Mexican towns. The main village was located between Calle del Rio on the north and Calle Campos Santo (the cemetery) on the south. From west to east, the north-south streets were Calle Calegio, Calle Lucas Alamán, Calle Antonio Martínez, Calle Baron de Bastrop, Calle Guadalupe Victoria, Calle Nicolás Bravo, Calle Vicente Guerrero, Calle Manuel Mier y Terán, Calle Luciano García, Calle Felix Trespalacios, and Calle de Hospicio. It is most interesting that the street names honored the courageous political leaders of the Mexican War of Independence and the new Republic and, also, individuals prominent in the history of Spanish-Mexican Texas. The east-west streets, on the other hand, were simply numbered roadways. To the west of the main village with blocks subdivided into lots, proposed streets and undivided blocks spanned the Arroyo Dulce as the town planners provided for possible expansion. In the center of the town, Calle Nicolás Bravo and Calle Vicente Guerrero bounded three plazas (or squares)—the Commercial, the Constitutional, and the Military plazas. To the east, the planners provided for an almshouse and orphanage.

While plans are one thing, reality is another. The little town of San Felipe was destined to remain a small (but significant) village. In 1828 José María Sánchez visited the settlement and recorded: "It was a scattered little town of [forty or fifty] little wooden houses built in the image of the forest and cabin life of the North American frontier, out of logs interlocked at the corners and chinked with mud plaster." Sánchez noted two wretched little stores where whiskey, rum, sugar, coffee, rice, flour, lard, and cheap cloth could be bought. Despite the elaborate plan of its founders, Sánchez remembered that, at the time of his observation, there was no coherent plan to the village and the houses were scattered at random over the low, rolling land.

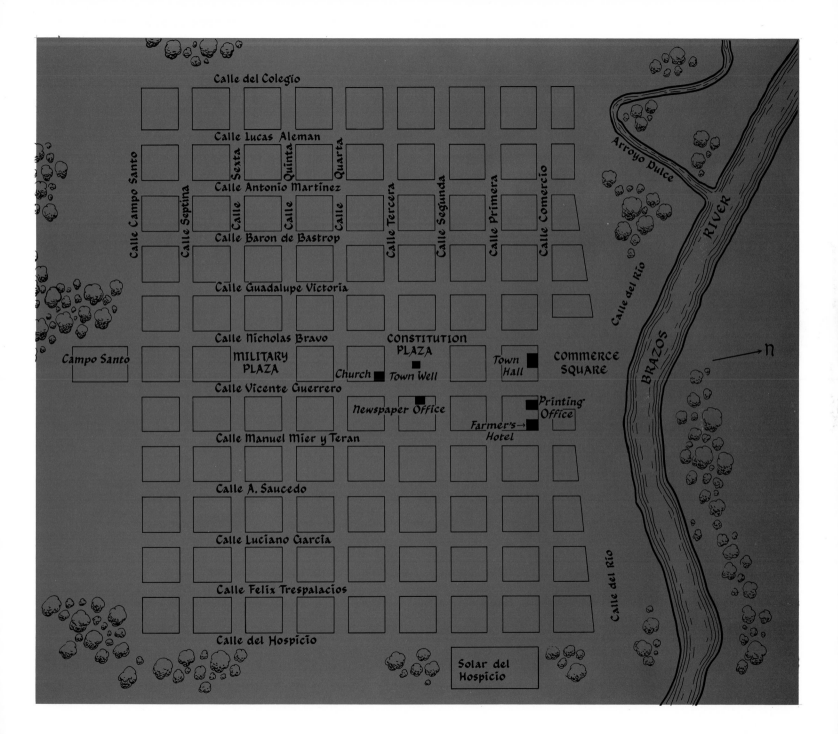

The best description of the village is that left by Noah Smithwick in his *Evolution of a State;* Smithwick paints a word picture of the village where, in 1828, he set up a blacksmith shop. Beginning with Stephen F. Austin's "headquarters something like a half a mile back from the river on the west bank of a little creek—Palmito [Dulce]—that ran into the Brazos just above the main village," Smithwick locates the farm of Joshua Parker, Seth and Ira Ingram's store, Hosea League's cabin, the law office of League and David G. Burnet, the "west end" residence of William (Buck) Pettus, and "going on down to the town proper," the Smithwick bachelor abode and blacksmith shop, Jonathan C. Peyton's tavern, the saloon of Cooper and Cheeves, Dinsmore's store, Walter White's store, the office of the "Cotton Plant," Godwin B. Cotten's residence, and the Whiteside Hotel.

Using the Smithwick description, Bob Abernathy of Waco drew a photographic map of San Felipe for Robert E. Davis' *The Diary of William Barret Travis;* an adaptation of this drawing appears on the preceding page with the town plat of 1824.

Robert E. Davis (ed.), *The Diary of William Barret Travis, August 30, 1833-June 26, 1834* (Waco, 1966).

Plan de Villa de Austin, 1 Julio de 1824, Archives, General Land Office, Austin, Texas.

Noah Smithwick, *The Evolution of a State* (Austin, 1900; reproduced, 1935).

# TEXAS, 1821-1836

 DURING the Mexican period, Texas was a land of opportunity for the thousands of people who felt oppressed in the more settled sections of the United States. The settlement of the lands beyond the Sabine, as has been so expertly pointed out by the late Eugene C. Barker, appeared as a lucrative adventure to the Anglo-American frontiersmen because of (1) the abolition of credit in the public land program of the United States, (2) the inflexible credit policy of the bank of the United States, (3) the economic depression known as the Panic of 1819, and (4) the rapid westward advance of the American frontier. Between 1821 and 1836, somewhere in the neighborhood of 30,000 to 35,000 Americans crossed the Sabine and Red rivers to settle in Mexican Texas.

These people settled in communities from Sabinetown and Bevilport on the east to Gonzales and San Antonio on the southwest. The principal settlements appear on the map: San Augustine, Nacogdoches, Liberty, and Anahuac in deep East Texas; Harrisburg, Velasco, Brazoria, Columbia, Washington, and San Felipe in present Southeast Texas; and Gonzales stands alone as the westernmost advance of the American colonist.

On the eve of the revolution, Texas was divided into three departments—the Department of Bexar, the Department of Brazos, and the Department of Nacogdoches. Each of these areas had one representative in the legislature of Coahuila and Texas at Saltillo, the state capital. In the light of future developments it is noteworthy that the northwestern line of settlement paralleled the Old San Antonio Road. Beyond this line

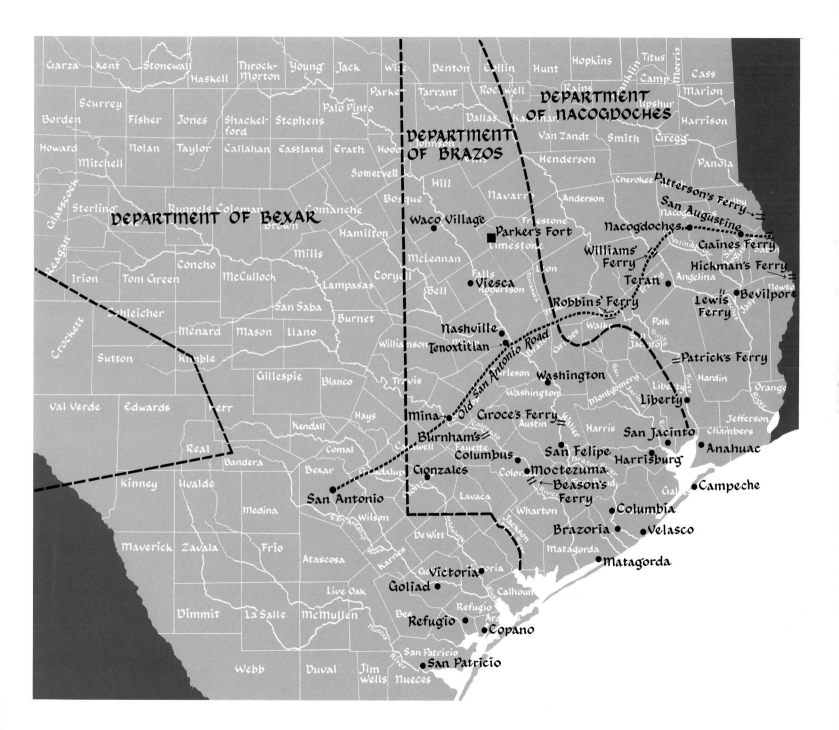

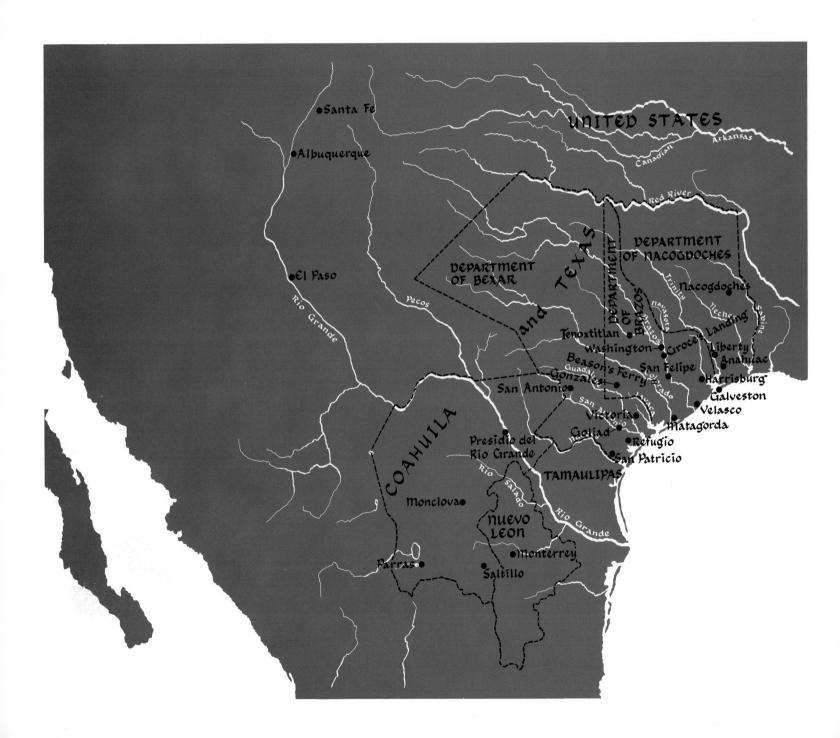

the only settlements were (1) at Wheelock, a block-house east of the Brazos River built by E. L. R. Wheelock in 1835; (2) at Nashville-on-the-Brazos, established on the right bank of the river by Sterling C. Robertson in 1835; (3) at Tenoxtitlán, a small settlement near the Brazos crossing of the Old San Antonio Road; and (4) at Parker's Fort, a blockhouse built near the headwaters of the Navasota River by Silas M. and James W. Parker for the protection of their families. These four settlements, however, were exceptions to the general rule; it can be said that in 1836 the frontier line of settlement lay southeast of the ancient road from Bexar to Nacogdoches.

# SAN ANTONIO IN THE 1830's

 IN THE LATE YEARS of the Mexican period, San Antonio de Bexar was, in the eyes of the Mexican people, the most significant settlement north of the Rio Grande. Explored by Domingo Terán de los Ríos, Father Damian Massanet, Father Antonio Olivares, and Father Isidro Espinosa, Martín de Alarcón established the mission San Antonio de Valero and the villa de Bexar in the spring of 1718; in March, 1731, the Canary Island colonists arrived, and in 1773 San Antonio de Bexar became the official seat of the Spanish government in Texas. On the eve of the Texas Revolution, a century and a quarter after its establishment, San Antonio had a population of 2400 and was the seat of local government for the Department of Bexar, state of Coahuila and Texas.

In 1834-35 San Antonio was centered about the horseshoe bend in the San Antonio River. Mission San Antonio de Valero (the Alamo) was located a short distance northeast of the river and north of La Villita. The streets in La Villita included the Calle a la Nueva Villa and the Calle de la Villita. The village was connected to the San Antonio de Valero complex by the Calle de la Mission. The Calle de la Alameda, an east-ward extension of the Camino Real al Presidio de Rio Grande, ran northeast into the Camino Real or Old San Antonio Road. To the southeast the Camino Real a la Bahía led into the open country in the direction of La Bahía and the settlements on the lower San Antonio River.

West of the river, the main section of town lay along the Camino Real al Presidio del Rio Grande and the Calle de la Soledad (the street of loneliness or solitude). It was here that the two main plazas—the Plaza de los Islas (Main Plaza), named in honor of the Canary Island settlers, and the Plaza de Armas (Military Plaza)—were located some two blocks apart between the Camino Real and Calle Dolorosa (street of sorrow). The Plaza de Armas was flanked by the Spanish governor's palace to the west and San Fernando church to the east. It is interesting to note that the plaza and cathedral were bordered by Dolorosa and Amarguras—sorrow and bitterness—two subjects falling within the sphere of clerical duties.

The north-to-south cross streets, in order from the Campo Santo cemetery on the west to the river on the east included the Camino Real a Laredo, Calle del

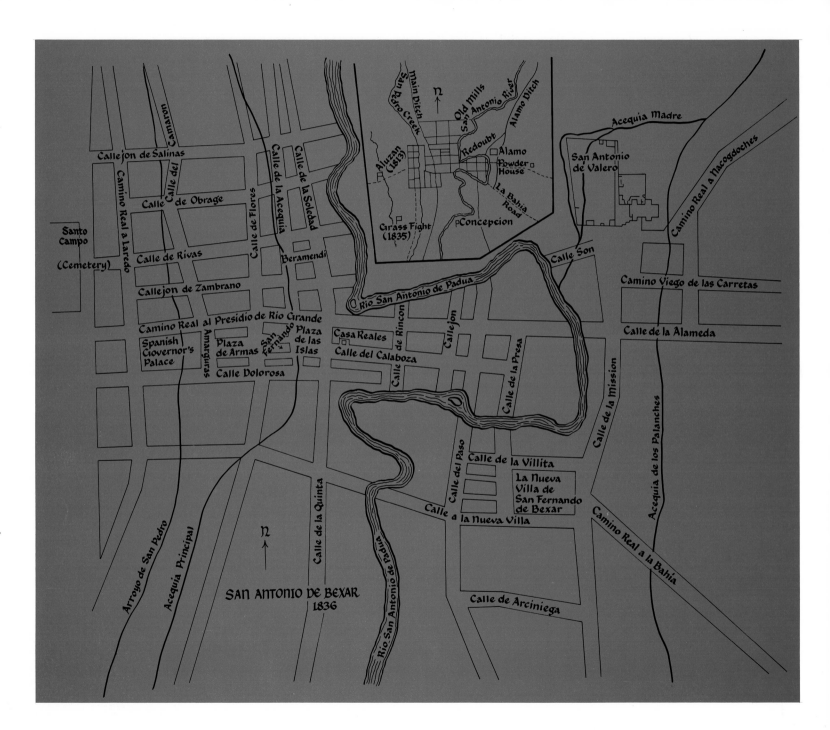

Callejon de Salinas
Calle del Camaron
Calle de Obrage
Calle de Flores
Calle de la Acequia
Calle de la Soledad
Camino Real a Laredo
Santo Campo
(Cemetery)
Calle de Rivas
Callejon de Zambrano
Camino Real al Presidio de Rio Grande
Spanish Governor's Palace
Plaza de Armas
San Fernando
Amarguras
Plaza de las Islas
Beramendi
Calle Dolorosa

Sierra Creek
San Pedro Creek
Main Ditch
San Antonio River
Old Mills
Alamo Ditch
N
Aluzan (1813)
Redoubt
Alamo
Powder House
La Bahia Road
Grass Fight (1835)
Concepcion

Acequia Madre
San Antonio de Valero
Camino Real a Nacogdoches

Rio San Antonio de Padua
Calle Son
Camino Viego de las Carretas
Calle de la Alameda

Casa Reales
Calle de Rincon
Callejon
Calle del Calaboza
Calle de la Presa
Calle de la Mission
Acequia de los Palanches

Calle del Paso
Calle de la Villita
La Nueva Villa de San Fernando de Bexar

Calle de la Quinta
Arroyo de San Pedro
Acequia Principal

N

Rio San Antonio de Padua
Calle a la Nueva Villa

SAN ANTONIO DE BEXAR
1836

Calle de Arciniega

Camino Real a la Bahia

Camarón (so-called because of the crayfish in San Pedro Creek), Calle de Flores, Calle de Acequia (near the main aqueduct), and Calle de Soledad—a street that became Calle de Quinta (street of the countryhouse) in the south part of town. The east-to-west streets, in order from north to south, included Calle Don de Salina, Calle de Obrage (street of arts and crafts), Calle de Rivas, Callejón de Zambrano, El Camino Real, and Calle Dolorosa—with the exception of the last two and the Calle de Obrage, all of these streets were named for families residing on them. Between the Plaza de Islas and the river, filling out the river bend, the Calle de Calaboza (street of the jail) parallels El Camino Real; the north-south cross streets included Calle de Rincón (street of the corner). This small town, whose residents were about to witness much fighting and bloodshed, was nothing more than a quiet, dignified village in the years 1833-1834—a symbol of Spanish-Mexican civilization north of the Rio Grande.

Hubert H. Brancroft, *A History of the North Mexican States and Texas* (San Francisco, 1889).

Charles Ramsdell, *San Antonio, A Historical and Pictorial Guide* (Austin, 1959).

Richard G. Santos, A Descriptive Map of San Antonio, Archives, Texas State Library, Austin, Texas.

# THE SIEGE & CAPTURE OF SAN ANTONIO: DECEMBER 1835

 THE SKIRMISH that signaled the beginning of the Texas Revolution took place in the foggy bottom of the Guadalupe River valley at Gonzales on October 2, 1835, when Captain Francisco Castañeda and about 100 men attempted to claim a small cannon. In the days that immediately followed, the Texas Army was organized with Stephen F. Austin as commander-in-chief assisted by a staff of Peter W. Grayson, W. D. C. Hall, William H. Wharton, Patrick C. Jack, and William T. Austin. John H. Moore, Edward Burleson, and Alexander Somervell were elected field commanders. On October 12, the small army crossed the Guadalupe and on the following day took up a line of march for San Antonio, the citadel of Mexican military power in Texas, where General Martín P. Cós commanded a sizable garrison of troops. While on the march, Austin did everything possible to convert his rugged individualists into an effective fighting force. The line of march carried the Texans to Cibolo Creek on October 16, Salado Creek on October 20, the Mission Espada on the San Antonio River on October 27, 1835—the siege of San Antonio began. Except for fighting near Mission Concepción on October 28-29, the siege of San Antonio continued throughout the month of November. As the Texan command (Stephen F. Austin had left the army to go on his mission to the United States) debated the possibility of abandoning the siege and returning to winter quar-

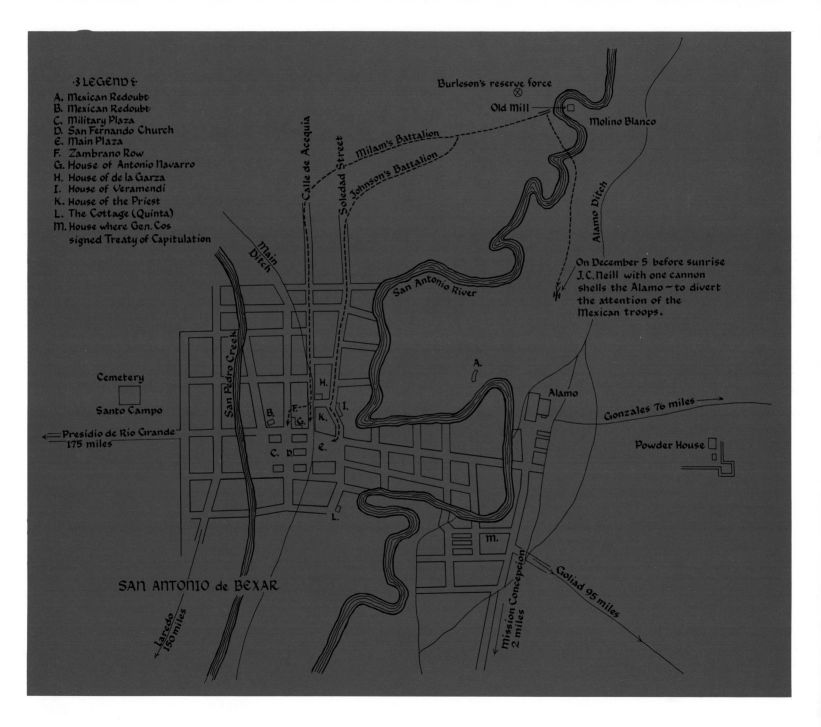

·3 LEGEND ⸙·
A. Mexican Redoubt
B. Mexican Redoubt
C. Military Plaza
D. San Fernando Church
E. Main Plaza
F. Zambrano Row
G. House of Antonio Navarro
H. House of de la Garza
I. House of Veramendi
K. House of the Priest
L. The Cottage (Quinta)
M. House where Gen. Cos
signed Treaty of Capitulation

Burleson's reserve force

Old Mill

Molino Blanco

Calle de Acequia

Soledad Street

Milam's Battalion

Johnson's Battalion

Alamo Ditch

On December 5 before sunrise
J.C. Neill with one cannon
shells the Alamo — to divert
the attention of the
Mexican troops.

Main Ditch

San Antonio River

San Pedro Creek

Cemetery

Santo Campo

A.

Alamo

Gonzales 76 miles

← Presidio de Rio Grande
175 miles

H.

I.

B.

F.

G.

K.

C. D.

E.

Powder House

L.

m.

SAN ANTONIO de BEXAR

Laredo
150 miles

Mission Concepcion
2 miles

Goliad 95 miles

ters, Frank W. Johnson and Benjamin R. Milam rallied the men to an attack on December 4, 1835; the assault on the city began on December 5.

In preparation for the battle, General Edward Burleson divided his small force into three divisions: the reserve force, under the command of Burleson, to remain outside the town for subsequent commitment where needed, and two assault forces commanded by Benjamin R. Milam and Frank W. Johnson. The troops under the command of Milam and Johnson were to make contact with the Mexican Army of General Martín P. Cós; the Mexican commander had concentrated his troops in the vicinity of the Alamo, east of the San Antonio River, and around Military Plaza due west of the river and the center of town. The Texas commanders assembled the attack force at the "Old Mill" on the San Antonio River north of town. From this point, Milam's battalion entered the first street (Calle de Acequia) "from the river running north from the plaza" with the occupation of the De la Garza house as its primary objective (actually the second street west of the river), while Johnson's battalion entered the street nearest the river (Soledad Street) with the home of the Veramendi family as the primary objective. From these two points of vantage,

the plan of battle called for an advance toward the plaza, fighting from house to house with the priest's house and Zambrano row as the final objectives of the Texans. On the morning of December 5, 1835, under cover of a diversionary artillery attack (one gun) on the Alamo, the initial parts of the plan were carried out with success. During the next four days (with Burleson's force standing in reserve at the "Old Mill"), house to house fighting was the main feature of the battle; on the afternoon of December 7, the venerable Ben Milam was killed by Mexican rifle fire; on the following morning (December 8) the Texans began their assault on Zambrano row; before nightfall this objective had been cleared of the enemy, and later in the evening the priest's house fell to the Texans. Faced with an untenable position, the Mexicans sent a flag of truce to the Texan positions on the morning of December 9, and on the following day, General Cós signed surrender terms—the San Antonio campaign had been a belated but complete success.

A. J. Houston, Military Maps of the Texas Revolution to accompany "Texas Independence, 1835-1836," Archives, Texas State Library, Austin, Texas.

Louis J. Wortham, A History of Texas (5 vols., Fort Worth, 1924).

# THE TEXAS REVOLUTION:
# THE MEXICAN INVASION OF 1836

THE BATTLES at Gonzales and San Antonio in the fall and early winter of 1835 constitute the first part of the military history of the Texas Revolution. The second and final phase centered around a massive invasion of Texas by a Mexican Army led by Antonio López de Santa Anna (ably assisted by generals Vicente Filisola, José Urrea, Martín P. Cós, Joaquín Ramirez y Sesma, Antonio Gaona, and others). After marching on Zacatecas in the spring of 1835 to defeat a group of provincial rebels led by Francisco Garcia, Santa Anna decided to put down the Federalist uprising in Coahuila and Texas himself. Despite the fact that conditions in Mexico pointed to instability, Santa Anna journeyed to San Luis Potosí in November, 1835, to organize his army. Once the problems of organization and training new recruits had been partially solved, Santa Anna began his march toward Texas and San Antonio de Bexar. He divided his troops into three divisions: The main army, commanded by Santa Anna in person, took the so-called upper road by way of Monclova and the Presidio de Rio Grande to San Antonio; a second group, under the direction of Joaquín Ramirez y Sesma moved from Saltillo in the direction of Laredo, and then to San Antonio; while a third, commanded by the efficient José Urrea, traveled by way of Ciudad Victoria and Matamoros to move eventually up the Texas Gulf Coast in support of the invaders' right flank.

Despite shortcomings in plans and organization, all went fairly well as Santa Anna and Ramirez y Sesma approached San Antonio de Bexar, their first objective.

After a few days delay in order to appraise the situation, this force destroyed the defenders of the Alamo on March 6, 1836. In the meantime José Urrea's troops moved from Matamoros to the Nueces River. Here they defeated and largely destroyed the Texan Matamoros expedition under the command of Frank W. Johnson and Dr. James Grant. After the victory at the Alamo, Santa Anna sent his army in the general direction of Gonzales in pursuit of the small force inherited by Sam Houston. In the third week of March, Urrea captured the entire command of James B. Fannin in the battle of Coleto Creek as the Texans attempted to evacuate the Goliad area. In the meanwhile, Sam Houston began his tactical "retreat" from Gonzales, to the Navidad, to Burnham's Crossing, to Beason's Crossing, to San Felipe, up the Brazos to Groce's Crossing and Donahue's plantation. The Mexican Army under Ramirez y Sesma and Santa Anna followed. While these events were taking place, Urrea's command moved, without serious opposition, to the Brazos River towns of Columbia and Brazoria. Having missed a battle with the Texans near Beason's Ferry, Santa Anna moved toward San Felipe, then down the west bank of the river to cross at Thompson's Ferry, near present Richmond. From there, he moved in haste to Harrisburg, and from Harrisburg to New Washington, a relatively new settlement on Morgan's Point. While these movements were taking place, Houston rested his forces at Donahue's place, and then he moved his rather small army to Harrisburg and the western shore of San Jacinto Bay. Thus the stage was set for the

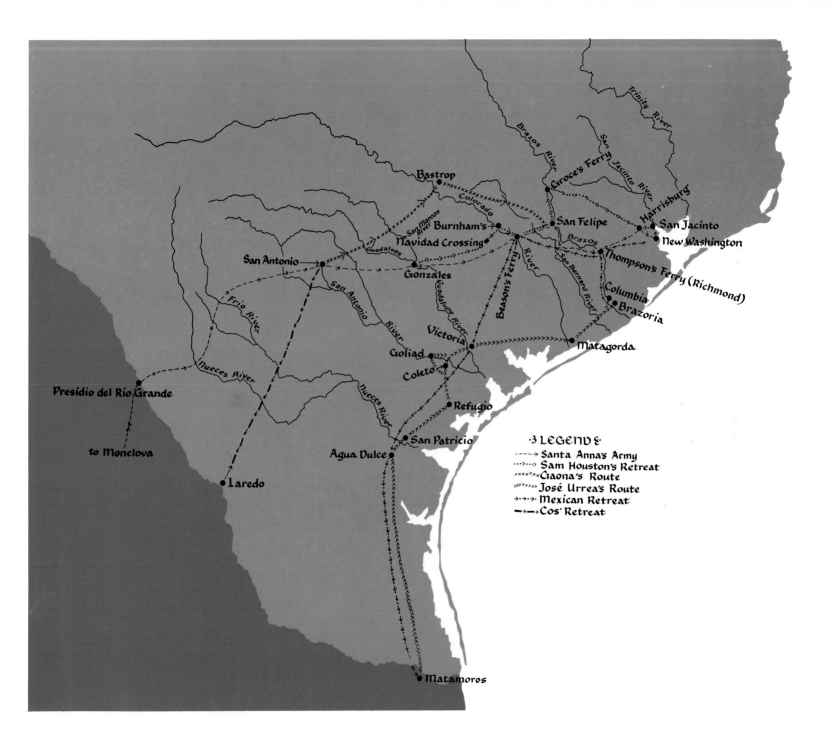

Bastrop

Groce's Ferry

Harrisburg

Trinity River

Brazos River

San Jacinto River

San Jacinto

San Felipe

New Washington

Burnham's

Navidad Crossing

San Marcos River

Colorado

San Antonio

Gonzales

Guadalupe

Thompson's Ferry (Richmond)

Brazos River

San Bernard River

Columbia

Brazoria

Guadalupe River

Beason's Ferry

Frio River

San Antonio River

Victoria

Matagorda

Goliad

Coleto

Nueces River

Presidio del Rio Grande

Refugio

to Monclova

Nueces River

San Patricio

Agua Dulce

Laredo

·3 LEGEND &·
---‣ Santa Anna's Army
·····‣ Sam Houston's Retreat
xxxxxx Gaona's Route
‣‣‣‣ José Urrea's Route
·‣·‣· Mexican Retreat
—‣— Cos' Retreat

Matamoros

deciding battle of the revolution—the battle of San Jacinto on April 21, 1836. After the destruction of Santa Anna's army and capture of Santa Anna, all the remaining Mexican forces could do (apparently) was to gather on the Colorado (after a short stay on the Brazos near Richmond) and, under the command of Vicente Filisola and José Urrea, begin their long retreat to the Rio Grande near Matamoros. The revolution had ended, but perhaps we should examine some of its parts in detail.

Carlos Castañeda (tr.), *The Mexican Side of the Texas Revolution* (Dallas, 1928).

Harbert Davenport, "The Men of Goliad," *Southwestern Historical Quarterly*, XLIII.

Amelia Williams, "A Critical Study of the Siege of the Alamo . . . .," *Southwestern Historical Quarterly*, XXXVI-XXXVII.

Louis J. Wortham, *A History of Texas* (5 vols., Fort Worth, 1924).

# THE ALAMO, MARCH 6, 1836

 ON THE EVE of March 6, 1836, General Antonio López de Santa Anna called his staff together for the final briefing concerning the assault on the Alamo—scheduled for the following morning. He told his senior officers that the infantry columns involved in the assault were to take position "at musket shot distance" from the first entrenchments and on a given bugle signal four columns commanded by General Martín P. Cós, Colonel Don Francisco Duque, Colonel José María Romero, and Colonel Juan Morales would move forward and attack the fortress. Santa Anna himself would command the reserve forces; Colonel Joaquín Ramirez y Sesma's cavalry units were "to scout the country, to prevent the possibility of an escape."

Reuben M. Potter, a resident of Matamoros who knew many of the officers involved and later questioned many of them about the particulars of the battle, reports that Santa Anna's plans were modified just before the initial assault so that five groups of in-

fantry were combined into three attacking columns. Santa Anna established his headquarters "about five hundred yards south of the Alamo near the old bridge." At the sound of a bugle the columns moved forward simultaneously in double quick time: Manuel Fernández Castrillón led the group attacking near a breach in the north wall; Martín P. Cós led the attack on the area including the chapel; while a third group, probably commanded by Juan Morales, attempted to scale the west barrier. All of the attacking forces were well equipped with ladders, crowbars, and axes; but their task was not easy. Castrillón's column was the first to arrive at the foot of the outer walls, but they were not the first to enter. The American guns, where Travis commanded, raked the north breach and brought Castrillón's column to a halt. Castrillón's troops passed through the breach shortly afterward, but in the meanwhile the column from the west crossed the barrier on that side at a point a little north of center. At the chapel, the troops under Cós were thrown back in

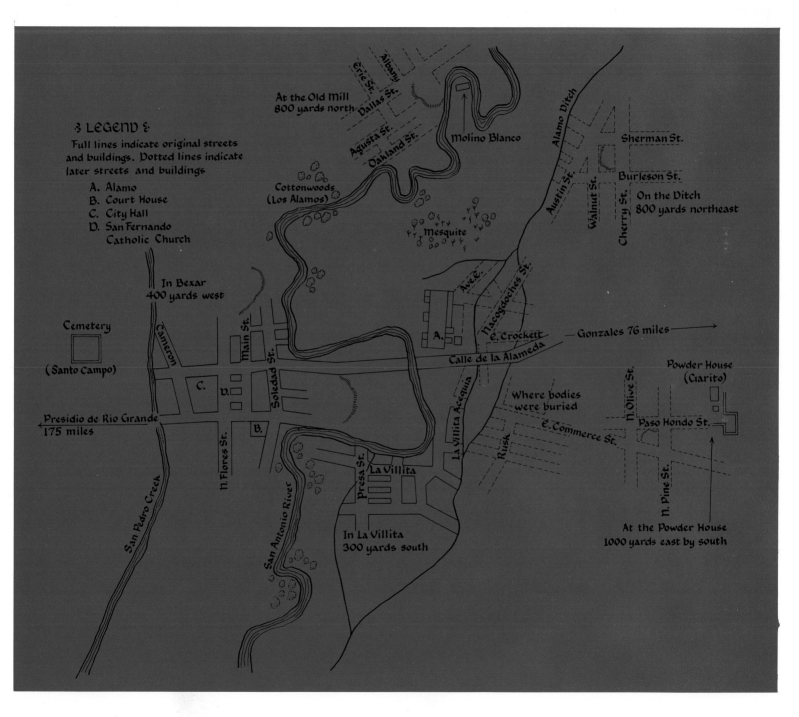

LEGEND

Full lines indicate original streets and buildings. Dotted lines indicate later streets and buildings

A. Alamo
B. Court House
C. City Hall
D. San Fernando Catholic Church

At the Old Mill
800 yards north

Molino Blanco

Erie St.
Albany
Dallas St.
Agusta St.
Oakland St.

Alamo Ditch

Sherman St.

Burleson St.

On the Ditch
800 yards northeast

Austin St.
Walnut St.
Cherry St.

Cottonwoods
(Los Alamos)

Mesquite

In Bexar
400 yards west

Cemetery

(Santo Campo)

Cameron

Main St.

Soledad St.

Ave. E.

Nacogdoches St.

A.

E. Crockett

Gonzales 76 miles →

Calle de la Alameda

Powder House
(Garito)

N. Olive St.

Where bodies
were buried

E. Commerce St.

Paso Hondo St.

C.

D.

Presidio de Rio Grande
175 miles

B.

N. Flores St.

La Villita Acequia

Rusk

Presa St.

La Villita

San Pedro Creek

San Antonio River

In La Villita
300 yards south

N. Pine St.

At the Powder House
1000 yards east by south

confusion and disorder to a point "behind the old stone stable and huts that stood south of the southwest angle"; there they were rallied and led inside the fortress by Juan Amador.

The outer walls and batteries were now abandoned by the defenders; the thinly manned outer defenses had crumbled and the Texans took refuge in the inner buildings, mainly in the long barracks—it was there that the main struggle took place, all of the defenders dying at their posts as room after room "was carried at the point of a bayonet." Some 180-odd Texans lay dead in the carnage, and the Mexican losses were extremely high.

Carlos Castañeda, *The Mexican Side of the Texas Revolution* (Dallas, 1928).

Richard G. Santos (ed.), *Santa Anna's Campaign Against Texas, 1835-1836* (Waco, 1968).

Amelia Williams, "A Critical Study of the Siege of the Alamo . . . ," *Southwestern Historical Quarterly,* XXXVI-XXXVII.

# THE BATTLE OF COLETO CREEK, MARCH 19-20, 1836

 ON MARCH 19, 1836, Colonel James Walker Fannin, Jr., and his command of some four hundred men began their leisurely retreat from Goliad toward Victoria. Fannin and his men knew that Mexican units under General José Urrea were in the area; indeed, most of the previous day had been spent in useless skirmishes with the enemy. It is possible, too, that the Texan commander had doubts about the fate of Amon B. King, who had been sent to Refugio on March 10 to extricate some stranded families and bring back some supplies, and William Ward, who, with his Georgia battalion, had been sent to the aid of King. Fannin had delayed in Goliad in hope of their return. Having moved some seven miles from Goliad, the entire party stopped for an hour to graze their oxen and to have breakfast. They had progressed another ten miles when they sighted the Mexican Army in their rear.

Believing that Fannin would remain in his Goliad fortification, Urrea was preparing to lay siege to the fort when he learned that the Americans had moved out. He immediately set out in pursuit with 370 infantry and 80 cavalry troops. When Fannin's soldiers saw the Mexicans approaching, they continued their march toward a densely wooded area ahead; however, their ammunition cart broke down while crossing a depression, and, completely cut off by the Mexican cavalry from both wood and water, the Texans were soon completely surrounded by the enemy.

In preparation for battle, Fannin arranged his men in a square or box; with, reports Ruby Cumby Smith, the Red Rovers and the New Orleans Grays in the front, John Duval's Mustangs in the rear, and his other troops on the sides. Urrea sent his cavalry troops to cut off the advance and deployed his infantry to complete the encirclement of the Texan forces. The battle

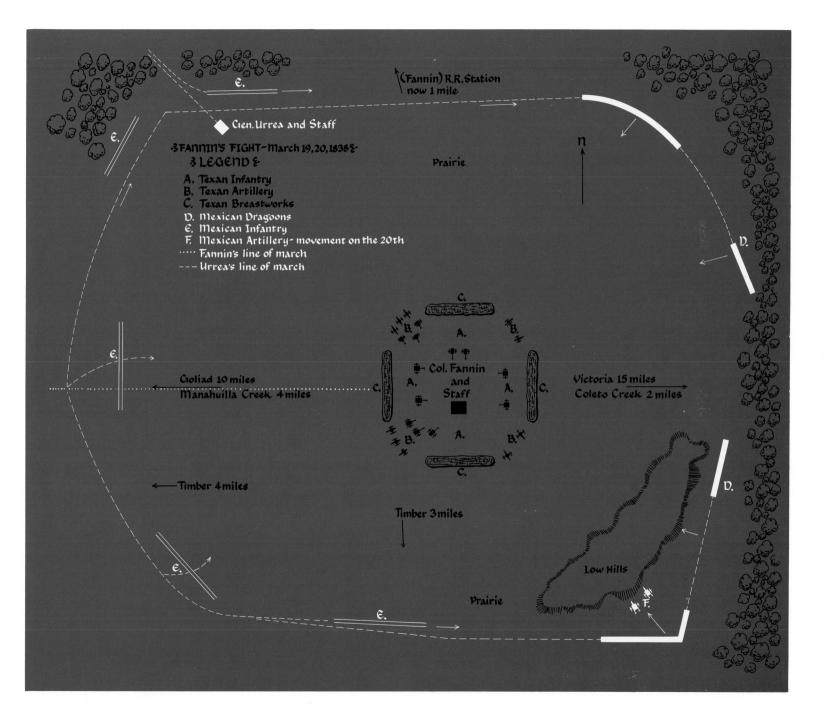

(Fannin) R.R.Station
now 1 mile

E.

n

Prairie

♦ Gen. Urrea and Staff

⅜ FANNIN'S FIGHT – March 19, 20, 1836 ⅜

⅜ LEGEND ⅜

A. Texan Infantry
B. Texan Artillery
C. Texan Breastworks
D. Mexican Dragoons
E. Mexican Infantry
F. Mexican Artillery – movement on the 20th
••••• Fannin's line of march
----- Urrea's line of march

E.

D.

C.

B.         A.         B.

A.         Col. Fannin         A.
           and
C.         Staff         C.

Goliad 10 miles
Manahuilla Creek 4 miles
B.         A.         B.
C.

Victoria 15 miles
Coleto Creek 2 miles

D.

← Timber 4 miles

Timber 3 miles

E.

Low Hills

F.

Prairie

E.

D.

lasted from mid-afternoon until dark; the Texas troops repulsed three Mexican attacks, and Urrea decided to wait for the arrival of his artillery before risking another assault. Sunset began a night of horror for Fannin and his men. The Texans were without lights, water, and provision, and they spent most of the night digging an entrenchment and in arranging their carts and carcasses of their dead animals in sort of a crude breastworks—escape was impossible.

Early the next morning (March 20) Urrea received a fresh supply of ammunition, two pieces of artillery, and reinforcements. A few rounds from Urrea's heavy guns and consideration of their hopeless position caused the Texans to deliberate on the possibility of surrender. Therefore, a white flag was raised and, following a conference, Fannin and his men signed an unconditional surrender. One historian writes "hunger, thirst, and tactical errors forced the Texans to surrender at discretion and at the mercy of the Mexican government, which meant the mercy of Antonio López de Santa Anna." The Texan casualties in the Coleto engagement were seven killed and sixty wounded; the Mexican losses have been set at 250 killed and an undetermined number wounded. These statistics are, no doubt, excessive with regard to the Mexican losses. José Urrea, in his *Diario*, records, "Nine pieces of artillery, three flags, more than a thousand rifles, many good pistols, guns, daggers, lots of ammunition, several wagons, and about 400 prisoners fell into the hands of our troops. There were ninety-seven wounded. . . . They had lost twenty-seven killed the day before. I lost eleven killed and forty-nine soldiers and five officers wounded."

Harbert Davenport, "The Men of Goliad," *Southwestern Historical Quarterly*, XLIII.

Ruby Cumby Smith, "James W. Fannin, Jr. and the Texas Revolution," *Southwestern Historical Quarterly*, XXIII.

José Urrea, "Diary of the Military Operations of the Division which under the Command of General José Urrea Campaigned in Texas," in Carlos Castañeda, *The Mexican Side of the Texas Revolution* (Dallas, 1928).

# THE BATTLE OF SAN JACINTO, APRIL 21, 1836

 ON LEARNING that General Santa Anna and a division of choice troops had burned Harrisburg and had moved in the direction of Lynch's ferry and New Washington (Morgan's Point), Sam Houston and the Texas Army moved east from Harrisburg on the morning of April 19; the line of march carried the Texans across the prairie lands south of Buffalo Bayou. On the morning of April 20, Texan scouts encountered the advance guard of Santa Anna's force; information was received that Santa Anna's command was encamped near New Washington and that the Mexican general planned to take up a line of march toward Anahuac the next day, crossing the San Jacinto River at Lynch's ferry. The Texan army halted in a grove of trees bordering the south banks of Buffalo Bayou and waited.

At sundown on the evening of April 20, the Texans were camped in the timber between the Lynchburg Road and Buffalo Bayou with the bend of the bayou and the adjacent marshes of the San Jacinto River to their left. The Mexican army had halted nearby the previous afternoon following a brief skirmish with the Texans. In his official report, Houston records that on April 20 "the enemy had occupied a piece of timber within rifle shot of the left wing of our army, from which an occasional interchange of small arms [fire] took place.... A short time before sunset, our mounted men, about eighty-five in number under the special command of Colonel Sherman, marched out for the purpose of reconnoitering the enemy. Whilst advancing they received a volley from the left of the enemy's infantry and after a sharp encounter with their cavalry . . . they retired in good order. All fell back in good order to our encampment about sunset, and remained without any ostensible action until the 21st at half past three o'clock."

On the morning of April 21, the final details of organization for battle were completed by both sides. As shown on the map, when the Texans left the protection of their wooded area, they formed a battle line along the Lynchburg Road with the small artillery positioned at the center and flanked by companies of infantry. Sidney Sherman's cavalrymen made their exit from the woods to the right of the main body of troops as they covered the Texan right flank to cut off possible escape routes to the south. Santa Anna resorted to a similar battle array; he stationed his artillery in the center of his line, flanked the field pieces with companies of infantry troops, and deployed his cavalry units to the left. About midmorning General Cós arrived at the Mexican camp to reinforce Santa Anna with some 500 choice troops, thus, according to Houston's subsequent report, increasing the Mexican effective force "to upwards of 1500 men whilst our aggregate force in the field numbered 783."

At 3:30 p.m. the Texans charged the Mexican defenses and the battle was on. In his concise description of what followed, Sam Houston writes, "Colonel Sherman with his regiment, having commenced the action upon our left wing, the whole line at the center and on the right, advancing in double-quick time . . . [in his joy and excitement, Houston confuses his left and right wings] received the enemy's fire and advanced within point blank shot before a piece was discharged from our lines. Our lines advanced without a halt, until they were in possession of the woodland and the breastwork. . . . The conflict lasted about eighteen minutes from the time of close action until we were in possession of the enemy's encampment, taking one piece of cannon (loaded), four stands of colors, all their camp equipage, stores, and baggage. Our cavalry had charged and routed that of the enemy . . . and [gave] pursuit to the fugitives. . . . The conflict at the breastworks lasted but a few moments. . . . The rout commenced at half past four, and the pursuit of the main army continued until twilight. . . . The enemy's loss was 630 killed . . . Wounded: 208 . . . Prisoners: 730; President-General Santa Anna, General Cós, four colonels, aides to General Santa Anna." General Santa Anna's account of the battle of San Jacinto (which he was confident of winning) agrees with the Houston report in all essentials.

Eugene C. Barker (ed.), *Readings in Texas History* (Dallas, 1929).

Carlos E. Castañeda, *The Mexican Side of the Texas Revolution* (Dallas, 1928).

Sue Flanagan, *Sam Houston's Texas* (Austin, 1964).

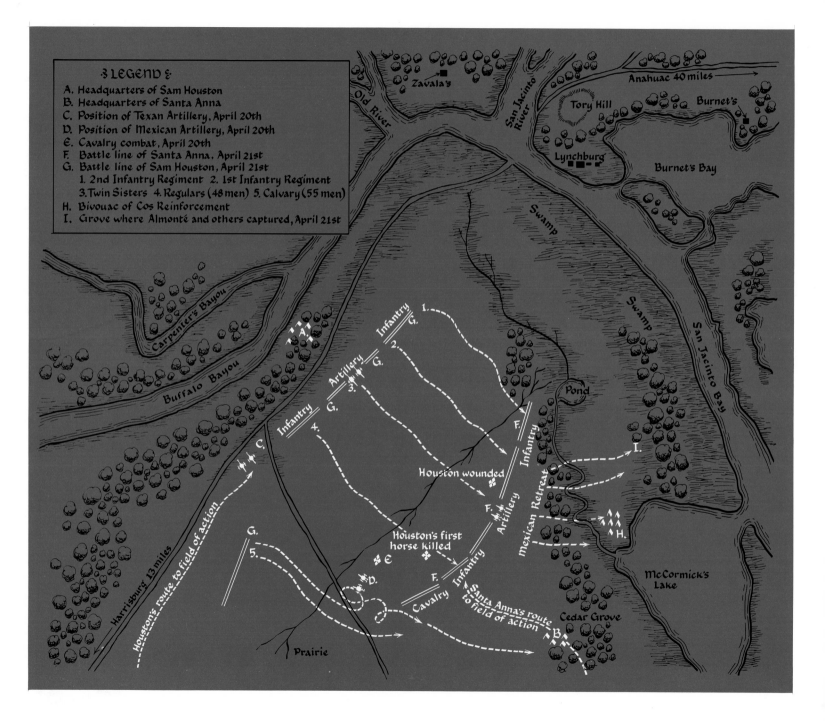

**LEGEND**

A. Headquarters of Sam Houston
B. Headquarters of Santa Anna
C. Position of Texan Artillery, April 20th
D. Position of Mexican Artillery, April 20th
E. Cavalry combat, April 20th
F. Battle line of Santa Anna, April 21st
G. Battle line of Sam Houston, April 21st
   1. 2nd Infantry Regiment  2. 1st Infantry Regiment
   3. Twin Sisters  4. Regulars (48 men)  5. Calvary (55 men)
H. Bivouac of Cos Reinforcement
I. Grove where Almonté and others captured, April 21st

Old River

Zavala's

San Jacinto River

Anahuac 40 miles

Tory Hill

Burnet's

Lynchburg

Burnet's Bay

Swamp

Carpenter's Bayou

Swamp

San Jacinto Bay

Buffalo Bayou

Infantry
G. 1.
Infantry
G. 2.
Artillery G.
3.
Infantry
G.
4.

Pond

F.
Infantry

I.

A

C

Houston wounded

Houston's route to field of action

Harrisburg 13 miles

G.
5.

G.

Houston's first horse killed

E

D

F. Artillery

F. Infantry

Mexican Retreat

H.

McCormick's Lake

Cavalry Infantry

Santa Anna's route to field of action

B

Cedar Grove

Prairie

IT IS a well-known fact that on December 19, 1836, the first Congress of the Republic of Texas adopted an act defining the southern and northwestern boundaries of the Republic to be the Rio Grande from its mouth to its source, then due north to the 42° parallel, east along the 42° parallel to the Adams-Oñis line, then south to the source of the Arkansas River, along the Arkansas to the 100° meridian, and south along that meridian to the Red River. This western and northern boundary line, adopted apparently on the suggestion of Stephen F. Austin and others, is almost beyond comprehension in its exaggerated final form; surely those responsible knew that the new republic had no justification at all for such a claim.

It is difficult for the student of southwestern history to realize just what we were claiming by virtue of this law. To set the record straight, a glance at a map of the present American West will reveal that the newly-born Republic claimed that its national domain extended from the mouth of the Rio Grande to its source; a claim that included approximately one half of New Mexico, a portion of the present Colorado high country west of Pueblo, Denver, and Ft. Collins, and a part of south central Wyoming. Also, the southwestern corner of present Kansas and the Oklahoma Panhandle were included within the boundaries fixed in 1836. At this time, the frontier line of settlement ran southward from a point on the Red River near old Jonesborough to Jefferson and Nacogdoches, then along the Old San Antonio Road to San Antonio de Bexar, and then parallel to the San Antonio River to the Gulf of Mexico near Copano Bay and Aransas Pass. Nevertheless, in 1841 Mirabeau B. Lamar launched the Texan Santa

Fe expedition in an effort to better establish the Texas claim to the lands around Santa Fe and Albuquerque, New Mexico. The valiant Texans on the trip, commanded by Colonel Hugh McLeod, Matthew Caldwell, William G. Cooke, José Antonio Navarro, and others, were defeated by the climate and topography of the High Plains long before they reached Santa Fe. The most amazing thing about this particular story is that the Texans were able, in one way or another, to hold on to their vague claims until the compromise settlement of 1850.

In 1841 the government of the Republic, eager to secure new settlers from the United States, embarked on a colonization scheme whereby contracts were granted to immigration agents for the settlement of new families in locations specified by the terms of the contract; in many respects, these colonization contracts were similar to the Mexican *empresario* agreements of the years prior to 1835. In the months that followed, contracts were signed with W. S. Peters and Associates (the Texas Emigration and Land Company), with Charles F. Mercer, with Henri Castro, and with Henry Fisher and Burchard Miller.

In the north, the contract with W. S. Peters and Associates, after several amendments, set aside more than 16,000 square miles of North Texas for the proposed Peters Colony. The company met with a variety of difficulties and in 1845 the attorney general instituted proceedings to cancel the agreement; however, the company did settle over 2000 families on its land between 1841 and 1848. Charles F. Mercer's contract called for the location of families on a large area of land lying east and south of the Peters' colony. Mercer ran into even more difficulty than did Peters and in

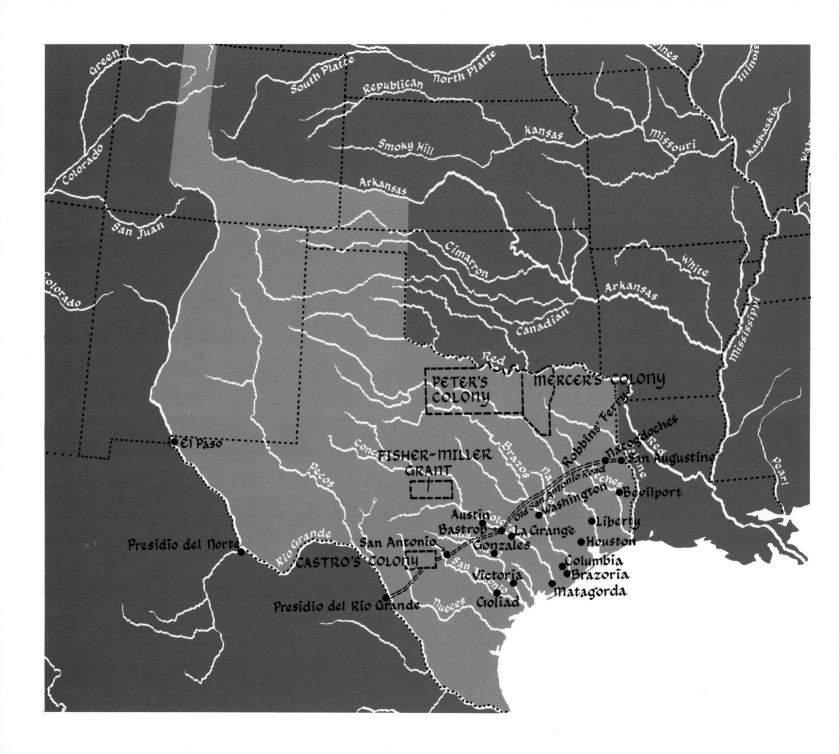

1848 Judge R. E. B. Baylor declared the Mercer contract null and void.

In South Texas, Henri Castro, a French colonizer, secured a contract to settle European families on two pieces of land south and west of San Antonio. In September, 1844, Castro established the town of Castroville and succeeded in bringing over 2000 colonists from France and Germany to the Castroville-D'Hanis-Hondo area. In the Texas Hill Country, Henry Fisher and Burchard Miller received a grant of land lying between the Llano and Colorado rivers. In 1844 Fisher sold an interest in the contract to the *Adelsverein,* a German colonization society destined to play a significant role in the colonization of the Texas Hill Country region; but that is a story to be sketched on a subsequent map.

# THE FRONTIER OF THE REPUBLIC, 1836-1846

 BY THE MID-YEARS of the history of the Republic, in spite of the swarm of immigrants entering Texas from the United States, the map is characterized mainly by vacant land.

As noted previously, with the exception of a few hardy souls that had pushed to the west, the frontier line ran from Jonesborough and Clarksville in the Red River valley southeast to the vicinity of Jefferson and Marshall, and then south to intersect the Old San Antonio Road in the vicinity of Nacogdoches. From Nacogdoches, the frontier followed the Old San Antonio Road to San Antonio and then on to the sea at Copano Bay. Established towns and communities in Northeast and East Texas included Clarksville, Boston, Jefferson, Marshall, Nacogdoches, Milam, San Augustine, Sabinetown, Bevilport, and Beaumont. Fort Johnson on the Red River, Fort English on Bois d'Arc Creek, and Fort Houston east of the Trinity provided a small measure of security for the area.

In the older section of the Republic—the former Anglo-American colonies of Mexican Texas—the increase in immigration was more noticeable. The new towns of Houston and Galveston appear on the map for the first time; other newly established communities included Columbus (Beason's), La Grange (Burnham's), Colorado, Texana Electra, Tidehaven, Lamar, Copano Landing, Seguin, Comanche (at the mouth of Onion Creek near Austin), and Austin, the new capital of the Republic. In Austin County, Friedrich Ernst established the first German settlement at Industry; New Ulm, a second German community, was established in 1845.

Beyond the pale of the settled area, small groups of individuals or families had established Port Sullivan, a few miles up the Brazos from Nashville, and Milam, a site of a blockhouse fort at the falls of the Brazos. On the Colorado, the new village of Austin and the communities of Hornsby Bend and Bastrop marked

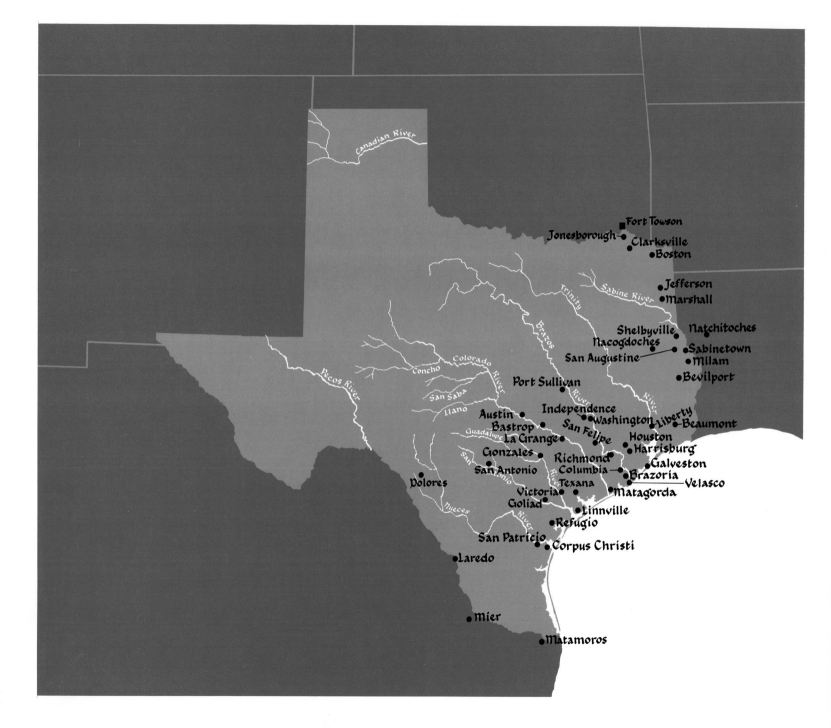

the western advance of settlement. While Henri Castro had been granted permission to establish a group of settlers from Alsace on lands west of San Antonio, his Medina River settlements did not get underway until 1844-1845. On the Guadalupe River east of San Antonio, Seguin was surveyed by Ben McCulloch in 1838 and first called Walnut Springs.

South of the San Antonio and Nueces rivers the land was referred to as El Desierto Muerto or the Wild Horse Desert. Except for the Mexican villages on the south bank of the Rio Grande, the entire region was populated by Mexican ranchers and their herds of cattle and horses: the ranchos of Viejo, Los Fresnos, Corrales, San Juan de Carricitos, Norias, Jaboncillos, Petronilla, Santa Margarita, Santa Gertrudis, Santa Rosa, and others. Near the north bank of the Nueces

River, San Patricio (founded in 1830) served as the county seat of San Patricio County. H. L. Kinney and William B. Aubrey engaged in ranching on a large scale near present Corpus Christi, a town that grew out of a trading post established by Kinney in 1840. To the west of Corpus Christi, the old town of Laredo flourished at one of the major river crossings into Mexico.

J. Bartholomew, "Texas and a Part of New Mexico," (Edinburgh, ca. 1850), Archives, University of Texas Library, Austin, Texas.

Seymour Connor, *Adventure in Glory, The Saga of Texas, 1836-1849* (Austin, 1965).

C. S. Williams, Map of Texas from the Most Recent Authorities (Philadelphia, 1847), Archives, University of Texas Library, Austin, Texas.

# AUSTIN, 1839-1845

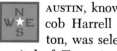 AUSTIN, known as Waterloo in the days of Jacob Harrell and William (Uncle Billy) Barton, was selected as the site of the permanent capital of Texas in 1839. In the spring of that year Edwin Waller surveyed the townsite and construction commenced on the public buildings. At an auction sale on August 1, 1839, over three hundred lots were sold; the officials of government arrived in October, the city was incorporated in December, and Edwin Waller was elected mayor in January, 1840.

Located on the north bank of the Colorado River, Austin, in the days of the Republic, was a tribute to Edwin Waller's skill as a surveyor and planner. The

street nearest the river, and parallel to the Colorado, was appropriately named Water Street. Between Water Street on the south and to North Avenue on the North (with the exception of College Street intersecting Capitol Square), the streets running from east to west, all named for principal trees of Texas, included Live Oak, Cypress, Cedar, Pine, Pecan, Bois d'Arc, Hickory, Ash, Mulberry, Mesquite, College, Peach, and Walnut streets. Between West Avenue and East Avenue, the east-west boundaries of Waller's plat, the streets running from north to south (with the exception of broad Congress Avenue in the center of the survey) were named after significant Texas rivers and

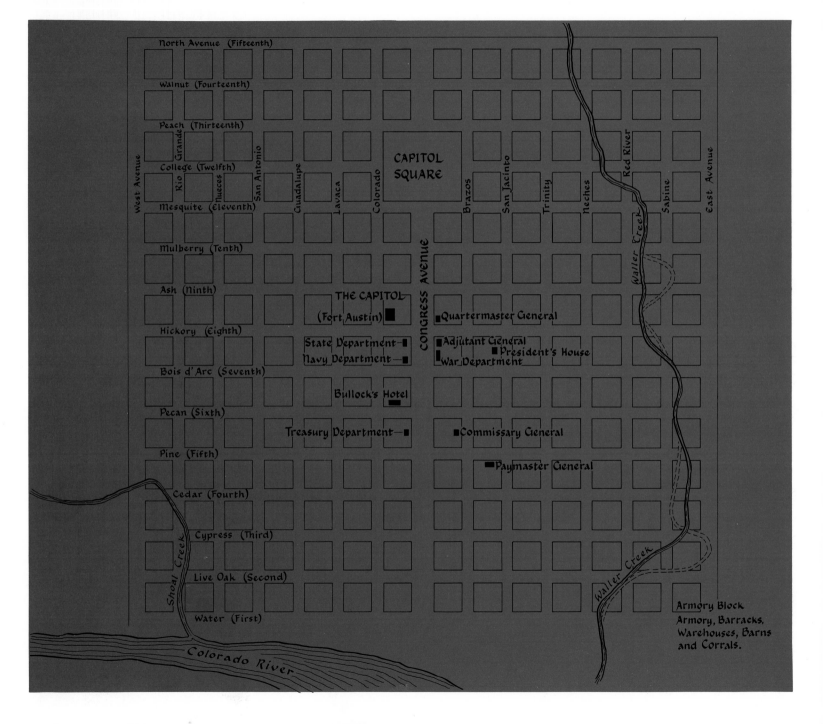

included Rio Grande, Nueces, San Antonio, Guadalupe, Lavaca, Colorado, Congress, Brazos, San Jacinto, Trinity, Neches, Red River, and Sabine streets.

While a "Capitol Square" was marked, the first capitol building, a typical dog-trot house surrounded by a stockade, was constructed on a hill west of Congress Avenue between Hickory and Ash streets. The State Department, the Navy Department, and the Treasury Department were located on the west side of Congress Avenue, while on the east side of the street, the War Department, the Adjutant General's office, and the Quartermaster General's office were found. The president's home was located two blocks east of Congress on San Jacinto Street between Bois d'Arc and Hickory streets. The armory, barracks, warehouses, barns, and corrals were clustered together on the southeast edge of town near the intersection of East Avenue and Water Street. The old Bullock Hotel dominated the center of town.

A number of excellent descriptions of early Austin have been left by the many travelers who visited Texas during the period of the Republic. Dr. Ferdinand Roemer, the German scientist who visited Texas in 1845-1846 and approached Austin from the general direction of Bastrop, described the beauty of the setting and reported: "This idyllic view from the distance is not wholly in keeping with the interior of the city. It was composed at this time of about one hundred to one hundred and fifty frame houses painted white and a few log houses. . . . A single short but broad street was lined with houses, other houses were scattered in irregular fashion in the prairie, although a very regular city plan had been outlined on the map." J. K. Holland recalled "When I first knew Austin, during the 1840's, it was a little country town on what was then the Texas frontier, and had only a few hundred inhabitants. Those were the log cabin days of the Republic. General Houston lived in one of the Austin log cabins, which he called his wigwam, and up and down Congress avenue on either side were scattered others in which were located the headquarters of the various departments of government. The Bastrop highway [ran along Pecan street]. The war-cry of the Indians could be heard in the nighttime within the very gates of the capitol. It was not safe for any man to go alone or without his gun beyond the limits of the town; for there was great danger of being shot or captured by the redskins who lay waiting in the mountains. Barton Springs and Mount Bonnell were the only places of resort. . . ."

But the city of Austin survived these early hardships, and, as the decades passed, wore well in the minds of Texans as the capital of the state.

Frank Brown, Annals of Travis County and the City of Austin, Archives, University of Texas Library, Austin, Texas.

J. K. Holland, "Reminiscences of Austin and Old Washington," *Quarterly of the Texas State Historical Association*, I (October, 1897).

Ferdinand Roemer, *Texas* (Oswald Mueller, tr., San Antonio, 1935).

# HOUSTON: CAPITAL OF THE REPUBLIC, 1837-1839

HOUSTON, the capital of the Republic for a brief span, was established in the summer of 1836 by Augustus C. and John K. Allen, two brothers who came to Texas from New York in 1832. The new town, named for General Sam Houston, was located on the south bank of Buffalo Bayou opposite its juncture with White Oak Bayou.

The map of Houston on the opposite page represents the village shortly after its founding, during the years 1837-1839, when Houston served as the temporary capital of Texas. At this time the town was built around Water Street and Main Street. Water Street followed the meanderings of the bayou and was intersected at right angles by Main Street at Commerce Square, a clearing on the south bank of Buffalo Bayou opposite White Oak Bayou. South of Water Street, the streets that ran, generally, in an east-west direction, included Commerce, Franklin, Congress, Preston, Prairie, and Texas streets. Intersecting the above-named streets at right angles and running generally north and south were Crawford Street (to the east), Lamar (La Branch), Austin, Carolina (Caroline), San Jacinto, Franklin, Main, Travis, Milam, Louisiana, Smith, and Brazos streets. The capitol building stood on the southwest corner of Main and Texas streets.

When President Mirabeau B. Lamar transferred the capitol and government offices to Austin in 1839, public indignation was expressed by the people of Houston. It is noteworthy, however, that the loss of the seat of government had very little effect on the growth of the new town. When Dr. Ferdinand Roemer arrived at night by riverboat from Galveston, he recorded: "When I awoke on the following morning and came upon deck, our steamboat was lying in the quiet water of the river, which was confined to its bed by banks thirty to forty feet high. Several large dilapidated buildings resembling storage sheds stood on top of the bank. A little beyond them many frame buildings were visible. . . . [I] started on foot to the 'Capitol,' which was the highsounding name of the reputedly best hotel in town. As soon as I had climbed the rather steep incline, I found myself on a straight street. . . . I was on the principal street of Houston. The houses were all of frame construction, similar in style to those of Galveston. . . . Nearly every house on Main Street was a store. The streets were unpaved and the mud bottomless. . . ." Despite the rather ordinary appearance of the town, Roemer observed that "Next to Galveston, it is the most important city of the State, numbering about three thousand inhabitants. It owes its rapid growth entirely to its location on Buffalo Bayou which is navigable for steamboats of considerable size. This circumstance will always assure it an important position in the future. . . ." Everyone must agree that Roemer was a keen and wise observer.

Max Freund (tr. and ed.) *Gustav Dresel's Houston Journal* (Austin, 1954).

Andrew F. Muir, "Diary of a Young Man in Houston, 1838," *Southwestern Historical Quarterly*, LIII.

Ferdinand Roemer, *Texas* (Oswald Mueller, tr., San Antonio, 1935).

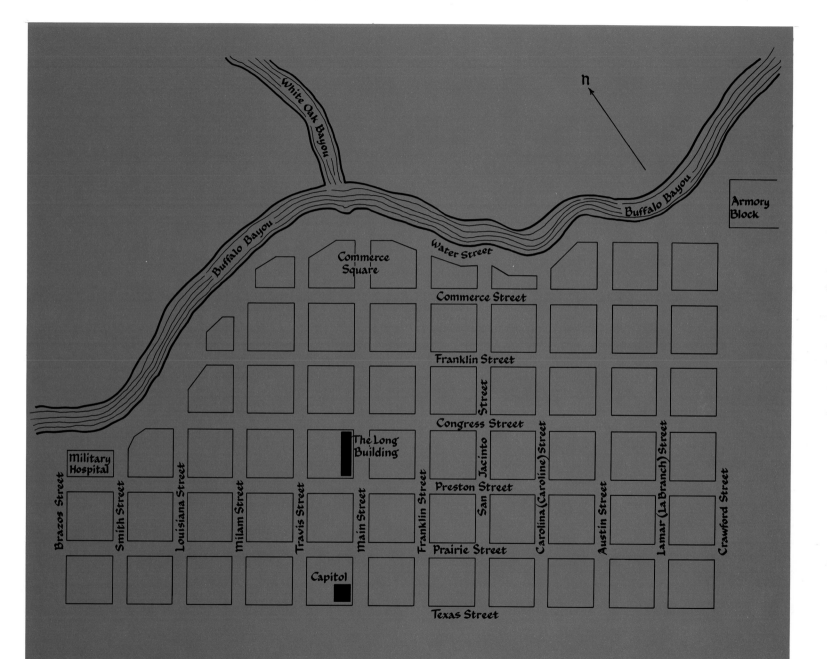

# WASHINGTON-ON-THE-BRAZOS

WASHINGTON-ON-THE-BRAZOS was established as an unnamed settlement in 1822 when Andrew Robinson began operating a ferry on the southwest bank of the Brazos just below the mouth of the Navasota River. John W. Hall laid out the townsite in 1830, but it was not until 1833 that John W. Kinney constructed the first residence. In 1834 several men, including John Hall, Asa Hoxey, and Thomas Gray, organized a townsite company and named the new town Washington. Joshua Hadley was elected alcalde in July, 1835, and according to the *Handbook of Texas*, by 1836 Washington-on-the-Brazos "had two hotels, some fifty houses, and a population of about one hundred."

After extensive research on Washington, R. Henderson Shuffler points out that "The only known plat of the town, 'Washington-on-the-Brazos, Texas,' in the times of Jim Johnson now fmn [freedman], then a slave, who lived there before the war, shows a well laid out town, with numerous intersecting streets and avenues, none of which, unfortunately, are labeled 'Main,' 'Brazos,' or 'Ferry.'" Nevertheless, because two roads came together at the top of a bluff and fed into the main north-south street of the town, Shuffler concludes, "It is quite logical to assume that the street beginning at the juncture of the ferry roads would be called 'Ferry Street' and it is also logical to assume that the wide intersecting street with the City Market in its center, would be 'Main Street.'"

Shortly after the Convention of 1836 assembled at Washington to write a Declaration of Independence and a Constitution for the Republic, William Fairfax Gray, a visitor from Virginia, described the frontier village: "laid out in the woods, about a dozen wretched cabins or shanties constitute the city; not one decent house in it, and only one well-defined street, which consists of an opening cut out of the woods. The stumps still standing. A·rare place to hold a national convention in. They will have to leave it promptly to avoid starvation." At the time of the Convention, however, the town served as a residence for either individuals or the families of White, McGathy, Nowall, Eddington, Johnson, McHall, Goldman, McFell, Captain Hatfield, Berkley, Cartmel, Emons, Pat Lust, Rucker, Bertram, Dr. Herd, Jno. Mathis, and Mrs. Griffin. In addition the village boasted a post office, a city market, and (in a short time) Independence Hall —reported to be a house (some record a blacksmith shop) owned by Noah Byars and Peter Mercer.

Several years later (1840), as the Texas Congress prepared to meet there, Dr. John Washington Lockhart records that "Washington in 1840 had a resident population of about 250 souls and a non-resident population of about 50 to 100 more, principally gamblers, horse racers, etc., for this was a great resort for such characters. . . . Of course barrooms were plentiful and did a good business. There were a few dry goods stores, which kept only a very inferior quality of goods, a few staple coarse goods, with an enormous price attached to them—so that only a few could afford to purchase them." Captain Charles Eliot, the British consul at Galveston, could not understand why "the President has convened Congress to assemble at Washington on the Brazos, where there are 12 or 13 wooden shanties, and to which place there are no means of getting except in an ox train or on a Bat horse. . . ."

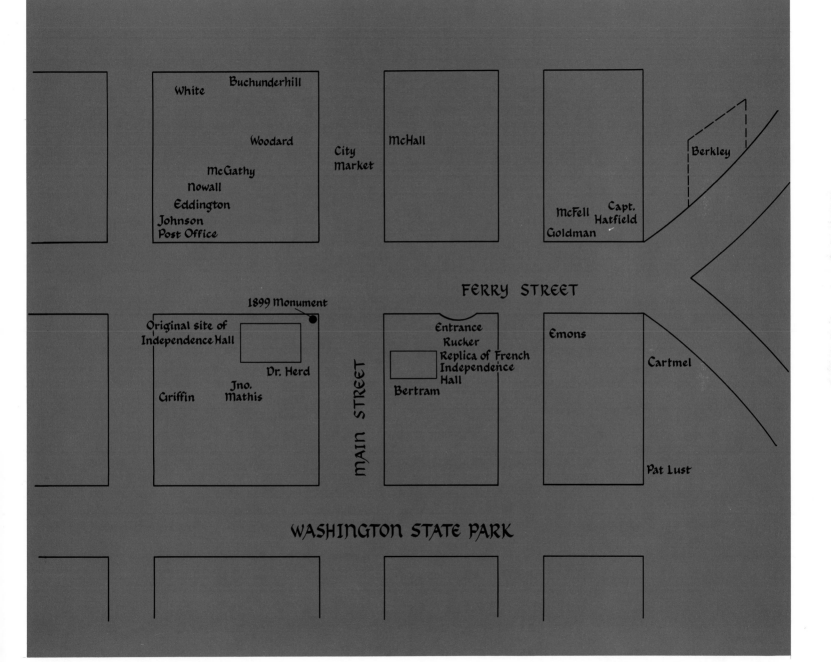

It is of considerable importance, however, that this much maligned village clustered around the corner of "Main" and "Ferry" streets played a large role in the early history of Texas.

Ephraim D. Adams, *British Diplomatic Correspondence Concerning the Republic of Texas* (Austin, 1917).

William F. Gray, *The Diary of Col. Wm. Fairfax Gray from Virginia to Texas, 1835-1836* (Houston, 1967).
John Washington Lockhart (Jonnie L. Wallis and L. L. Hill, eds.), *Sixty Years on the Brazos* (Los Angeles, 1930).
R. Henderson Shuffler, "The Signing of Texas' Declaration of Independence: Myth and Record," *Southwestern Historical Quarterly,* LXV.

# THE TEXAS NAVY

THE TEXAS NAVY came into being on November 25, 1835, when the General Council of the provisional government passed a bill providing for the purchase of four schooners. In January, 1836, the Navy actually came into being with the purchase of the 60-ton *William Robbins* (renamed the *Liberty*), the 125-ton *Invincible*, the 125-ton *Independence*, and the 125-ton *Brutus*. In March, David G. Burnet appointed Captain Charles E. Hawkins commodore in command of the fleet. The first Texas Navy lasted until the middle of 1837; all of the small ships having been lost by that time: The *Liberty* had to be sold in New Orleans because the Texas government could not pay the repair bill; the *Independence* was captured by the Mexican Navy in April, 1836; the *Invincible* ran aground while under fire near the entrance to Galveston harbor; and the *Brutus* was lost in a storm in 1837.

The second Texas Navy resulted from an authorization of the Texas Congress in 1836 as supplemented by another bill which was passed in 1837 appointing a commissioner to go to Baltimore to contract for the building of six ships costing $280,000. As a result, Texas acquired the *Zavala*, the 170-ton schooner *San Jacinto*, the 170-ton schooner *San Antonio*, the 170-ton schooner *San Bernard*, the 400-ton brig *Wharton*, the 600-ton sloop-of-war *Austin*, and the 400-ton brig *Archer*. President Mirabeau B. Lamar appointed Edwin Ward Moore commodore of the fleet.

In 1840 the small Texas fleet saw considerable service in the Gulf of Mexico between the port of New Orleans to the east and Yucatan peninsula to the south. As the result of an alliance between Texas and the rebellious Indians of Yucatan, in 1841 Lamar ordered the fleet to depart for the peninsula area. Leaving Galveston on December 13, 1841, with the *Austin, San Bernard,* and *San Antonio,* Commodore Moore sailed for Yucatan. The expected conflict, however, did not develop, and the Texas Navy returned home to await future developments. After experiencing a mutiny in port in New Orleans, the *San Antonio* departed for Yucatan in September, 1842, and was never heard from again (presumably lost in a tropical storm). The *Zavala* (acquired in November, 1838), in the meanwhile, had been allowed to rot due to a lack of funds for repair and was run aground to be scrapped. Commodore Moore, ordered to return to Galveston from New Orleans (where financial difficulties blocked

Brazos

Navasota

Trinity

Neches

Sabine

Red

Mississippi

Pearl

Colorado

New Orleans

Guadalupe Lavaca

Harrisburg

Galveston

San Antonio

Velasco

Matagorda

Nueces

Rio Grande

Matamoros

### TEXAS NAVY
### 1835-36

—— Flash
– – – Wm. Robbins (Liberty)
–·–·– Flora
–··–··– San Felipe
········ Ocean

Ft. Jerez

Tampico

Lobos Is.
Tuxpan

Tecolutin

Gutierrez
Zamora
Vega de Alatorre

Vera Cruz

Alvarado

Tlacotalpan
Puerto Mexico

Paraiso

San Pedro

Frontera

Sisal

Progresso
Puerto Morales
Cozumel Is.

Ascencion
Bay

Campeche

Espiritu Santo
Bay

Champoton

San Juan Bautista

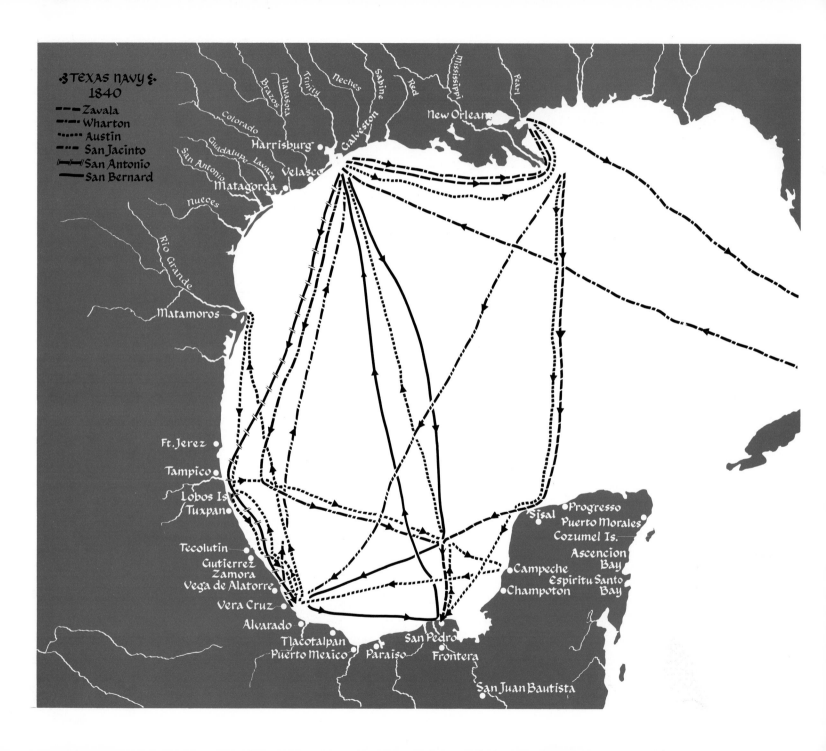

TEXAS NAVY
1840
--- Zavala
-·-· Wharton
···· Austin
-··- San Jacinto
|—|—| San Antonio
—— San Bernard

New Orleans

Colorado
Brazos
Navasota
Trinity
Neches
Sabine
Red
Mississippi
Pearl

Harrisburg
Galveston
Guadalupe
San Antonio
Lavaca
Velasco
Matagorda

Nueces

Rio Grande

Matamoros

Ft. Jerez

Tampico
Lobos Is.
Tuxpan

Tecolutin
Gutierrez
Zamora
Vega de Alatorre
Vera Cruz

Alvarado
Tlacotalpan
Puerto Mexico
Paraiso
San Pedro
Frontera

San Juan Bautista

Sisal
Progresso
Puerto Morales
Cozumel Is.
Ascencion
Bay
Campeche
Espiritu Santo
Champoton
Bay

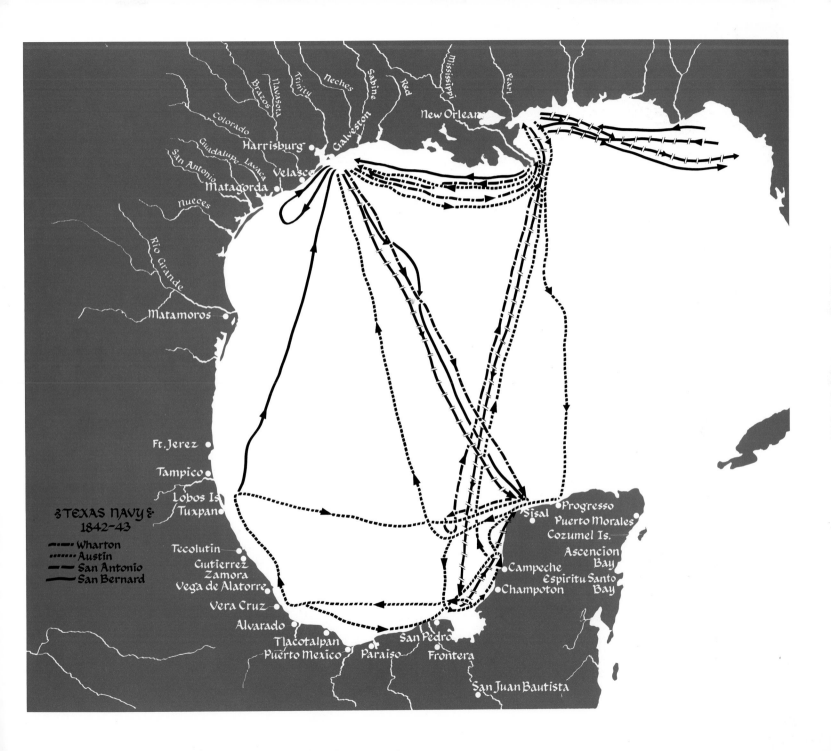

Neches

Sabine

Red

Mississippi

Pearl

Brazos

Navasota

Trinity

Colorado

New Orleans

Guadalupe

Galveston

Harrisburg

Lavaca

San Antonio

Velasco

Matagorda

Nueces

Rio Grande

Matamoros

Ft. Jerez

Tampico

Lobos Is.

Tuxpan

Sisal

Progresso

Puerto Morales

Cozumel Is.

Ascencion
Bay

TEXAS NAVY
1842-43

Wharton

Austin

San Antonio

San Bernard

Tecolutin

Gutierrez

Zamora

Vega de Alatorre

Vera Cruz

Alvarado

Tlacotalpan

Puerto Mexico

Paraiso

San Pedro

Frontera

Campeche

Espiritu Santo
Bay

Champoton

San Juan Bautista

necessary repairs), finally sailed instead for Yucatan, where several engagements were fought with units of the Mexican Navy. Despite the fact that President Sam Houston's Congress ordered the remaining ships of the fleet (the *Austin, Wharton, Archer,* and *San Bernard*) to be sold at public auction, the sale was blocked by the citizens of Galveston, and the small fleet survived to be transferred to the United States Navy in June, 1846.

The naval operations of the Texas fleet are shown on the three preceding maps as follows: (1) the operations of 1835-1836, (2) the operations in the Gulf of Mexico, 1840, and (3) the voyages of 1842-1843.

Alexander Dienst, "The Texas Navy," Mss. in the Elliott Collection, Library, Southwest Texas State College, San Marcos, Texas.

——, "The Navy of the Republic of Texas," *Quarterly of the Texas State Historical Association,* XII-XIII.

Jim Dan Hill, *The Texas Navy in Forgotten Battles and Shirt Sleeve Diplomacy* (Chicago, 1937).

Tom Henderson Wells, *Commodore Moore and the Texas Navy* (Austin, 1960).

# THE INDIAN FRONTIER, 1837-1845

AS SPAIN and Mexico discovered in prior decades, the government of the Republic of Texas found the Indian problem demanding a lion's share of attention. As the public officials attempted to establish an Indian policy, two opposing philosophies emerged: that of Sam Houston and the so-called Houston party, and that of Mirabeau B. Lamar and his followers. The first, exemplified by Houston, counseled moderation, honesty, and leniency; while the second, boldly asserted by Lamar, was more aggressive and severe. In the cauldron of local frontier politics in the decade that followed San Jacinto, the net result was a policy characterized by inconsistency, confusion, broken promises, a lack of understanding, and a general reluctance to meet the problem.

It is impossible to chart on a map all of the significant locations of events, massacres, depredation, and battle relating to early Texas Indian affairs. The year 1836 witnessed numerous Indian attacks on settlers and settlements at Dolores (the Beales's colony) on the Rio Grande, at Parker's Fort in Limestone County, and at many isolated locations all along the frontier. The Texas Congress responded by creating a battalion of "mounted gunmen," known also as "rangers," and by authorizing a line of blockhouse forts along the Texas frontier, but President Houston had neither the time nor the funds to effect the plan. In 1837, however, Houston did establish the foundations of what was to become the Texas Rangers; in addition, blockhouse forts were built on Walnut Creek in present Travis County, at the Three Forks of Little River, and at Fort Houston, located east of the Trinity near present Palestine.

In 1838 Vicente Cordova, an intelligent and respectable resident of Nacogdoches, entered into an alliance with Chief John Bowl of the Cherokees. Establishing

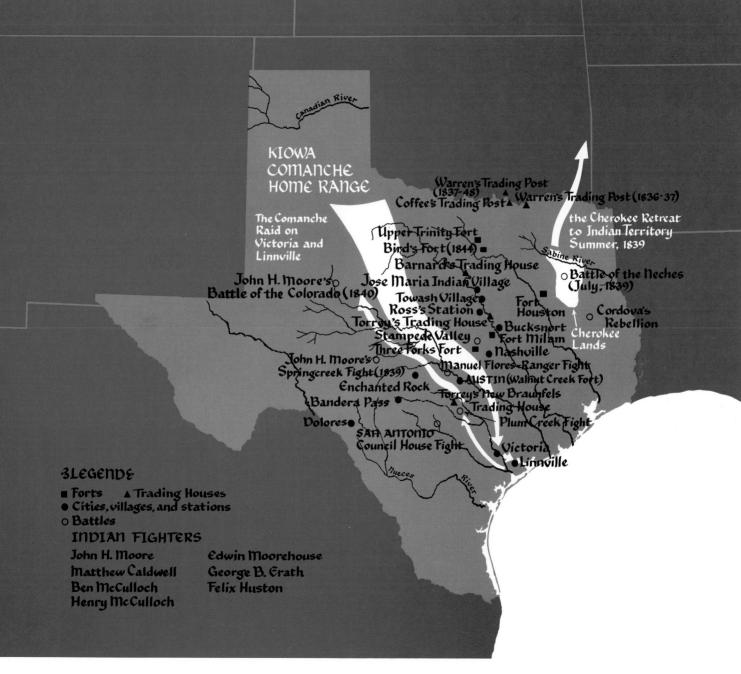

KIOWA
COMANCHE
HOME RANGE

Canadian River

The Comanche
Raid on
Victoria and
Linnville

Warren's Trading Post
(1837-48) ▲
Coffee's Trading Post ▲   ▲ Warren's Trading Post (1836-37)

the Cherokee Retreat
to Indian Territory
Summer, 1839

Sabine River

Upper Trinity Fort
Bird's Fort (1844) ■
Barnard's Trading House ▲

○ Battle of the Neches
(July, 1839)

John H. Moore's ○
Battle of the Colorado (1840)
Jose Maria Indian Village
Towash Village ●
Ross's Station ●
Torrey's Trading House
Stampede Valley
Three Forks Fort

Fort ■
Houston
● Bucksnort
■ Fort Milam
● Nashville

○ Cordova's
Rebellion

Cherokee
Lands

John H. Moore's ○
Springcreek Fight (1839)
Enchanted Rock
Bandera Pass ●
Dolores ●

○
Manuel Flores-Ranger Fight
■ AUSTIN (Walnut Creek Fort)
Torrey's New Braunfels
▲ Trading House

SAN ANTONIO
Council House Fight ○
Nueces

Plum Creek Fight

● Victoria
● Linnville

River

**LEGEND:**
- ■ Forts    ▲ Trading Houses
- ● Cities, villages, and stations
- ○ Battles

INDIAN FIGHTERS

John H. Moore        Edwin Moorehouse
Matthew Caldwell     George B. Erath
Ben McCulloch        Felix Huston
Henry McCulloch

himself on an island in the Angelina River, Cordova led an open rebellion against the government. Of short duration, the Cordova Rebellion was but a prelude to the more serious strife of 1839—the year that saw the death of Manuel Flores near Austin and the subsequent ruthless expulsion of the Cherokees from their East Texas lands following their defeat in the Battle of Neches. The Council House Fight took place in 1840 and was followed by the Comanche raid on Victoria, Linnville, and the Texas Gulf Coast.

In the months that followed John H. Moore, Matthew Caldwell, Ben McCulloch, Henry McCulloch, Jack Hays, Edwin Morehouse, George B. Erath, and others gained considerable fame as Indian fighters. Holland Coffee, Abel Warren, George Barnard, and the Torrey brothers established Indian trading posts on the Red and Brazos rivers. Blockhouses were built on the upper Trinity, on the West Fork of the Trinity (Bird's Fort), at the confluence of the Brazos and Bosque rivers (Ross's Station), at the falls of the Brazos (Fort Milam), and, as previously mentioned, at Three Forks and on Walnut Creek. Dozens of other temporary forts were established for brief periods. Under the Lamar administration, Jack Hays and John H. Moore carried the fight into Indian territory and fights took place at Bandera Pass, Enchanted Rock, Spring Creek, and along the upper Colorado River. During all this time, Joseph C. Eldridge, Thomas Western, and R. S. Neighbors rendered valuable service to the Republic as Indian agents.

Dorman Winfrey, *Texas Indian Papers* (2 vols., Austin, 1959-1960).

# THE MEXICAN INVASION, 1842, & THE SOMERVELL EXPEDITION

ON SEPTEMBER 11, 1842, General Adrian Woll, a Frenchman in the employ of the Mexican Army, appeared on the outskirts of San Antonio with an army of 1400 men. Three members of Congress and the entire membership of the district court (then in session) were among the prisoners taken by Woll as he took the city without resistance. Following on the heels of an earlier invasion the previous March, Woll's army crossed the Rio Grande at the old Presidio Crossing downstream from present Eagle Pass. Leaving the river, the army traveled north across the Nueces and through the Anacacho Mountain region to the Frio River. Crossing the Frio near the base of the Balcones escarpment, Woll moved almost due east to enter San Antonio from the west.

Sam Houston declared a national emergency, volunteer soldiers poured into San Antonio, and W. H. Daingerfield was sent to the United States to seek men, money, and supplies. General Woll held San Antonio nine days, inflicted losses on the Texan volun-

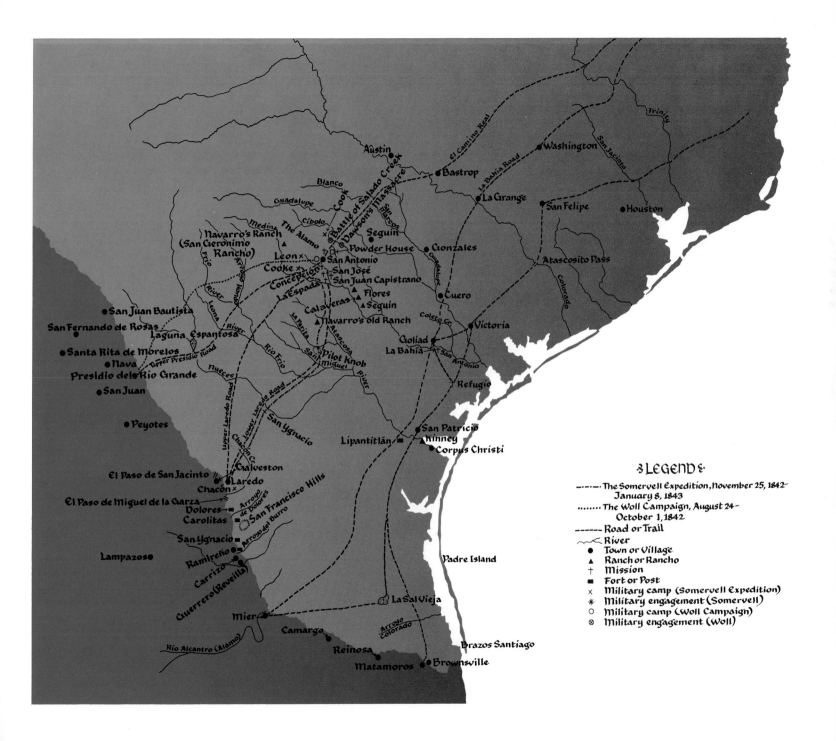

Austin

Washington

Trinity

Blanco

Bastrop

El Camino Real

Guadalupe

Cook

La Bahía Road

San Jacinto

La Grange

San Felipe

Houston

Navarro's Ranch
(San Geronimo
Rancho)

Medina

The Alamo

Cibolo

Battle of Salado Creek

Dawson's Massacre

San Marcos

Seguin

Powder House

Gonzales

Leon

San Antonio

Guadalupe

Atascosito Pass

Frio

Cooke

San José

Concepción

San Juan Capistrano

Colorado

La Espada

Flores

Cuero

Hondo

Calaveras

Seguin

San Juan Bautista

River

Leona

Navarro's old Ranch

Coleto Cc.

Victoria

San Fernando de Rosas

Laguna Espantosa

La Parita

Pilot Knob

Goliad

La Bahía

San Antonio

Santa Rita de Morelos

Nava

Upper Presidio Road

Rio Frio

Atascosa

Saint Miguel River

Presidio del Rio Grande

Nueces

Refugio

San Juan

Peyotes

Lower Laredo Road

San Ygnacio

Lipantitlán

San Patricio

Kinney

Corpus Christi

El Paso de San Jacinto

Galveston

San Francisco Hills

Upper Laredo Road

Chacón Cc.

Laredo

Chacón

El Paso de Miguel de la Garza

Arroyo de Dolores

Dolores

Carolitas

San Francisco Hills

Padre Island

San Ygnacio

Arroyo del Burro

Lampazoso

Ramireño

Carrizo

Guerrero (Revdilla)

La Sal Vieja

Mier

Arroyo Colorado

Camargo

Rio Alcantro (Alamo)

Reinosa

Brazos Santiago

Matamoros

Brownsville

## ❧ LEGEND ❧

--·--·-- The Somervell Expedition, November 25, 1842–
January 8, 1843

············ The Woll Campaign, August 24–
October 1, 1842

------ Road or Trail

∿∿ River

● Town or Village

▲ Ranch or Rancho

† Mission

■ Fort or Post

✕ Military camp (Somervell Expedition)

✳ Military engagement (Somervell)

○ Military camp (Woll Campaign)

⊗ Military engagement (Woll)

teer militia in the battle of Salado Creek and the Dawson fight, and retired toward the Rio Grande with a number of prisoners.

Long after Woll's departure, a Texan army was gathered together by Alexander Somervell, Jack Hays, Matthew Caldwell, and others for the purpose of pursuing the retreating Mexicans. Ordered to scout the country between San Antonio and Laredo but not to cross the Rio Grande, Alexander Somervell and his command (the Southwestern Army of Operation) of some 750 troops departed San Antonio on November 25, 1842; their destination was the Rio Grande at Laredo, not the Presidio Crossing further upstream. Somervell traveled by way of the Navarro ranch, the Atascosa River, La Parita Creek, and Pilot Knob to the Frio River. Intersecting the lower Laredo Road near Pilot Knob, Somervell's army followed the road across the Frio and Nueces rivers to Laredo (December 8, 1842). The town was taken without anything resembling a fight, and a few days later, when Somervell abandoned the project, about three hundred men refused to obey the order to return home. These troops, organized after a fashion by Colonel W. S. Fisher, marched down the Rio Grande in search of Mexicans. At the village of Mier they attacked a superior Mexican Army on Christmas Day, 1842. On the following afternoon, the Texans surrendered to General Pedro Ampudia and were subsequently marched to Castle Perote. After an attempt to escape at Salado on February 18, 1843, the "black beans" were drawn and seventeen men were executed.

Joseph Milton Nance, *Attack and Counter-attack, The Texas Mexican Frontier, 1842* (Austin, 1964).

# THE WAR WITH MEXICO, 1846-1848

 RUPERT N. RICHARDSON writes, "The War with Mexico, which grew out of the annexation of Texas, concerned the people of Texas vitally." During the negotiations concerning annexation, General Zachary Taylor and a strong force of United States troops moved from Fort Jessup, Louisiana, to the north bank of the Nueces River in the vicinity of Corpus Christi Bay. Thus Taylor camped on the north bank of the stream that had been fixed by Mexico as the boundary between Texas and Nuevo Santander. The United States, however, sustained the claim of Texas, and when the Slidell mission failed, James K. Polk decided to move Taylor's army from the Nueces to the north bank of the Rio Grande opposite the old city of Matamoros. Taylor reached the Rio Grande on March 23, 1846. On April 24 and May 8-9, Mexican forces crossed the river and attacked Taylor's troops in the opening battles of the Mexican War at Palo Alto and Resaca de la Palma. The American Army hastily constructed Fort Brown on the north bank of the river and laid siege to Matamoros. After the capture of Matamoros, Taylor refused to move forward until he had received reinforcements and supplies. After men and ammunition arrived, his army advanced to Monterrey (Nuevo León) by way of Camargo and Mier. Taylor's troops captured Monter-

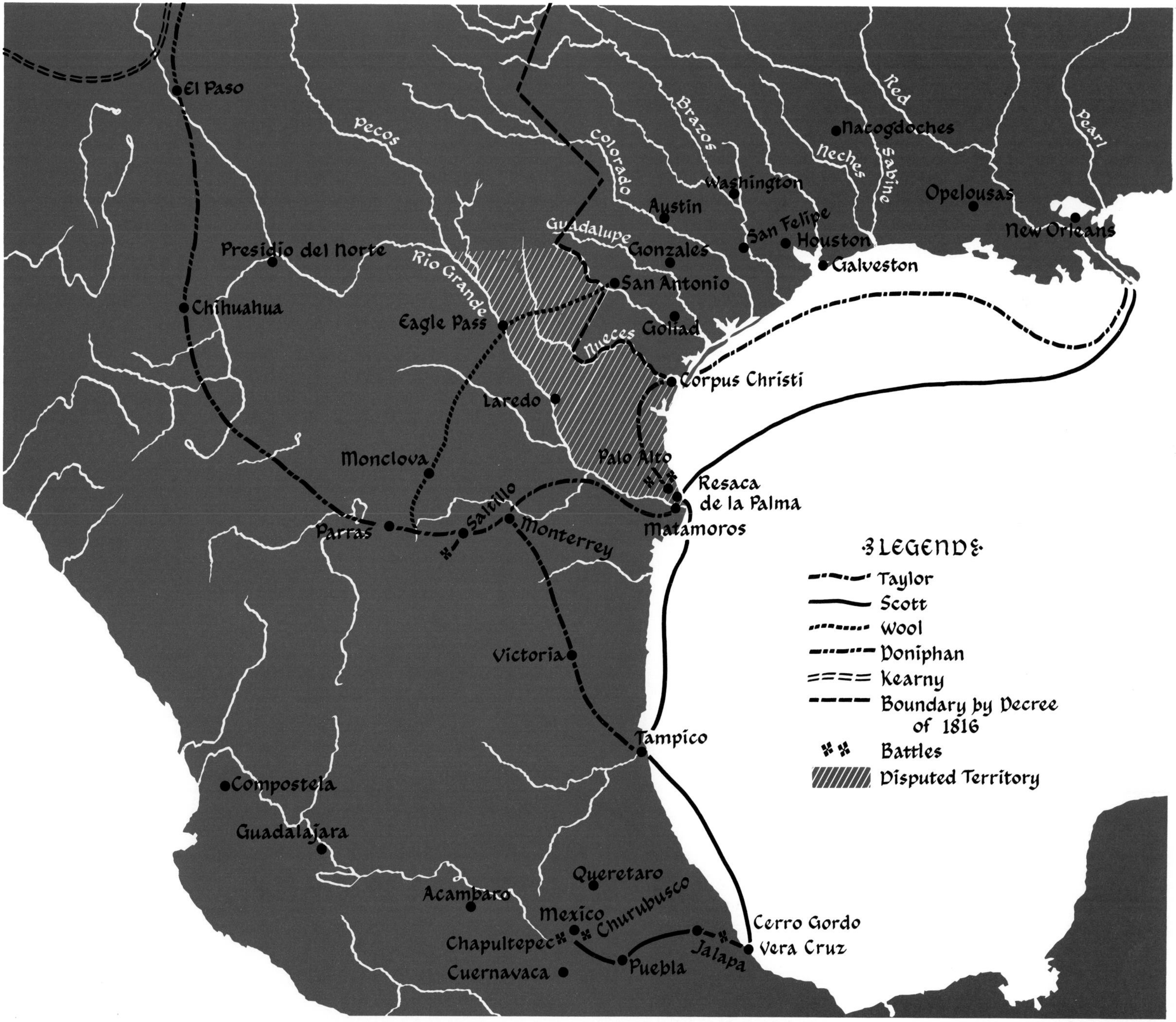
El Paso
Pecos
Colorado
Brazos
Red
Pearl
Nacogdoches
Neches
Sabine
Washington
Austin
Opelousas
New Orleans
Guadalupe
San Felipe
Houston
Presidio del Norte
Rio Grande
Gonzales
Galveston
San Antonio
Chihuahua
Eagle Pass
Goliad
Nueces
Corpus Christi
Laredo
Palo Alto
Monclova
Resaca
de la Palma
Saltillo
Parras
Monterrey
Matamoros
LEGENDE
Taylor
Scott
Wool
Doniphan
Kearny
Boundary by Decree
of 1816
Battles
Disputed Territory
Victoria
Tampico
Compostela
Guadalajara
Queretaro
Acambaro
Churubusco
Mexico
Cerro Gordo
Chapultepec
Vera Cruz
Jalapa
Puebla
Cuernavaca

rey after a three-day battle, September 21-23, and moved on to Saltillo and a major victory at Buena Vista. There General Taylor was side-tracked by a jealous James K. Polk, who turned to General Winfield Scott and a plan to invade Mexico at Vera Cruz with Mexico City as the chief objective. In the summer of 1847 General Scott achieved a brilliant victory in a series of skirmishes and battles in the environs of Mexico City; the Mexican capital fell to the invaders, and the war came to an end.

In the meantime, Stephen W. Kearny marched an army from Fort Leavenworth, Kansas, across the American Southwest to California. Kearny, with the help of the United States Navy, completed the conquest of California.

Texans made a significant contribution to the campaign in northern Mexico as several thousand men volunteered for service with Taylor's army. Special distinction came to a group of Texas Rangers commanded by John C. (Jack) Hays, Ben McCulloch, Samuel H. Walker, and John S. (Rip) Ford. These experienced rangers, equipped with Colt revolvers, served as scouts with Taylor's forces. They did such an excellent job that, in 1847, they were transferred to Winfield Scott's command for the invasion at Vera Cruz.

By the terms of the Treaty of Guadalupe Hidalgo, February 2, 1848, Mexico ceded to the United States Texas (with the Rio Grande as the boundary), New Mexico (including present Arizona), and upper California (including San Diego)—in short, all of Mexico's possessions west of the 100° meridian, south of the 42° parallel, and north of the traditional southern boundary of New Mexico along the Gila and Colorado rivers. In return for this vast territorial cession, the United States assumed the unpaid claims of American citizens against Mexico and paid Mexico $15,000,000.

The legacy of the war left perplexing questions concerning both the western boundary of the state of Texas (Did the Treaty of Guadalupe Hidalgo verify the Texas claim to eastern New Mexico?) and the status of Negro slavery in the newly won territory. Both questions were to be involved in the compromise settlements of 1850.

Seymour V. Connor, *Adventure in Glory: The Saga of Texas, 1836-1849* (Austin, 1965).

Justin H. Smith, *The War with Mexico* (2 vols., New York, 1919).

Walter P. Webb, *The Texas Rangers* (New York, 1935).

# TEXAS & THE COMPROMISE OF 1850

 THE WAR with Mexico brought a series of developments that threatened the territorial rights of Texas in the territory of New Mexico. In August, 1846, Stephen W. Kearny and the Army of the West occupied Northern New Mexico and established a civil government there without regards to the claim of the state of Texas. The federal government approved of Kearny's action, and when Governor J. Pinckney Henderson reminded James Buchanan, the United States secretary of state, of the

Texas claim to the region, Buchanan replied that the matter would have to be settled by Congress. Fearful over the possible loss of this vast territory, the Texas legislature, on March 15, 1848, created Santa Fe County with extensive boundaries covering practically all of the eastern and northeastern part of the state. After the residents of New Mexico petitioned for territorial organization (November, 1848), the Texas legislature, on December 31, 1848, fixed new boundaries for Santa Fe County, added the counties of Worth, Presidio, and El Paso, and sent Robert S. Neighbors to organize the new local governments. In New Mexico, the Texan efforts met the hostility of the people of New Mexico and of President Zachary Taylor. In the year 1850 the United States Congress inherited the problem.

Plans suggesting a settlement of the dispute were presented to Congress by Senator Thomas H. Benton of Missouri, Senator John Bell of Tennessee, a compromise committee of thirteen headed by Henry Clay and Senator James A. Pearce of Maryland—the Pearce plan was finally adopted by Congress and the boundary of Texas became a part of the famous Compromise of 1850 as the Texas and New Mexico Act, September 9, 1850, which provided "Texas will agree that her boundary on the north shall commence at the point at which the meridian of one hundred degrees west from Greenwich is intersected by the parallel of thirty-six degrees thirty minutes north latitude, and shall run from said point due west to the meridian of one hundred and three degrees west from Greenwich; hence her boundary shall run due south to the thirty-second degree of north latitude; thence on the said parallel of thirty-two degrees of north latitude to the Rio Bravo del Norte, and thence with the channel of said river to the Gulf of Mexico."

Also, Texas relinquished all of her claims to territory "exterior to the limits and boundaries" described above; the state also relinquished "all claims against the United States for liability of the debts of Texas," and the United States promised to pay Texas "the sum of ten million dollars in a stock bearing five per cent interest, and redeemable at the end of fourteen years."

An earlier resolution, a section of eight resolves introduced by Henry Clay on January 29, 1850, specified "that the western boundary of the State of Texas ought to be fixed on the Rio del Norte, commencing one marine league from its mouth [5.56 kilometers or 3.4 miles] and running up that river to the southern line of New Mexico; . . ."

Thus it was in this fashion that the southern, western, and northern limits of Texas were fixed by law. The historian must conclude that Texas made a good bargain considering the absence of documents to back up her claims.

Henry Steele Commager (ed.), *Documents of American History* (New York, 1948).

## PLANS FOR BOUNDARY ADJUSTMENTS, 1850

A Benton's plan of January 16
---- provision made for later division into two states

B Bell's plan of February 28
---- provision made for later division into three states

C Plan of Committee of Thirteen, April 17

D Pearce's plan of August 5 established by Congress, 1850

E Boundary dispute with New Mexico in Constitution of 1850

Area claimed by New Mexico in 1850

Present state of New Mexico

Territory to be relinquished

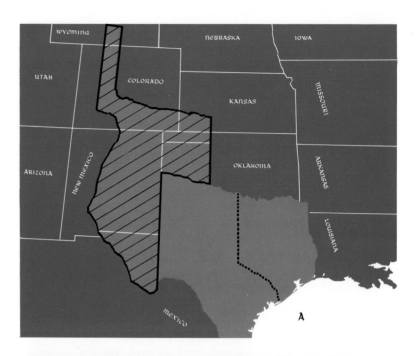

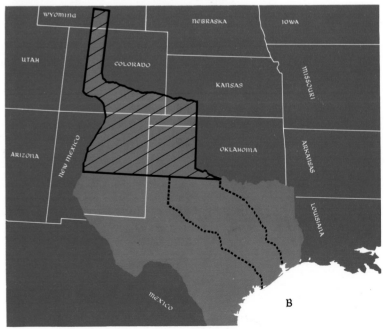

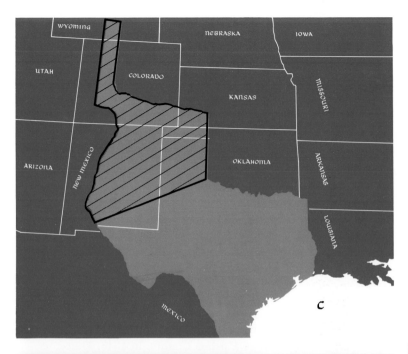

c

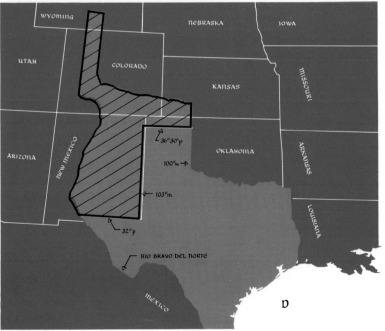

36° 30' p

100°m

103°m

32° p

RIO BRAVO DEL NORTE

D

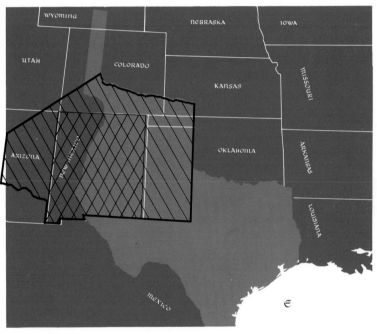

E

# THE NORTHEAST TEXAS FRONTIER, 1836-1860

IN HIS STUDY of immigration and extension of settlement in *Texas, The Lone Star State,* Professor Rupert N. Richardson points out that "the old Texans had hardly returned from the army or from the 'runaway scrape' before their kinsmen from east of the Sabine began to join them. . . . Poor crops in the United States, the panic of 1837, and the business stagnation that followed combined to send a swarm of immigrants to Texas in 1837." This rising tide of migration continued, with minor setbacks, throughout the years of the Republic and increased sharply after annexation. New settlements and western expansion are, therefore, the major theme of the two decades, 1840-1860.

The Northeast and East Texas area was the region of the most rapid frontier advance during the years of the Republic. It was here, following such hunters and traders as Silas Colville, Holland Coffee, and Abel Warren, that the pioneers pushed westward from the older settlements around Pecan Point, Jonesborough, Clarksville, Boston, and Jefferson into the post oak forests and blacklands along the Sulphur, Sabine, and upper Trinity rivers and into the unoccupied lands nearest the Arkansas and Louisiana borders. New communities westward along the Red River valley included Bonham, first known as Bois d'Arc, established in present Fannin County near Fort English as a direct result of Bailey English's interest in the area; Warren's Trading Post (also known as Old Warren), constructed on a bend of the Red River by Abel Warren in 1836-37; Preston, also known as Coffee's Station be-cause of Holland Coffee's trading post, established on the south bank of the Red in 1837; and the town of Sherman, surveyed and established in present Grayson County in 1846. Colbert's Ferry was located eight miles downstream from Preston and became one of the most prominent immigrant crossings into Texas. In 1847 William Fitzhugh built Fitzhugh's Station three miles southeast of present Gainesville; Gainesville, in present Cooke County, was settled in 1850 by persons who had started over the California Trail.

Between Sulphur River and the Trinity, new settlements grew up at Tarrant, a small town that became the county seat of Hopkins County in 1846; Gilmer, the first county seat of Upshur County, in 1846; Quitman, settled in the early 1840's and named the county seat of Wood County in 1850; Tyler, incorporated in 1846; Mount Pleasant, established in 1846 by John Binion, Richard Moore, and L. Gilbert; Grand Saline, first called Jordan's Saline because John Jordan and A. T. McGee pioneered the salt mines there in 1845; Buffalo, founded in 1846 in northwest Henderson County at John P. Moore's ferry across the Trinity River; Kaufman, first known as Kingsboro for Dr. William P. King, established as the county seat of Kaufman County in 1851 (Kaufman and Kingsboro appear on the Texas maps of the 1850's as separate places); Greenville, established as the county seat of Hunt County in 1846 (the town had grown up around the homes of H. M. Wright and Fred Ende); Athens, surveyed by Samuel Huffer in 1850; and Mount Vernon, established by Stephen Keith in 1849.

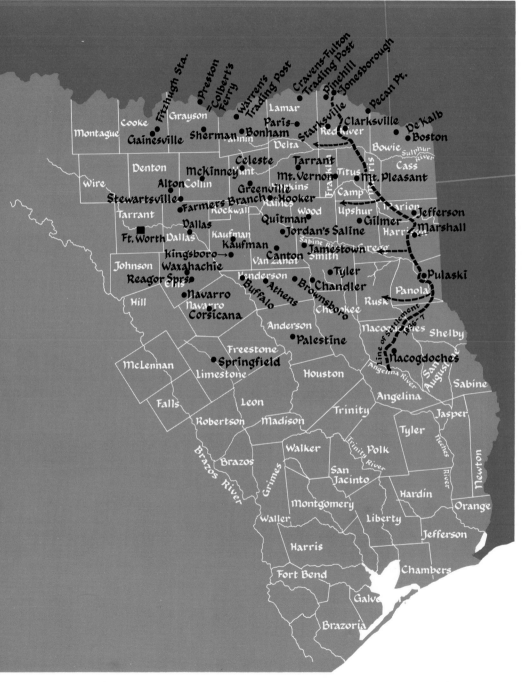

West of the Trinity the first settlements were at Corsicana and Navarro. Corsicana grew up around the McKinney Inn, built by Hampton McKinney in 1849; Navarro, located to the northwest of Corsicana, was a thriving settlement by the 1850's. Near the junction of the three forks of the Trinity, the settlement of Dallas had its origin in 1842 when John N. Bryan persuaded a few families from Bird's Fort to move to the site of his cabin on the east bank of the Trinity. To the south, Ellis County (organized in 1849) grew out of early settlements at Reagor Springs and near present Forreston.

North and northwest of Dallas, William S. Peters and associates pioneered and settled the lands of Grayson, Collin, Denton, Tarrant, and Dallas counties. McKinney, named for Collin McKinney, was settled in 1845 near the home of Dr. William E. Throckmorton. Alton, originally surveyed by the Peters' company, and Pinckneyville were, in the late 1840's, the two principal settlements in Denton County; the new community of Denton was established in 1857. When secession and the Civil War came, Gainesville (Fitzhugh's) and Denton were on the rimland of the north Texas frontier. While new counties had been created to the west, these areas were largely unpopulated.

# SOUTHEAST TEXAS, 1837-1867

 WHILE the coastal plains of Southeast Texas and the pine forests of the Sabine and Neches river basins have received prior coverage on several maps, perhaps we need to look at this older region again in the light of new settlements and frontier expansion during the years of the Republic and early statehood. While it is true that the vast majority of Anglo-Americans who came to Texas before 1837 settled in this region, thousands of acres of vacant land remained to be claimed; and shortly after the establishment of the Republic, there were sufficient people to claim the land.

Along the Sabine River, Sabine City was settled on the southwest shore of Sabine Lake. Upstream, Orange was first known as Green's Bluff and Madison before a final name change in the late 1850's. Further upstream, Booths Mills or Salem appears on the early maps of the region. Belgrade was founded by William McFarland at a point where the Coushatta Trace crossed the Sabine River; north of Belgrade, Burkeville (apparently known as New Columbia for awhile) was established in 1844 on Little Cow Creek by John R. Burke.

In the Neches River valley, Beaumont (very early known as Tevis Bluff) was founded by the Thomas Huling Company in 1835. Quite a distance upstream, and on the Angelina River, Old Zavala was founded in 1834 at the Beef Trail Crossing of the Angelina. Woodville, on the forks of Turkey Creek, was located by a Tyler County election in 1846; and Livingston was established in 1839 by Moses Choate. It is interesting that the 1857 Topographical Engineer map of this Big Thicket and Piney Woods area carries such descriptive notes as "difficult swamp," "pine forest," "low flat country covered with pine forest [between Jasper and Belgrade]," and "country very hilly, hills covered with thick scrubby oaks [south of Milam and Sabine town]." Also, all ferries were marked such as "west Liberty ferry" at Liberty on the Trinity; "crossing good by ferry" between Woodville and Jasper and at several other locations, and "river 80 yards, crossing good" at New Columbia on the Sabine.

On the Trinity River upstream from Liberty, the early town of Smithfield, where there was a "good crossing by ferry" has apparently been lost to most Texas historians. Upstream from Smithfield, Swartwout was established in 1838 on the Trinity at the site of an Alabama-Coushatta Indian village by James Morgan, Arthur Garner, and Thomas Bradley; the new village was named for Samuel Swartwout, the New York financeer and "prince of thieves" during the Andrew Jackson administration. Upstream from Swartwout, the communities of Carolina and Alabama apparently left little or no trace. In between the latter two, however, Cincinnati, located on the Trinity in present Walker County, was founded by James C. De Witt in 1838; Cincinnati was a well-known river port in this region until 1853, when an epidemic of yellow fever virtually destroyed the town. South of Cincinnati, Huntsville was established in 1836-37 by Pleasant and Ephriam Gray as an Indian trading post. To the north of Cincinnati (and to the northeast of "lost" Alabama), Crockett was surveyed in 1838-39 by A. E. Gossett (two families resided on the site in 1839). To the west of the Alabama settlement,

Leona was founded when Moses Campbell built a store on the site in 1845; Leon County was created in 1846 with Leona as the first county seat.

West of the Trinity, in counties carved from the old Stephen F. Austin grant (and the danger of repetition increases), new communities would include the following: Rutersville, established by Martin Ruter in 1838 east of the Colorado River and La Grange; Boonville, located two miles northeast of present Bryan, established by Mordecai Boon, John Millican, and John H. Jones in 1841 as the county seat of Brazos County; Cypress City, established on Cypress Creek in the early 1850's; Bellville, founded in 1848 and named for Thomas Bell, who built a home on the site in 1838; Montgomery, founded in 1837 by W. W. Sheppard, James Mitchell, and Dr. Charles B. Stewart, became the first county seat of Montgomery County; and Anderson, a town in Grimes County that traces its origin to the Fanthrop Inn of 1834, became an actual settlement in 1835 with Henry Fanthrop as postmaster.

The communities of Old Franklin, Caldwell, and Springfield were located on the hither edge of (and, one suspects, were surrounded by) free land in the 1850's.

J. Bartholomew, "Texas, part of New Mexico" (Edinburg, 1850), Elliott Collection, Library, Southwest Texas State College, San Marcos, Texas.

Map of Texas and part of New Mexico, 1857, Bureau of Topographical Engineers, Washington, D.C.

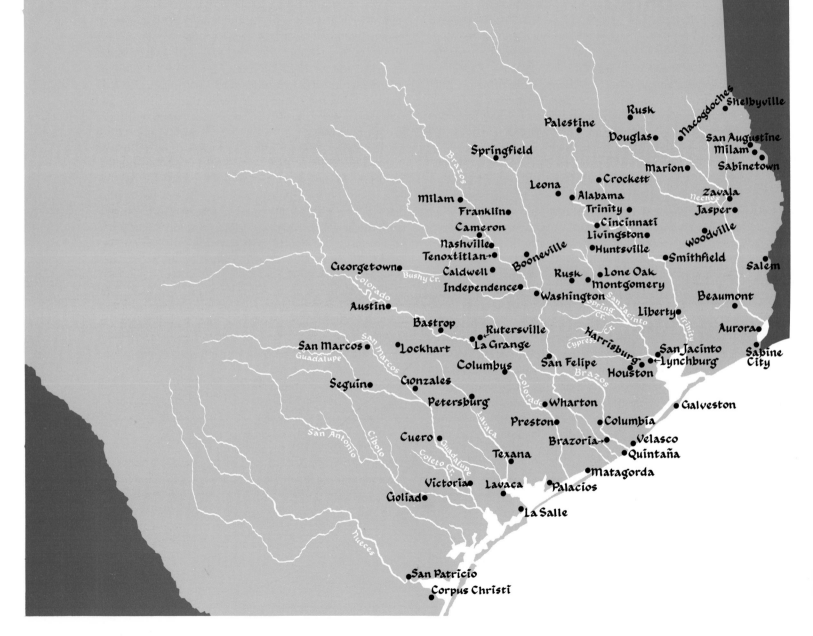

Rusk •     • Nacogdoches    • Shelbyville

Palestine •

Douglas •     • San Augustine

Springfield •     • Milam

Marion •    • Sabinetown

Leona •     • Crockett

Milam •    • Alabama    Zavala •

Franklin •    Trinity •    Jasper •

Cameron •    Cincinnati •

Nashville •    Livingston •   Woodville •

Tenoxtitlan→   Booneville •   Huntsville •

Georgetown •    Caldwell •   Rusk •   Lone Oak •    Smithfield •

Independence •   Montgomery •    Salem •

Austin •    Washington •

Bastrop •    Liberty •    Beaumont •

Rutersville→   Harrisburg    Aurora •

San Marcos •   Lockhart •   La Grange •   San Jacinto •   Sabine City

Columbus •   San Felipe   Lynchburg ←

Seguin •   Gonzales •    Houston •

Petersburg •    Wharton •   Galveston •

Preston •   Columbia •

Cuero •    Brazoria→   Velasco •

Texana •    Quintaña •

Victoria •   Lavaca    Matagorda •

Goliad •    Palacios •

La Salle •

San Patricio •

Corpus Christi •

WEST OF THE TRINITY in the area of the old Sterling C. Robertson Colony (or the Austin-Williams "upper" colony) the western advance was necessarily slow because of the fear of Indian attack. At the close of the Texas Revolution the only settlements northwest of the Old San Antonio Road were Nashville-on-the-Brazos, Wheelock, and Sarahville de Viesca, and only a few families lived at these three places. During the years 1840-1860, however, the westward advance was rather rapid as pioneer settlers moved into the region along the Brazos River from both the east and the southeast.

To the east of the Brazos, along the watersheds of the Navasota and Trinity rivers, the earliest settlements included Dunn's Fort (1834), Old Franklin (1838), and Owensville in present Robertson County. Fort Boggy (1840), Leona (established at Moses Campbell's store in 1846), and Centerville (1851) were the first settlements in present Leon County.

To the west of the Brazos, the older settlements of Nashville and Port Sullivan became temporary stops for many families bound for the river bottom lands along Little, Lampasas, Cowhouse, Leon, and Bosque rivers. As the frontier moved to the northwest, new settlements were established at Bryant's Station, a blockhouse fort built by Benjamin Bryant on the north bank of Little River in 1840; Cameron, surveyed by James M. Smith in 1846 as the county seat of Milam County; the Three Forks settlement, a community near an old ranger station built by George B. Erath at the confluence of the Lampasas, Leon, and Cowhouse rivers in 1836; and Marlin (first known as Adams Spring and Bucksnort), established a few miles east of the falls of the Brazos near the old John Marlin settlement in 1850. In this region, Milam County, growing out of the Milam Land District, was created in 1836, Bell County in 1850, and Falls County in 1850. The pioneers of Bell County included the families of Goldsby Childers, Robert Davidson, John Fulcher, Moses Griffin, John Needham, William Taylor, Michael Reed, and O. T. Tyler.

In 1845 Neil McLennan built a cabin on the South Bosque River west of present Waco. The following year the families of Abram Richardson, John Rhoads, Jesse Sutton, Shapley P. Ross, and Thomas Barron moved into the region near the confluence of the Brazos and Bosque rivers. Waco was surveyed and established by George B. Erath in the spring of 1849 and McLennan County was created in 1850. To the north and west, the families of Ewell Everett, L. H. Scrutchfield, William Barton, J. L. Sears, and Sam Barnes pioneered the present Bosque County settlements along Hog Creek (Searsville and Valley Mills) and the Kimball Bend region of the Brazos River. In 1853-54 Ole Canuteson, Jens Ringness, and Kleng Peerson were instrumental in establishing the Norwegian colony in western Bosque County. Meridian was surveyed (and the county created) in 1854. To the east of the Brazos River, W. H. Kirkpatrick, John Caruthers, Bynum Fancher, and Jack Boiles pioneered the Hill County area, 1849-1854. Brandon, Towash, and Jacks Branch were among the pioneer settlements; Hill County was created in 1853.

Along the Leon and Cowhouse rivers, Fort Gates led to the establishment of Gatesville and the organization of Coryell County in 1854. Robert Carter and family, followed by James Rice and Henry Standefer pioneered the Hamilton County area in 1855; the coun-

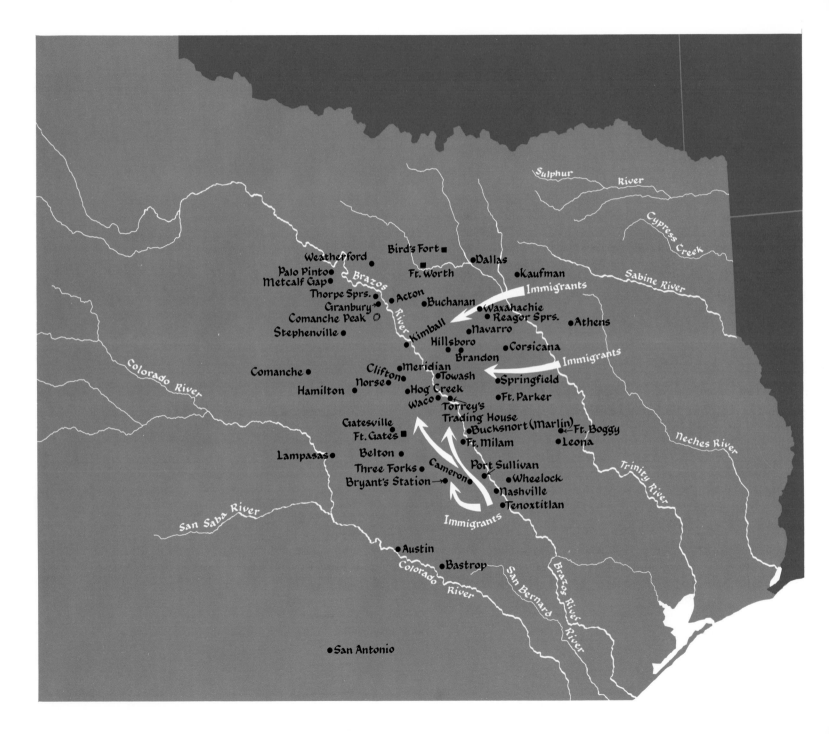

ty was created in January, 1858. In the meanwhile John M. and William F. Stephens had established Stephenville in 1854; Erath County (named for George B. Erath) was organized in 1856. Further north, George R. Bevers settled near the Flat Rock crossing of the Big Keechi Creek in 1854. Oliver Loving, Reuben Vaughan, John Hittson, and Charles Goodnight moved to the region in 1856. Palo Pinto County was created in 1856 with Golconda (Palo Pinto) as the county seat. The first Hood County settlements were made near the old Acton community in 1853-54 under the leadership of W. J. Richardson, William Robinson, Gideon Mills, and Robert Crockett; the county was organized in 1866. To the south of the Hood territory, Johnson County was created and organized in 1854 with Buchanan as the county seat.

The settlements along the mid-Brazos were aided greatly when the United States government established its first line of frontier forts in 1849; this line of defense (to be traced in detail later) included Fort Worth, on the south bank of the Trinity; Fort Graham, on the east bank of the Brazos in present Hill County; and Fort Gates, on the Leon River a few miles south of present Gatesville.

Lila M. Batte, *A History of Milam County*, (San Antonio, 1958).

Jacob de Cordova, New Map of the State of Texas (New York, 1849), Archives, University of Texas Library, Austin, Texas.

William C. Pool, *The Bosque Territory, A History of an Agrarian Society* (Kyle, Texas, 1964).

————, *Texas in 1856*. J. H. Colton and Company, New York, Elliott Collection, Library, Southwest Texas State College, San Marcos, Texas.

O. T. Tyler, *A History of Bell County* (San Antonio, 1936).

C. S. Williams, State of Texas from the Latest Authorities (Philadelphia, 1847), Archives, University of Texas Library.

# THE HILL COUNTRY FRONTIER, 1836-1860

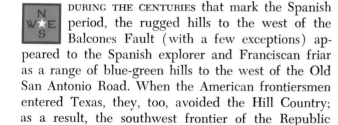 DURING THE CENTURIES that mark the Spanish period, the rugged hills to the west of the Balcones Fault (with a few exceptions) appeared to the Spanish explorer and Franciscan friar as a range of blue-green hills to the west of the Old San Antonio Road. When the American frontiersmen entered Texas, they, too, avoided the Hill Country; as a result, the southwest frontier of the Republic followed the Old San Antonio Road from San Antonio to the Colorado River.

San Marcos was founded in 1846-47 and Hays County organized in 1848. To the southwest of San Marcos, New Braunfels was established at Comal Springs in 1845 by Carl of Solms-Braunfels and German immigrants sent to Texas by the *Adelsverein*. In the early 1840's, San Antonio and the settlements at New Braunfels, San Marcos, Lockhart, Austin, and the Brushy Creek communities stood on the eastern edge of free land and faced the hills beyond.

In 1842 the Texas Congress granted the land between the Llano and Colorado rivers to Henry Fisher and Burchard Miller. The Fisher-Miller grant was soon transferred to the *Adelsverein*. Under the leadership of Prince Carl of Solms-Braunfels and John O.

Meusebach, the *Adelsverein* established Fredericksburg in 1846 as the first permanent settlement west of the Balcones Fault. Other settlements followed the success at Fredericksburg (including the Mormon Colony of Zodiac), and Gillespie County was organized in 1848. In 1847 the *Adelsverein* established Castell and Bettina on the Llano River; Llano County was organized in 1856 with the new town of Llano as the county seat. Northeast of the Colorado, San Saba County was created and organized in 1856; Lampasas County (with Burleson, a community near where Moses Hughes had settled in 1853) was organized in 1856. The name of Burleson, located near Hancock Springs, was changed to Lampasas a few months later. East of Llano County, Samuel E. Holland's residence, Henry E. McCulloch's ranger station, and Fort Croghan represented the vanguard of the frontier in present Burnet County (created in 1852 and organized in 1854).

West of Austin, San Marcos, and New Braunfels, the pioneer settlers followed the meanderings of the Blanco, Guadalupe, and Pedernales rivers into the heartland of the Texas hills. James H. Callahan located a homestead on the upper reaches of the Blanco River in 1853. The Pittsburgh Land Company, owned by Callahan and John D. Pitts, established the town of Blanco (first called Pittsburgh) in 1853-54. When Blanco County was organized in the spring of 1858, the name Pittsburgh became Blanco City. Shortly after the organization of Blanco County in 1858, the brothers Andrew Jackson, Jesse Thomas, and Sam Ealy Johnson, Sr., pioneered the settlement of the Pedernales River valley.

Further west, Kerrville (known originally as Brownsborough and Kerrsville) was established by a group of cypress shingle makers in 1846 near the Guadalupe River cabin of Joshua D. Brown. Comfort was founded by Ernst Altgelt and a small group of German settlers in 1854, and Kerr County was organized in 1856. Kendall County remained a part of Blanco, Bexar, and Comal until 1862, although Boerne (1851) and Sisterdale (1847) had been founded earlier. It was in this immediate region, north of the Guadalupe, that George Wilkins Kendall introduced sheep to Texas.

To the northwest of Fredericksburg and Gillespie County, the frontier town of Mason grew up around Fort Mason; the adjacent territory was populated by German settlers, and Mason County was organized in 1858. To the south of Fredericksburg and Kerrville, Bandera was surveyed on the Medina River by John James, John H. Herndon, and Charles de Montel in 1853; Bandera County was created and organized in 1856. Just below the southern rim of the Balcones Fault, Castroville (1844), D'Hanis (1847), Quihi (1845), and Vandenburg (1847) were all settled by Henri Castro. Uvalde was settled in 1853 by R. W. Black and Nathan Stratton, and Uvalde County was organized in 1856.

In the 1850's the Hill Country frontier received protection from Fort Inge, Camp Verde, and Fort Mason. While Raleigh Gentry had moved to the North Llano in Kimble County and other pockets of pioneers existed beyond, a line running south from the vicinity of Fort Mason, through western Kerr County to Uvalde would have represented the frontier in 1860; much of the Edwards Plateau lay beyond.

THE RIO GRANDE PLAIN may be loosely defined as lying south of San Antonio and between the northern rim of the Nueces River drainage basin, the northern bank of the Rio Grande, and the Gulf of Mexico. Covered with a dense growth of prickly pear, cactus, mesquite, dwarf oak, catclaw, huajillo, huisache, blackbrush, cenizo, and other wild shrubs, the plain is drained by the Rio Grande and Nueces and their tributaries. This region was secured to Texas by the terms of the Treaty of Guadalupe Hidalgo, and its history—Spanish, Mexican, and American—is shown on the map from the lower Pecos River valley to the Gulf.

Beginning at a point on the Rio Grande near the mouth of the Pecos River and looking at the region as it existed prior to the Civil War, one notices that only geographical terms break the monotony of the map: streams such as Rio San Pedro, Arroyo Zoquete, Arroyo de las Piedras Pintas (the painted rocks of the native Indian tribes), Arroyo Salado, Mavericks and Las Moras Creeks; meaningful notations such as "Indian trail," "no water," "good route"; and also notes to the effect that Lieutenant F. F. Bryan and Lieutenant Nathaniel Michler of the Corps of Topographical Engineers had explored the country and blazed new trails in 1853.

It was in this region that Dr. John Charles Beales established his short-lived colony of Dolores at the head of Las Moras Creek in 1834. In 1850 Eagle Pass (El Paso de Aguila) was established by Henry Matson on the north bank of the Rio Grande between old Camp Duncan and Camp California, the latter being a resting place on the California trail. According to local historians, Matson borrowed a tent and set up

a saloon just outside Fort Duncan. Shortly thereafter John Twohig (a San Antonio landowner and banker) surveyed and named the new community. In 1853 W. G. Freeman visited the location of Fort Duncan and reported: "Immediately above and separated from it only by a deep ravine, is the settlement or town called Eagle Pass, in which there are three or four stores for the sale of goods principally adapted to the Mexican market. This place contains some eight or ten good buildings, and the same number of mud hovels occupied by the lower order of Mexicans, with a population of from 80 to 100, of whom not more than twelve or fifteen are Americans." The town of Eagle Pass appears on more than one pre-Civil War map as "Kinney's Court House," signifying the county seat of Kinney County, created in 1850.

Downstream a short distance from Eagle Pass and Cazneau's ranch, two crossings on the Rio Grande stand out in early Texas history—the Paguache or Upper Crossing and Paso de Francia or Lower Crossing. During the Spanish-Mexican period, these two fords, flanking the Presidio San Juan Bautista, were significant crossings leading into Texas from the interior of Mexico. Old Camp Pendencia stood near the Presidio Crossing, Kingsbury's Rapids, and the "Coal Beds" that give the name Piedras Negras, the Mexican counterpart to Eagle Pass.

South, or downstream from the Presidio Crossing, the country between forts Duncan and McIntosh is described by W. G. Freeman as "most unpromising. It is scantily watered and will probably always remain a dreary waste." Laredo, in Webb County (1848), was established in 1755 by Tomás Sánchez, who was given permission by José Escandón to form

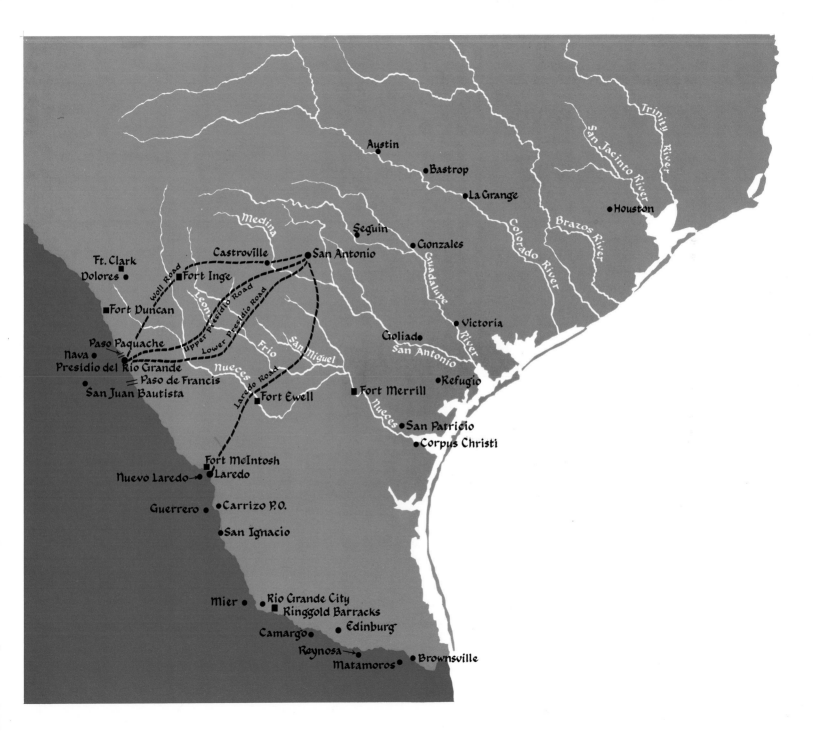

Trinity River

San Jacinto River

Brazos River

Colorado River

Houston

La Grange

Bastrop

Austin

Seguin

Gonzales

Medina

Castroville

San Antonio

Guadalupe River

Victoria

Ft. Clark

Dolores

Woll Road

Fort Inge

Leon

Upper Presidio Road

Lower Presidio Road

Fort Duncan

Goliad

San Antonio River

Paso Paquache

Frio

San Miguel

Nava

Nueces

Refugio

Presidio del Rio Grande

Paso de Francis

Laredo Road

Fort Ewell

Fort Merrill

San Juan Bautista

San Patricio

Nueces

Corpus Christi

Fort McIntosh

Nuevo Laredo → Laredo

Guerrero

Carrizo P.O.

San Ignacio

Mier

Rio Grande City

Ringgold Barracks

Camargo

Edinburg

Reynosa →

Matamoros

Brownsville

a settlement there. When Webb County was organized in 1848, Laredo became the county seat. In describing the location of Fort McIntosh in 1853, Freeman reports "to the south and one mile distant is the old Mexican town of Laredo, containing a population of from 800 to 1000, of which number not more than forty are Americans. . . . a small town has sprung up on the west bank of the river, nearly opposite, called New Laredo."

South of Laredo and Webb County, the Texas legislature created Starr, Hidalgo, and Cameron counties in 1848. Downstream villages in the late 1850's included San Ignacio, Carrizo Post Office (opposite Guerrero), Roma (a short distance from Mier), Rio Grande City (opposite Camargo), Edinburg (opposite Reynosa), and Brownsville (opposite Matamoros).

Between the Rio Grande and the Nueces River, the map still (as it did in Spanish-Mexican days) reflects the names "Mustang Prairie" and "wild horses and cattle." Corpus Christi, where the Nueces empties into the Bay, was founded by H. L. Kinney in 1840; Nueces County was established in 1846 with Corpus Christi as the county seat. Upstream from Corpus Christi and San Patricio, Fort Merrill was established in 1850 on the right bank of the river; and, further upstream Fort Ewell was established in 1852 on the south bank of the river in present La Salle County. Roads from the Rio Grande communities to Corpus Christi and San Antonio traversed the "mustang prairie." Fort Inge (1849) and Fort Clark (1852) guarded the sparse settlements along the upper Nueces.

# THE EXPLORATION OF WEST TEXAS, 1849-1850

DURING THE YEARS of the Republic (except for Dr. Henry Connelly's Chihuahua Trail of 1839-1840, a little known and little used road from Presidio to Horsehead Crossing, to Big Spring, and northeast to the Red River), not much consideration was given to that part of Texas that lay to the west of the line of settlement. As a result, when Texas entered the United States in 1845-46, large areas of the far western section of the state were largely unknown and unexplored; explorations carried on by the state government and the Corps of Topographical Engineers of the United States Army between 1848 and 1860 were of great aid in the eventual establishment of roads and in the general development of the country. The following map shows the route of six of these western explorations, all between the years 1848 and 1850.

1. In the summer of 1848 Captain John C. (Jack) Hays led an expedition from San Antonio to the German community of Castell on the Llano River, then either up the Llano to its source or north to the San Saba River (accounts conflict), and then southwest

to the headwaters of the Nueces. From the Nueces headwaters, the expedition moved to Las Moras Creek, San Pedro (Devils) River, the Pecos River, and, having become thoroughly lost in the Trans-Pecos region, finally arrived at the Presidio del Norte and Ben Leaton's fort. From Leaton's fort, Hays returned to San Antonio by way of Horsehead Crossing of the Pecos and a rather direct route.

2. In 1849 Robert S. Neighbors and John S. Ford led an expedition from San Antonio and Austin to El Paso by way of Torrey's Trading House, the North Bosque River, Old Owls Camp near Stephenville, south to the Colorado River, west along Brady's Creek across the South Concho, then by way of Castle Mountain and Horsehead Crossing to the Pecos, west across the headwaters of Limpia and Toyah creeks to the Rio Grande at a point downstream from the Quitman Mountains, and then up the Rio Grande to El Paso. On the return trip, the expedition traveled by way of Guadalupe Pass, Delaware Creek, the Pecos River, Horsehead Crossing, Castle Mountain, Mustang Water Hole, Green Mountain (Tom Green County), the headwaters of the San Saba, Mason, Fredericksburg, and Boerne.

3. In the spring of 1849, William F. Smith and Lieutenant W. H. C. Whiting of the Topographical Engineers led an expedition from San Antonio to El Paso. Leaving San Antonio on February 12, Whiting and Smith traveled the "Old Pinto Trail" to the headwaters of the South Fork of the San Saba River, and then to El Paso by way of Live Oak Creek, the Pecos River, Comanche Spring (Fort Stockton), the Davis Mountains, the Van Horn Mountains, and the Rio Grande. Searching for better water on their return, Whiting and Smith blazed what came to be known as the "lower route" from El Paso to San Antonio—by way of the Rio Grande, across country to the Pecos River, down the Pecos for 60 miles, across to Devils

River, and then to San Antonio by way of Las Moras Creek, the Nueces, Frio, and Seco rivers.

4. Returning from the Rio Grande in September, 1849, Captain Randolph B. Marcy left Donna Ana, New Mexico, and established the famous Marcy Trail across West Texas. Marcy traveled by way of the salt lakes, Guadalupe Pass, Delaware Creek, the Pecos River, overland to "Bigspring," the Colorado River, the Clear Fork of the Brazos, Double Mountains (Stonewall County), the Brazos River near New Castle in present Young County, following the Wichita rivers, and then across present Jack, Clay, Montague, and Cooke counties to Preston on the Red River; Marcy then continued to Fort Smith, Arkansas.

5. In the fall and early winter of 1849, Lieutenant Nathaniel Michler explored the territory between the Red and Pecos rivers. Leaving Fort Washita in November, Michler paralleled the Big and Little Wichita rivers to the Brazos country, then went to the headwaters of the Clear Fork of the Brazos, and the "Bigspring" of the Colorado River (Big Spring, Texas), then to Horsehead Crossing, and, finally, to San Antonio along Lt. Francis T. Bryan's route.

6. In the summer of 1849, Lieutenant Francis T. Bryan of the Topographical Engineers was ordered to explore the country between San Antonio and El Paso. Leaving San Antonio, Bryan traveled by way of Fredericksburg, Kickapoo Creek, Dove Creek, Horsehead Crossing, Delaware Creek, and Guadalupe Pass.

Other explorations of these years include W. H. C. Whiting's establishment of the "military road" from Fort Lincoln (Seco Creek) to Martin Scott, Bandera Pass, Fort Croghan, Fort Gates, Fort Graham, and Fort Worth; Joseph E. Johnston's retracing of the "lower route" from San Antonio to El Paso; and Nathaniel Michler and M. L. Smith's establishment of a road from San Antonio to Fort Ringgold on the Rio Grande in 1850.

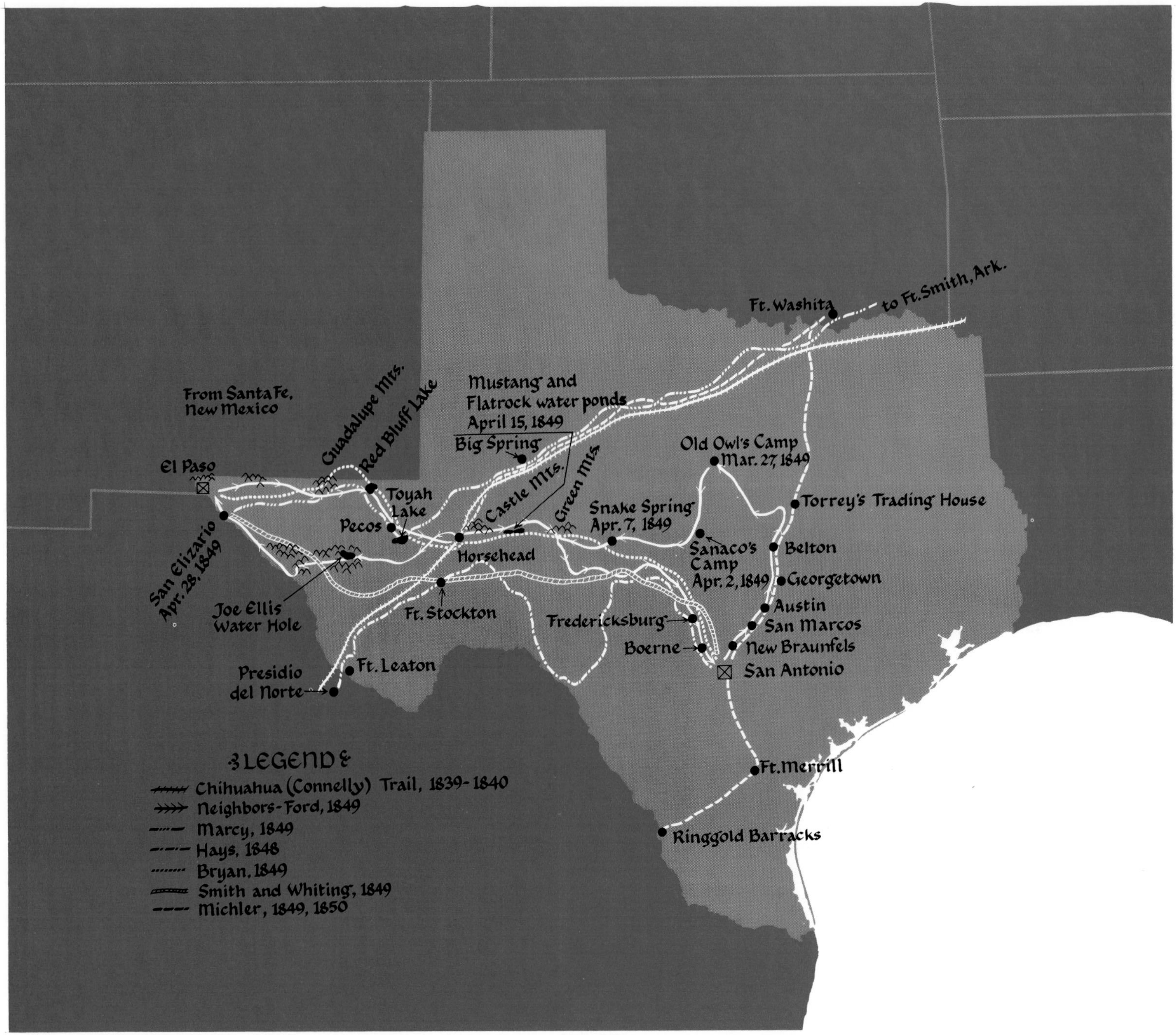

Ft. Washita ⋯⋯ to Ft. Smith, Ark.

From Santa Fe,
New Mexico

Guadalupe Mts.

Red Bluff Lake

Mustang and
Flatrock water ponds
April 15, 1849

Big Spring

Old Owl's Camp
Mar. 27, 1849

El Paso

Toyah
Lake

Castle Mts.

Green Mts.

Snake Spring
Apr. 7, 1849

Torrey's Trading House

San Elizario
Apr. 28, 1849

Pecos

Horsehead

Sanaco's
Camp
Apr. 2, 1849

Belton

Georgetown

Joe Ellis
Water Hole

Ft. Stockton

Fredericksburg

Austin

San Marcos

Boerne

New Braunfels

Presidio
del Norte

Ft. Leaton

San Antonio

Ft. Merrill

⋰LEGEND⋱

〉〉〉〉 Chihuahua (Connelly) Trail, 1839–1840
⟩⟩⟩⟩ Neighbors-Ford, 1849
╌ ╌ ╌ Marcy, 1849
╌·╌·╌ Hays, 1848
⋯⋯⋯ Bryan, 1849
▦▦▦ Smith and Whiting, 1849
╌╌╌ Michler, 1849, 1850

Ringgold Barracks

J. Bartholomew, "Texas and a Part of New Mexico," Edinburg, n.d., Elliott Collection, Library, Southwest Texas State College, San Marcos, Texas.

A. B. Bender, "Opening Routes Across West Texas, 1848-1850," *Southwestern Historical Quarterly*, XXXVII.

William H. Goetzmann, *Army Exploration in the American West, 1830-1863* (New Haven, 1959).

Map of Texas and a Part of New Mexico, 1857, Topographical Engineers, Washington, D. C.

Joseph C. McConnell, *The West Texas Frontier* (Jacksboro, 1933).

Kenneth F. Neighbours, "The Expedition of Major Robert S. Neighbors to El Paso, 1849," *Southwestern Historical Quarterly*, LVIII.

# FRONTIER FORTS, 1846-1867

 WHEN TEXAS was annexed to the Union in 1845-46, the United States government acquired an additional burden of border and frontier defense. Colonel William S. Harney was in San Antonio with no army to command. When the Comanches began their raids, acting Governor Albert C. Horton asked for troops; he received several companies of state militiamen who were to serve temporarily under the United States Army. The companies were located at (1) Conner's Station on Richland Creek in southern Navarro County, (2) Ross's Station on the North Bosque River, probably in present McLennan County, (3) McCulloch's Station on Hamilton Creek in present Burnet County, (4) Medina Station on the Medina River in present Medina County, (5) Fredericksburg in Gillespie County, and (6) two companies were stationed in Austin. This feeble and inadequate beginning marks the first real line of defense in Texas.

In 1849 the United States Army established the first line of federal forts staffed and manned by federal troops. This line of defense included the following: (1) Fort Worth, on a bluff overlooking the confluence of the Clear Fork and West Fork of the Trinity River on the site of the present city of Fort Worth; (2) Fort Graham, on the east bank of the Brazos River near the site of the old José María Indian village south of present Blum in Hill County; (3) Fort Gates, on the north bank of the Leon River above its junction with Coryell Creek east of present Gatesville; (4) Fort Croghan, on Hamilton Creek in present Burnet County three miles south of the town of Burnet; (5) Fort Martin Scott, on Baron's Creek in present Gillespie County about two miles south of Fredericksburg; (6) Fort Lincoln, on the west bank of Seco Creek a mile north of D'Hanis in present Medina County; (7) Fort Inge, on the east bank of the Leona River in present Uvalde County; (8) Fort Duncan, on the east bank of the Rio Grande at present Eagle Pass; and (9) Fort Bliss, at present El Paso.

In addition to the above posts, the 1849 line of defense included the border posts of Fort McIntosh at Laredo, Fort Ringgold (or Ringgold Barracks) at Rio Grande City (known also as Davis' Landing), and Fort Brown at Brownsville.

Within a few months the 1849 posts proved inadequate. After a study of the problem the War Department began the construction of a second line of defense posts further west, extending eventually to

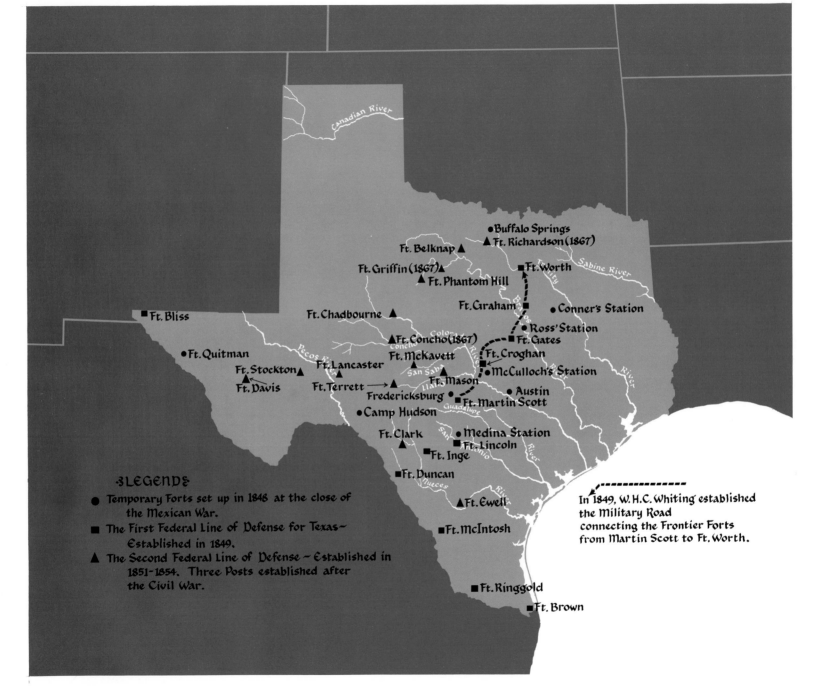

Buffalo Springs
●Ft. Richardson (1867)▲
Ft. Belknap ▲
Ft. Griffin (1867)▲
Ft. Phantom Hill ▲
■Ft. Worth
Ft. Graham ■  ●Conner's Station
Ft. Chadbourne ▲
●Ross' Station
Ft. Bliss ■
Ft. Concho (1867)▲
■Ft. Gates
Ft. McKavett
●Ft. Quitman
Ft. Lancaster
→Ft. Croghan
Ft. Stockton ▲
●McCulloch's Station
Ft. Davis ▲
Ft. Terrett →▲
Ft. Mason
Fredericksburg ●Austin
■Ft. Martin Scott
Camp Hudson
●Medina Station
Ft. Clark
■Ft. Lincoln
▲
■Ft. Inge
■Ft. Duncan

▲Ft. Ewell

■Ft. McIntosh

▲ LEGEND ▲
● Temporary Forts set up in 1848 at the close of
    the Mexican War.
■ The First Federal Line of Defense for Texas~
    Established in 1849.
▲ The Second Federal Line of Defense ~ Established in
    1851-1854.  Three Posts established after
    the Civil War.

In 1849, W.H.C. Whiting established
the Military Road
connecting the Frontier Forts
from Martin Scott to Ft. Worth.

■Ft. Ringgold

■Ft. Brown

El Paso. These forts were built during the 1850's with the exception of Richardson, Concho, and Griffin— the three completed after the Civil War in 1867. This second line (with dates) included the following: (1) Fort Richardson (1867), at Jacksboro in lieu of an earlier site at Buffalo Springs in southern Clay County; (2) Fort Belknap (1851), on the Brazos River ten miles upstream from its confluence with the Clear Fork; (3) Fort Griffin (1867), on the Clear Fork of the Brazos in northeastern Shackelford County near present Fort Griffin; (4) Fort Phantom Hill (1851), between the headwaters of the Elm and Clear Fork of the Brazos north of present Abilene in Taylor County; (5) Fort Chadbourne (1852), on the east bank of Oak Creek three miles above its junction with the Colorado River in present Coke County; (6) Fort Concho (1867), at the junction of the North and South Concho rivers in present San Angelo; (7) Fort McKavett (1852), on the right bank of the San Saba River at the present town of Fort McKavett in Menard County; (8) Fort Mason (1851), two miles west of Comanche Creek near the present town of Mason in Mason County; (9) Fort Terrett (1852), on the northeast bank of the North Fork of the Llano River near its source in present Sutton County; (10) Fort Clark (1852), on the right bank of Las Moras Creek near its head at the present town of Brackettville; (11) Fort Ewell (1852), on the right bank of the Nueces River at the crossing of the San Antonio-Laredo road in present La Salle County; (12) Fort Lancaster (1855), on the "old military road" from San Antonio to El Paso near the confluence of Live Oak Creek and the Pecos River in present Crockett County; (13) Fort Stockton (1850), at Comanche Springs and the crossing of the San Antonio-El Paso road with the Old Comanche Trail in present Pecos County; and (14) Fort Davis (1854), at present Fort Davis in Jeff Davis County.

In addition to the above-named posts, Camp Hudson was established in 1857 on the west bank of Devils River (at San Pedro Creek) forty miles upstream from present Del Rio, and Fort Quitman was established in 1858 on the north bank of the Rio Grande some seventy miles downstream from El Paso. In addition, the border posts of Bliss, Duncan, McIntosh, Ringgold, and Brown were continued.

M. L. Crimmins (ed.), "Freeman's Report on the Eighth Military Department," *Southwestern Historical Quarterly*, LI-LII.

Robert W. Frazer, *Forts of the West, Military Forts and Presidios and Posts Commonly Called Forts West of the Mississippi River to 1898* (Norman, 1965).

"Report of Inspector General J. F. K. Mansfield," *Southwestern Historical Quarterly*, XLII.

Ernest Wallace, *Texas in Turmoil* (Austin, 1965).

Walter Prescott Webb, *The Texas Rangers* (Austin, 1965).

# NATURALISTS OF THE TEXAS FRONTIER, 1820-1880

PROFESSOR SAMUEL WOOD GEISER has pointed out "while the naturalists of the Texas frontier are of interest to the historian of science primarily because of their work in extending the bounds of knowledge in various fields of natural science, their careers must be considered always in the light of their social environment as well. . . . While their achievements were due largely to traits of character inherent in the men themselves, their failures were due in almost every case to the environment." Some of the pioneer scientists in Texas and the areas in which they worked are as follows: (1) Jacob Boll (1828-1890), a Swiss naturalist and entomologist, came to Texas in 1869 and worked primarily in the North Texas region; (2) Jean Louis Berlandier (1805-1851), a Swiss naturalist, came to Mexico in 1826 and explored for plants and animals in Texas, 1828-1834, primarily along the lower Rio Grande and in the New Braunfels-Comal County area (although he spent time in several other localities); (3) Thomas Drummond (1790-1835), the Scottish botanical collector, came to Texas in 1833-34 and did extensive collecting in the Stephen F. Austin colony and on Galveston Island; (4) John J. Audubon, the distinguished ornithologist, came to Texas in 1837 and explored the Texas coast in the vicinity of Galveston Bay and Houston; (5) Louis C. Ervendberg (1809-1863), the distinguished German scientist, lived in Texas from 1839 until 1855 and was interested in plant collecting and experimental agriculture near New Braunfels; (6) Ferdinand Jakob Lindheimer (1801-1879), arrived in Texas in 1836 and from 1843 to 1852 collected plants for Asa Gray; Lindheimer worked primarily in the German communities of Gillespie, Comal, Fayette, and Austin counties; (7) Ferdinand Roemer, the distinguished German scientist, came to Texas in 1845 and toured the new state from Houston and La Grange on the coastal plains to New Braunfels, San Antonio, Fredericksburg, the Llano River country, and the Brazos River as far north as Torrey's Trading Post; on returning home, Roemer wrote of his travels and observations in two books and six articles; (8) Charles Wright came to Texas in 1837 and collected plants for Asa Gray from 1844 to 1852 in many localities ranging from the lower Sabine River region to Del Rio and El Paso to the southwest; (9) Dr. Gideon Lincecum resided at Long Point in Washington County, 1848-1874, and did extensive work in this region; (10) Julien Reverchon, a French scientist, came to Dallas in 1856 as a colonist at La Réunion; he explored for plants extensively in the Dallas-Fort Worth area and also to the west along the old military road from Fort Belknap south to Fort Inge; and (11) Gustav Wilhelm Belfrage, a Swedish entomologist, arrived in Texas in 1867 and worked chiefly in Bosque and McLennan counties.

In addition to the scientists listed above, mention should be made of William H. Emory, an officer in the Corps of Topographical Engineers, and John Russell Bartlett, the New England historian and ethnologist, both of whom made extensive explorations of Southwest Texas as members of the Mexican Boundary Survey Commission. Of more significance to the pure

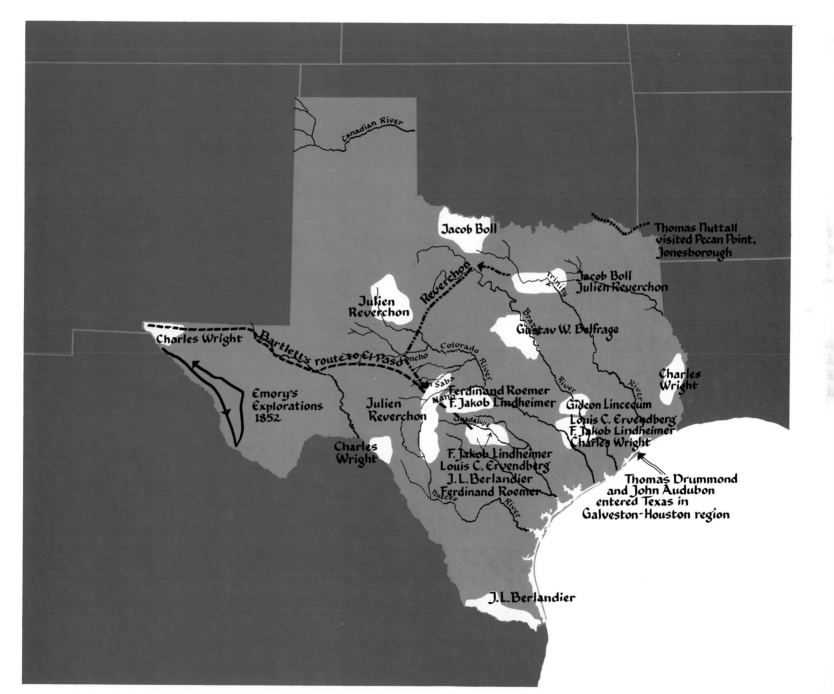

Canadian River

Jacob Boll

Thomas Nuttall
visited Pecan Point,
Jonesborough

Jacob Boll
Julien Reverchon

Reverchon

Julien
Reverchon

Trinity

Gustav W. Belfrage

Brazos

Charles Wright

Charles Wright

Bartlett's route to El Paso

Colorado

River

Concho

River

San Saba

Emory's
Explorations
1852

Julien
Reverchon

Llano

Ferdinand Roemer
F. Jakob Lindheimer

Gideon Lincecum

Louis C. Ervendberg
F. Jakob Lindheimer
Charles Wright

Guadalupe

Charles
Wright

F. Jakob Lindheimer
Louis C. Ervendberg
J. L. Berlandier
Ferdinand Roemer

Thomas Drummond
and John Audubon
entered Texas in
Galveston-Houston region

Nueces

River

J. L. Berlandier

scientist, however, would be the work of Dr. John Milton Bigelow, the botanist who worked under Bartlett, and Dr. Thomas Hopkins Webb, a zoologist who made a remarkable collection of fish, reptiles, and insects as a member of the Boundary Survey Commission staff.

Samuel Wood Geiser, *Naturalists of the Frontier* (Dallas, 1948).

# EARLY TRADE & TRAVEL ROUTES

PRIOR TO THE CIVIL WAR, many wilderness roads traversed Texas and among the more significant of these early trade and travel routes were the following: (1) the route running from the Rio Grande at present Brownsville to Goliad and San Antonio; this road, one of the earliest, was known as the Matamoros Road to Goliad (used by Urrea's army in 1836), Taylor's route (traversed by Zachary Taylor's troops in 1846), and the Brownsville to San Antonio State route; (2) the old Salt Trail (to the salt lakes) or the old military road from Fort Brown to Ringgold Barracks and eventually to Fort McIntosh at Laredo; (3) the Goliad Road, also known as the Victoria Road, and also known as the Atascosito Road; (4) the Brownsville to San Antonio stage route; (5) a continuation of the Atascosito Road from Victoria to Beason's Crossing at Columbus and on to Atascosito Post or Liberty; this, of course, was one of the most important trails of the Anglo-American period of Mexican history; (6) the Salt Grass Trail from Washington-on-the-Brazos and Brenham to Lynchburg, Harrisburg, and Houston; (7) the La Bahía (Labberdee) Road from Goliad on the south to its intersection with the Old San Antonio Road at the Trinity River; (8, 8a, 8b, and 8c) El Camino Real or the Old San Antonio Road, the historic trail blazed by St. Denis, Diego Ramón, and Marquis de Aguayo from the Presidio of the Rio Grande to San Antonio and on to Nacogdoches and the Sabine River frontier; (9) Trammel's Trace, running north from Nacogdoches to present Jefferson, present Hughes Springs, and on into Arkansas; (10) the Jonesborough-Nacogdoches Road, connecting the early Red River settlements with Nacogdoches; (11) the Caddo Trace or Jefferson Road, beginning at Jefferson and the head of Caddo Lake and running northwest to Preston on the Red River; (12) the Central National Road connecting Dallas with Jonesborough; (13) the Caddo Trace, a relatively short trail from Dallas to Fort Houston in Anderson County and on into the East Texas region; (14) the Comanche Road, connecting Fort Houston and vicinity with Fort Graham on the Brazos River; (15) Preston Road, a trail and stage route traversing the length of Central Texas from Austin to Dallas to Preston on the Red River; (16) the Military Road from Fort Lincoln to forts Martin Scott, Croghan, Gates, Graham, and Worth (the trail laid out by Lieutenant William Henry Chase Whiting in 1849); (17) the Phantom Hill Road from Bell County to Buffalo Gap and Fort Phantom Hill; (18) the so-called Upper Road from San Antonio to El Paso, also known as the Upper California Road; (19) the road from San Antonio to San Felipe Springs (Del

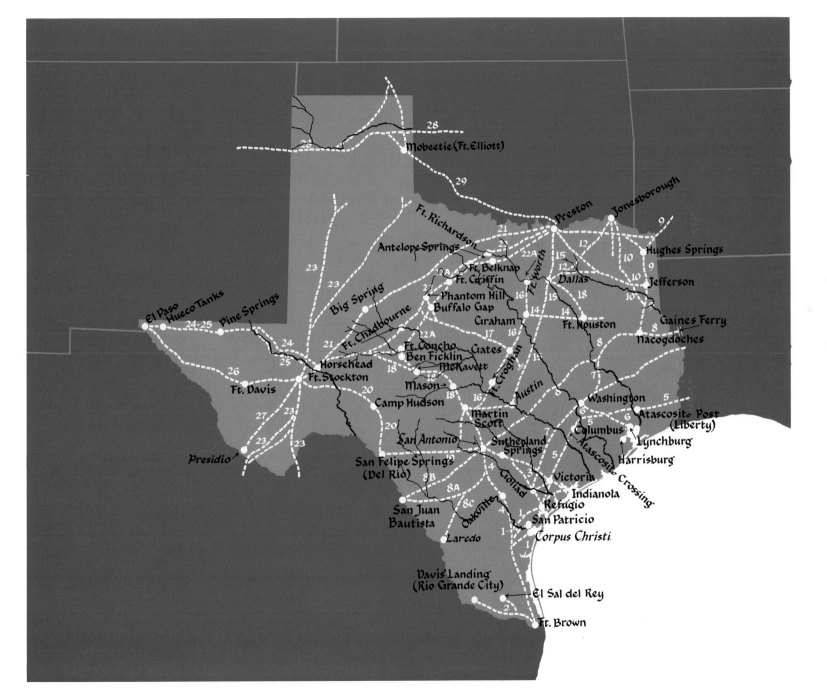

Rio), also a section of the San Antonio-San Diego stage route (the Jackass Mail); (20) the San Antonio-San Diego stage road, or the Chihuahua Road, from Devils River and the Rio Grande to Fort Stockton and El Paso; (21) the Marcy Trail or the Chihuahua Road, a trail traversing West Texas from Preston on the Red River to Horsehead Crossing on the Pecos, and then to El Paso by way of Delaware Creek and Guadalupe Pass (the road traveled by Randolph B. Marcy in 1849); (22 and 22a) the Butterfield Stage Route, also known as the Upper California Road and the Southern Overland Mail route; the parallel route, the Preston to El Paso Road, also traversed the breadth of West Texas by way of the frontier forts; (23) the Comanche War Trail, a historic route leading from the plains of the Panhandle region into Mexico which was used extensively by the Comanche Indians on their raids into the ranch country of northern Mexico; (24) the Emigrant Route to California; this section of the road is nothing more than the Pecos River extension of the Marcy or Upper California Trail to El Paso; (25) the Pecos to El Paso section of the Butterfield Stage route, followed the right bank of the river to Delaware Creek to join the California Trail; (26) the San Antonio-San Diego Mail Route—the Fort Stockton to El Paso section of the trail; (27) the Chihuahua Trail, a historic trade route leading into Mexico from the Fort Stockton-Comanche Springs junction with other western trails; (28) the Marcy Road or the Great Spanish Trail from Fort Smith on the Arkansas River along the Canadian River into northern New Mexico (Santa Fe); and (29) the Preston-Mobeetie section of the Great Spanish Road.

During the decades preceding and following the Civil War, the travel routes shown on this map were used extensively, as were many other lesser known (but no less important) connecting roads.

# THE VOTE ON SECESSION, 1861

ON FEBRUARY 23, 1861, in a campaign marked by intimidation, intolerance, and violence, the people of Texas voted 46,129 to 14,697 to secede from the United States. The opposition to secession came largely from two areas—the western counties centering around Austin and San Antonio (including the area of substantial German population) and the North Texas counties along the Red River. Along the Red River, eight counties—Montague, Cooke, Grayson, Fannin, Lamar, Collin, Wise, and Jack—accounted for a large percent of the vote against secession. In this region, a part of the old Peters' Colony, James W. Throckmorton and others were powerful voices counseling moderation and compromise. To the south, ten counties along the Colorado River and in the Hill Country opposed secession; the counties of Fayette, Bastrop, Travis, Williamson, Burnet, Blanco, Gillespie, Mason, Uvalde, and Medina. In this region the anti-secessionist majority resulted from such factors as the leadership of persons like Sam Houston, A. J. Hamilton, E. M. Pease, and John Hancock; the determined opposition of the newspaper press in Austin and the

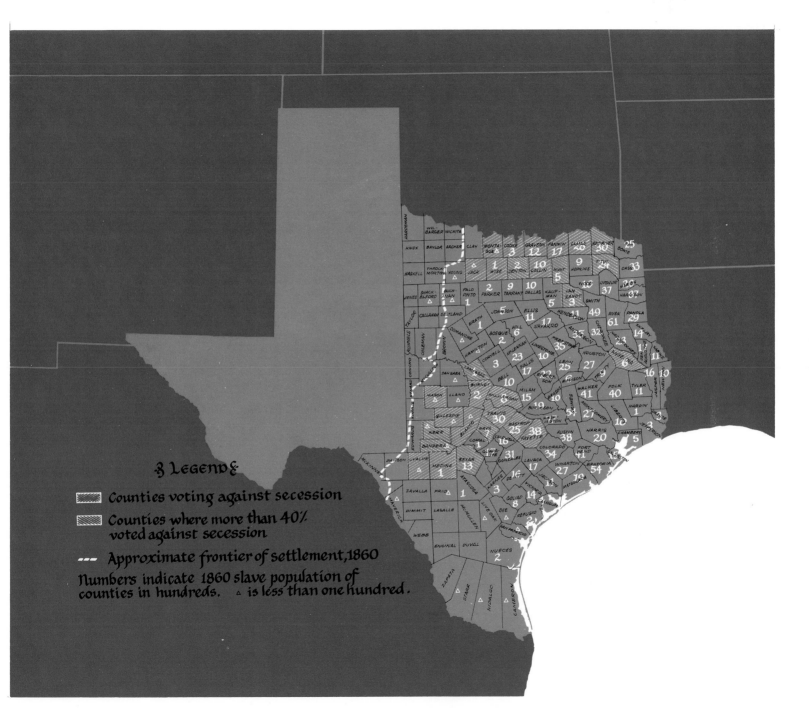

LEGEND

Counties voting against secession

Counties where more than 40% voted against secession

--- Approximate frontier of settlement, 1860

Numbers indicate 1860 slave population of counties in hundreds. △ is less than one hundred.

fact that the emigrants from Sweden and Germany were constitutionally and morally opposed to slavery are given as traditional reasons for the Union sentiment. In his *Texas in Turmoil*, Ernest Wallace points out that "The entire frontier voted 46.7 percent against secession; with only one fourth of the state's population, it tallied almost half of the vote in opposition. Several factors contributed . . . the origins of the population, the economic status of the settlers, and the fear of less adequate protection against Indian depredations."

Regardless of the reasons for opposition, the vote in 1861 indicated that Texas in the Confederacy would be faced with a rather severe problem relative to Union sentiment and Union sympathizers. The late

Claude Elliott points out that "Texas was not ripe for revolution in 1861. . . . They [the people] had voted for secession supinely hoping that the step they took did not mean war. . . . When . . . all hopes of avoiding war were dashed to earth by the Sumter incident, the people of Texas were dazed and stood bewildered as they faced the storm. . . . It is extremely doubtful, therefore, whether more than one-third of the people of Texas actively supported the Confederacy."

Claude Elliott, "Union Sentiment in Texas," *Southwestern Historical Quarterly*, L.
Frank H. Smyrl, "Unionism in Texas, 1856-1861," *Southwestern Historical Quarterly*, LXVIII.
Ernest Wallace, *Texas in Turmoil: The Saga of Texas, 1849-1875* (Austin, 1965).

# THE CIVIL WAR

 A GLANCE at a Civil War map of Texas reveals that the state escaped the heavy fighting that brought destruction to large areas of the South east of the Mississippi River. In fact, it was the age-old problem of frontier defense against the Indians of the Great Plains that occupied the energies and talents of a majority of the Texans in military service.

In the spring of 1861, Colonel W. C. Young led some two thousand troops across the Red River to capture forts Arbuckle, Cobb, and Washita. During the summer of 1861, Colonel John R. Baylor extended Confederate authority over New Mexico, and the following year (1862) three regiments of Texans under the command of General H. H. Sibley marched from San Antonio to El Paso and then north along the Rio

Grande. Sibley's army was so depleted by the rigors of campaigning and stubborn Federal resistance at Valverde and Glorietta that the commander decided in late March to abandon New Mexico. The retreat, under Federal pressure from Edward R. Canby's army, became a rout as the Texans fled toward the security of El Paso—it was a long trek from El Paso back to San Antonio.

Late in 1862 Galveston was captured by a Federal force, only to be recaptured by the Confederates under General John B. Magruder on January 1, 1863. In September, 1863, a Federal invasion of Texas was turned back with heavy losses at Sabine Pass by Lieutenant Richard Dowling and a very small group of soldiers under his command. In November, 1863,

General N. P. Banks and a Federal army captured Brownsville and adjacent points in the lower Rio Grande valley; Banks's troops pushed up the Texas coast to take Fort Esperanza and Indianola. In the summer of 1864, Colonel John S. Ford recaptured Brownsville, but the mouth of the Rio Grande remained in Federal hands until the close of the war.

Both the Confederate government at Richmond and the state government at Austin realized the necessity of protecting the frontier settlers from Indian attack, but by the fall of 1861 it became clear that Texas would have to provide for its own protection against the Indians. As a result, the state legislature (in November, 1861) provided for ten companies, known as the Frontier Regiment, under the command of Colonel James M. Norris, assisted by Alfred T. Obenchain and J. E. McCord. The Frontier Regiment was then scattered along the Texas frontier in sixteen camps: Camp Cureton in Archer County; Old Fort Belknap in Young County; Camp Breckenridge in Stephens County; Camp Salmon in northeast Callahan County; Camp Pecan in southern Callahan County; Camp Collier in Brown County; Camp McMillan on Richland Creek in San Saba County; Camp San Saba on the Mason-San Saba county line; Camp Llano on the Llano River in Mason County; Camp Davis on White Oak Creek in Gillespie County; Camp Verde in southern Kerr County; Camp Montel on Seco Creek in Bandera County; Camp Dix in Uvalde County; Camp Nueces on the Nueces River in present Zavala County; Camp Rabb in the southwestern corner of present Zavala County; and Fort Duncan on the Rio Grande at Eagle Pass.

Late in 1863 the troops of the Frontier Regiment were transferred to the Confederate Army by Governor Pendleton Murrah; the regiment was to remain in Texas but not necessarily on the frontier. As a result of this loss, the state legislature, on December 15, 1863, provided that all men in a tier of frontier counties from the Red River to the Rio Grande should be organized into companies of state troops; at least one fourth of these men were to be in the field at all times, with the remainder on call. The counties selected were Cooke, Wise, Parker, Johnson, Bosque, McLennan, Lampasas, Burnet, Blanco, Kendall, Bandera, Medina, Atascosa, Live Oak, La Salle, Dimmitt, and Maverick. The northern division, with headwaters at Decatur, was under the command of a Major Quayle; the central division, with headquarters at Gatesville, was commanded by Major George B. Erath; and the southern division, with headquarters at San Antonio, was commanded by J. D. McAdoo.

This system of a "home guard" worked very well, probably because the Indians were relatively quiet in 1864 and 1865. In January, 1865, several companies from the central Texas counties, assisted by Confederate troops (the old Frontier Regiment) attacked and defeated a group of Kickapoo Indians in the battle of Dove Creek, a small tributary to Spring Creek in present Tom Green County. It is of significance, however, that these "volunteer" troops were often called on to make extended Indian scouting treks into the wilds of West Texas. Poorly equipped and poorly supplied, these journeys became real ordeals, and the student of history must sympathize with one old veteran of these Civil War scouting parties, who, after facing one bitter Texas norther after another, recorded in his diary: "Norther blew up last night very cold pack up the meat At day light March and froze to Phantom Hill Commences snowing in the evening Snow on to midnight Slept under a green buffalo hide froze stiff in the Morning" and, after reaching the end of the trail "Camp at Meridian in Bosque Co. big rain all got drunk." About time!

At times the Confederate state government could be intolerant and despotic. Elise Waerenskold, a Nor-

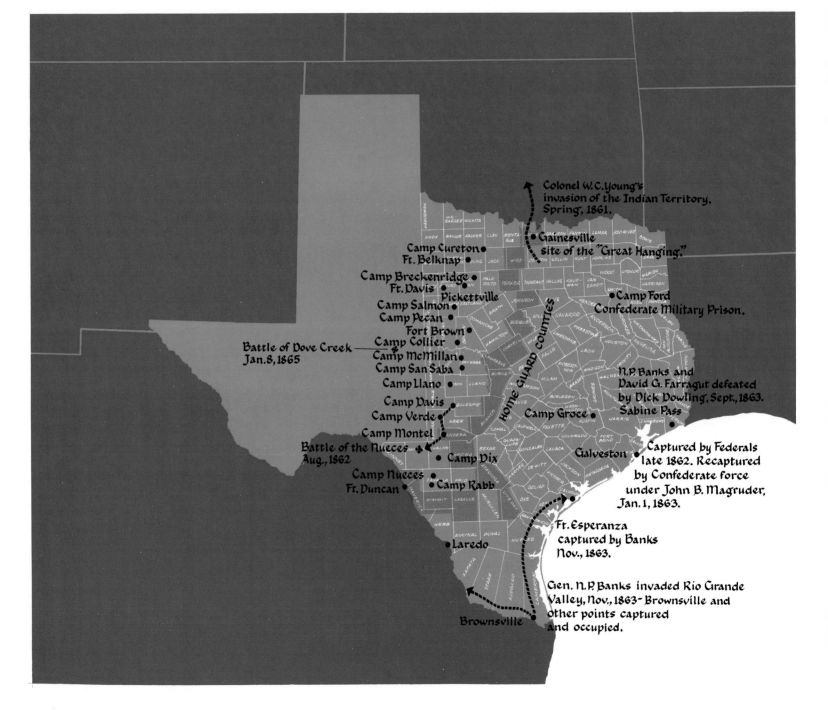

Colonel W.C. Young's invasion of the Indian Territory, Spring, 1861.

Gainesville site of the "Great Hanging."

Camp Cureton

Ft. Belknap

Camp Breckenridge

Ft. Davis

Pickettville

Camp Salmon

Camp Pecan

Fort Brown

Camp Collier

Battle of Dove Creek Jan. 8, 1865

Camp McMillan

Camp San Saba

Camp Llano

Camp Davis

Camp Verde

Camp Montel

Battle of the Nueces Aug., 1862

Camp Dix

Camp Nueces

Ft. Duncan

Camp Rabb

Laredo

Camp Ford Confederate Military Prison.

Home Guard Counties

N. P. Banks and David G. Farragut defeated by Dick Dowling, Sept., 1863. Sabine Pass

Camp Groce

Galveston

Captured by Federals late 1862. Recaptured by Confederate force under John B. Magruder, Jan. 1, 1863.

Ft. Esperanza captured by Banks Nov., 1863.

Gen. N. P. Banks invaded Rio Grande Valley, Nov., 1863- Brownsville and other points captured and occupied.

Brownsville

wegian emigrant living at Brownsboro during the war wrote in 1865: "Our government was despotic and dishonest. . . . Those who would not fight for the rebel government were in danger of their lives and were subjected to all sorts of torture when caught." While acts of atrocity were everyday occurrences, the two that stand out above all the others were the great hanging at Gainesville in 1862 and the Battle of the Nueces, August, 1862, where German Unionists were attacked by a Confederate ranger force; in the battle that followed, nineteen were killed and nine wounded, and, a few days later, six more were killed as they attempted to cross the Rio Grande. It is reported that during the weeks that followed the Battle of the Nueces, Captain James Duff, a Texas Ranger, "hanged about fifty men and killed a number of others in Gillespie County." Military prison camps were established at Camp Groce, on the Brazos River near Hempstead, and at Camp Ford, near Tyler. When the Confederacy collapsed in the spring of 1865, near anarchy prevailed until General Gordon Granger landed at Galveston in June with a United States Army of Occupation.

Claude Elliott, *Leathercoat: The Life of James W. Throckmorton* (San Antonio, 1938).
Allen W. Jones, "Military Events in Texas during the Civil War, 1861-1865," *Southwestern Historical Quarterly*, LXIV.
Robert W. Shook, "The Battle of the Nueces, August 10, 1862," *Southwestern Historical Quarterly*, LXVI.
Ernest Wallace, *Texas in Turmoil, The Saga of Texas, 1849-1875* (Austin, 1965).

# TEXAS, 1865-1870

 IT MAY BE SAID that at the close of the Civil War, Texas was representative of (1) the Indian frontier, (2) the ranchers' frontier, and (3) the farmers' frontier. Long ago Frederick Jackson Turner defined the American frontier as "the margin of that settlement which has a density of two or more to the square mile." It may be assumed that Rupert N. Richardson had the Turner definition in mind when he wrote, "In 1870 the western limit of settlements was a line running approximately from Henrietta, near the Red River and the ninety-eighth meridian, to Junction and hence southwestward to the Rio Grande. . . . This line was the cattlemen's frontier. A line drawn east of it from 30 to 150 miles . . . may be designated as the farmers' frontier." It is significant that during the five-year period immediately following the Civil War, two distinct frontier lines can be drawn from north to south across West Texas—to the west lay the "free lands" of the Indian frontier.

The farmers' frontier, 1865-1870, ran from the Cooke-Montague County boundary on the Red River south, in irregular fashion, by way of Parker County and Weatherford, Erath County and Stephenville, Hamilton County and Hamilton, Lampasas, San Saba, Llano, Fredericksburg, Bandera, and Castroville-D'Hanis; from the latter point, the frontier curved southeasterly to the Coastal Bend at Corpus Christi Bay. The average farmer-stockraiser had progressed to this western

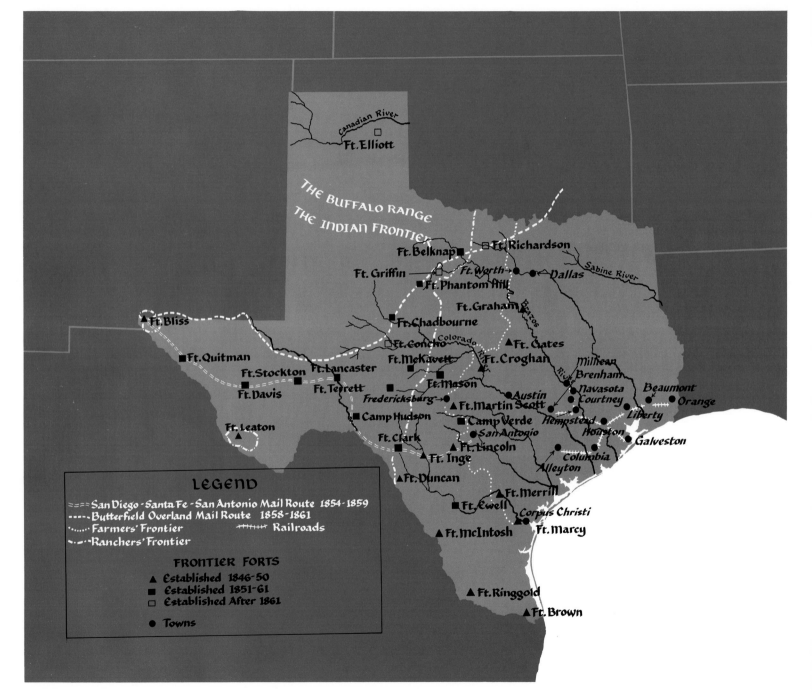

Canadian River
Ft. Elliott

THE BUFFALO RANGE
THE INDIAN FRONTIER

Ft. Belknap ■ □ ■ Ft. Richardson
Ft. Griffin — □ Ft. Worth → ● Dallas
■ Ft. Phantom Hill
Sabine River
Ft. Graham

Ft. Bliss ▲
Ft. Quitman ■
Ft. Chadbourne ■
Ft. Concho □ Colorado R.
Ft. McKavett ■ ▲ Ft. Gates
Ft. Croghan ▲
Ft. Stockton ■ Ft. Lancaster ■
Millican ●
Brenham ●
Ft. Mason ■
Ft. Terrett ■
Navasota ● Beaumont ●
Ft. Davis ■
Austin ● Courtney ● Orange ●
Fredericksburg →
Ft. Martin Scott ▲
Hempstead ● Liberty
Ft. Leaton ▲
Camp Hudson ■
Camp Verde ■
Houston ●
Ft. Clark ■
San Antonio ●
Galveston ●
Ft. Inge ▲
Ft. Lincoln ▲
Columbia ●
Ft. Duncan ▲
Alleyton ●
Ft. Merrill ▲
Ft. Ewell ■
Corpus Christi ●
Ft. Marcy ▲
Ft. McIntosh ▲

Ft. Ringgold ▲

Ft. Brown ▲

LEGEND
≋≋≋ San Diego - Santa Fe - San Antonio Mail Route 1854-1859
------ Butterfield Overland Mail Route 1858-1861
········ Farmers' Frontier          ┼┼┼┼┼ Railroads
-·-·- Ranchers' Frontier

FRONTIER FORTS
▲ Established 1846-50
■ Established 1851-61
□ Established After 1861

● Towns

limit prior to the war. It will be noted that the farmers' frontier paralleled roughly the 98° meridian; the advance beyond would be slower and more difficult.

Between the farmers' frontier and the ranchers' frontier, the absolute limit of settlement, lay the narrow domain of the cattlemen, an industry still in its infancy in 1870. Adventurous frontiersmen had pushed into this region in the years just prior to the Civil War but their hold upon the land was precarious at best, as select examples from *The Handbook of Texas* point out. In Clay County, where the population stood at 109 in 1860, "the temporary county organization of 1861 had to be abandoned in 1862 because of inadequate frontier protection during the Civil War. The Census of 1870 gave no figures for Clay County, although a few ranchers remained along the Red River after most of the settlers had removed eastward." To the south, in Brown County, "the country was in open range" prior to 1880. On the Edwards Plateau, Kimble County was a land where "from 1857 through the early 1880's the settlements were harassed by the Indians and in many instances were broken up by Indian massacres or by settlers moving to better protected areas. While R. F. Tankersley, who moved his herd of Longhorn cattle to the South Concho in present Tom Green County in 1864, was an exception to the rule, the McCulloch County region remained an area where "not until the 1870's were the buffalo hunted off the prairies and scattered ranches established." In 1870, however, the cattle industry (with a sea of grass stretching north and west before it) was on the eve

of a period of rapid expansion, not only over all of West Texas, but over a considerable part of the American West as well.

During the period of expansion for the cattlemen, the farmers' frontier remained relatively static as water, transportation, fencing, and other temporarily insurmountable problems held the agricultural frontier back. Before either the rancher or the farmer could occupy West Texas, however, the Indian problem had to be solved and the buffalo removed from the range.

Before moving to these two problems, however, it is also significant to note that railroad mileage in Texas in 1865 consisted of the few hundred miles of the Texas and New Orleans; the Houston Tap and Brazoria; the Houston and Galveston; the Houston and Texas Central; and the Buffalo Bayou, Brazos, and Colorado railroads. All of these short lines radiated out from Houston and Harrisburg; only the Houston and Texas Central had penetrated into the interior of the state— to Brenham and Millican. Like the cattle kingdom, the railroads in 1865 stood on the eve of their "golden age" and rapid expansion would be their story for the next quarter of a century.

Colton's New Map of the State of Texas, G. W. and C. B. Colton Company, n.d., Archives, University of Texas Library, Austin, Texas.

Augustas Mitchell, County Map of Texas (Philadelphia, 1866), Archives, University of Texas Library, Austin, Texas.

Frederick J. Turner, *The Frontier in American History* (New York, 1920).

# THE INDIAN CAMPAIGNS, 1872-1874

IN 1859 the Comanche Indians of Texas were moved to a reservation in the Indian Territory. After the removal, however, conditions along the Texas frontier grew worse instead of better. Now joined by their wild kinsmen of the Northern Comanche divisions, the Kiowa, and occasionally the Cheyenne, the Penateka Comanche warriors made repeated raids against the frontier of the hated Texans. During and immediately following the Civil War, the Indians took many captives, killed scores of frontier residents, stole hundreds of horses, and drove back the West Texas settlers. Ernest Wallace, in summarizing the situation after the close of the Civil War writes, "Beginning in the spring of 1866, the Comanche and Kiowas entered the settlements in droves. A Waco newspaper in April, 1866, reported that the Comanches swarmed all through the country, and not more than one fifth of the ranches were left occupied." Many petitions came to Governor James W. Throckmorton pleading for help. Defense along the northern frontier was negligible as the United States military attempted to establish peace by treaty-making rather than force, a policy climaxed by negotiation of the Treaty of Medicine Lodge in October, 1867. The terms of this treaty provided that the Comanche-Kiowa tribes would accept an agency, schools, and farms on a reservation in southwestern Oklahoma. The raids into Texas, however, continued with an increased fury as many of the Comanches refused to move into the reserve.

In the meantime the frontier forts were reestablished by the military and Ranald S. Mackenzie assumed command at Fort Concho in February, 1871. Between 1871 and 1875 Mackenzie was occupied by a series of campaigns which removed the Indians from Northwest Texas. The highlights of this extended effort include the fight on McClellan Creek, September, 1872; an invasion of Mexico in the spring of 1873 in search of the Kickapoo; and a final campaign against the Kiowa, Comanche, and Cheyenne in 1874.

The plan of attack for the 1874 campaign consisted of four separate troop movements: (1) Colonel Mackenzie was to move northward along the eastern edge of the Cap Rock from Fort Concho and Fort Griffin, (2) Major W. R. Price was to move east from Fort Union, New Mexico, to scout the Canadian River country, (3) Colonel Nelson Miles was to advance to the south from his post at Fort Dodge, Kansas, and (4) Lieutenant Colonel John R. Davidson was to depart from Fort Sill, Oklahoma, and move westward. The objective of this merciless campaign was to round up all of the Comanche and their allies found off the Oklahoma reserve. The campaign was a success; the Indians were "rounded up," (their villages burned, their horses "liberated," and many of the warriors who resisted were killed). Mackenzie's destruction of the Indian villages in Palo Duro Canyon (and their horse herd) on September 29, 1874, was the last major Indian fight in Texas. The power of the Comanche and Kiowa Indians had been broken forever. The vast plains of West Texas were now open.

R. C. Carter, *On the Border with Mackenzie* (Washington, D. C., 1935).

W. J. Hughes, "Rip Ford's Indian Fight," *Panhandle Plains Historical Review*, XXX.

Norman Leckie, *The Military Conquest of the Southern Plains* (Norman, 1963).

Ernest Wallace, *Ranald S. Mackenzie on the Texas Frontier* (Lubbock, 1964).

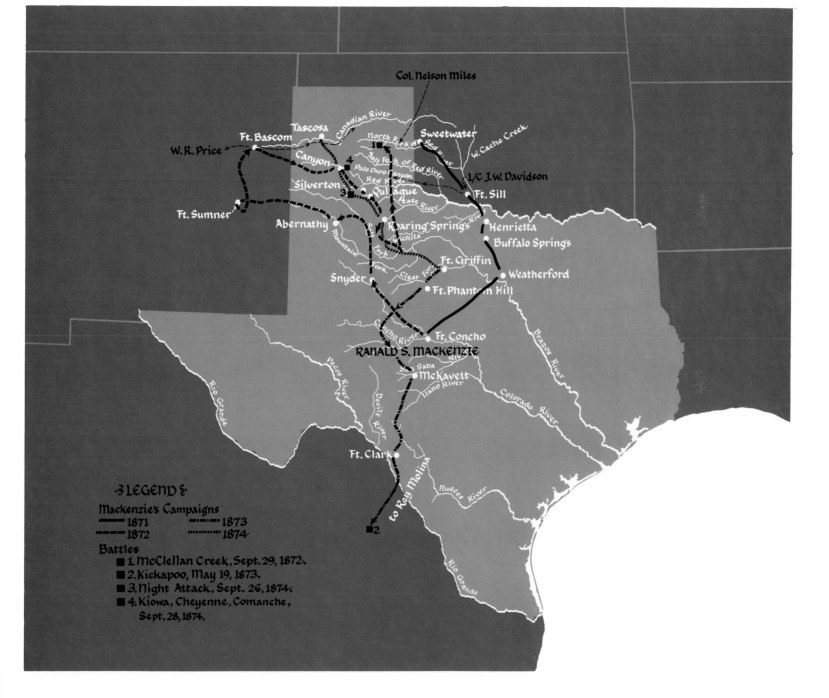

Col. Nelson Miles

W.R. Price

Ft. Bascom
Tascosa
Canyon
Silverton
Ft. Sumner
Abernathy
Snyder

Sweetwater
North Fork off Red River
Salt Fork of Red River
Palo Duro Canyon
Red River
Pease River
Waring Springs
Wichita
North Fork
Clear Fork
Ft. Griffin
Ft. Phantom Hill

Canadian River
W. Cache Creek
L/C J.W. Davidson
Ft. Sill
Henrietta
Buffalo Springs
Weatherford

Quitaque
Mountain

1
4
3

Concho River
Ft. Concho

RANALD S. MACKENZIE

Saba River
McKavett
Llano River

Pecos River
Devil's River

Brazos River
Colorado River

Rio Grande

Ft. Clark
Nueces River
to Rey Molina

Rio Grande

·3 LEGEND &
Mackenzie's Campaigns
—— 1871       —·— 1873
——— 1872      ······ 1874
Battles
■ 1. McClellan Creek, Sept. 29, 1872.
■ 2. Kickapoo, May 19, 1873.
■ 3. Night Attack, Sept. 26, 1874.
■ 4. Kiowa, Cheyenne, Comanche,
    Sept. 28, 1874.

# THE BUFFALO RANGE

THE COMMERCIAL HUNTING of buffalo began in Kansas in 1872 and lasted until about 1881. The Texas, or southern herd was slaughtered between 1874 and 1878.

Late in the summer of 1873, J. Wright and John Webb Mooar, hearing of large herds of buffalo in the Texas Panhandle, rode down from the Cimarron country to see for themselves. According to Wayne Gard, "Before they reached the breaks of the South Canadian, they found buffaloes in an almost solid mass as far as they could see. There were hundreds of thousands of them, fattening on the upland grass." In the fall of 1873 the Mooar outfit (led by J. Wright and John W. Mooar) traveled south to establish their camp on the South Canadian River; several other outfits followed the Mooar wagons. The hunters found the hunting good, and, in the spring of 1874, a large caravan of hunters left Dodge City for the Texas High Plains. The stockaded outpost of Adobe Walls, built by dealers in provisions and hides, was established to serve as a headquarters for the hunters along the Canadian. On June 27, 1874, the Indians attacked the post of Adobe Walls, and the post was abandoned.

In the spring of 1875, the Mooar brothers came to Texas by way of the Shawnee Trail, Denison, and Fort Griffin. From Fort Griffin they traveled southwest to the plains of present Nolan, Fisher, and Mitchell counties. The hunting was excellent along the divide between the Brazos and Colorado, and the Mooars returned to the area in the years that followed. The Mooar brothers were among the more successful of the thousands of hunters and skinners who took to the buffalo range in the late 1870's and early 1880's. Wright Mooar estimated that he killed 6500 buffalo with his fourteen-pound Sharps rifle and 14,000 with his eleven-pounder. Among the two brothers and their associates, the outfit marketed tens of thousands of hides.

In 1876 Charles Rath loaded a wagon train with kegs of powder, tobacco, whiskey, and other supplies and pushed south from Dodge City to blaze the Rath Trail across West Texas. Rath paused near Fort Elliott to establish Hidetown or Rath's Trading Post (later Mobeetie); from Fort Elliott, he continued south across Salt Fork, the Red River, and the Brazos to a location known as Rath City. Subsequently, hundreds of thousands of hides were freighted northward over the Rath Trail to the Dodge City railhead.

Other locations of significance on the buffalo range included Pete Snyder's supply camp and trading post (known as Robbers Roost) on the location of present Snyder in Scurry County; Teepee City, founded in 1879 near the South Pease River in northern Cottle County as a repair and supply station for wagon trains; and Fort Griffin, the community along the "flats" of the Clear Fork of the Brazos near the military post.

Frank Eben Conrad came to Texas in 1868 as the post trader at Fort McKavett, two years later he moved to Fort Griffin. Conrad's store did a thriving business during the years of the Indian campaigns, and, once the buffalo slaughter got underway, the store supplied the hunters with guns, ammunition, and supplies of all kinds. In partnership with Charles Rath, Conrad moved the store to the town of Fort Griffin in 1879. Both Conrad and Rath enjoyed great financial success as merchants in the West Central Texas area.

On the outer edge of the buffalo range, Sherman, Denison, and Fort Worth prospered as supply points for the westward-bound hunters.

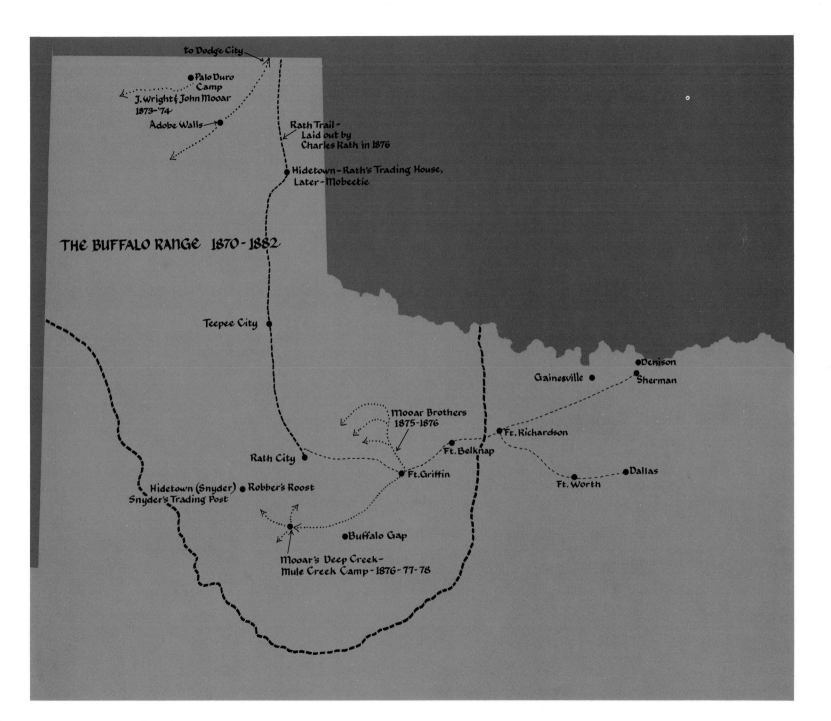

to Dodge City

● Palo Duro Camp

J. Wright & John Mooar 1873-'74

Adobe Walls ➤

Rath Trail — Laid out by Charles Rath in 1876

● Hidetown — Rath's Trading House, Later — Mobeetie

THE BUFFALO RANGE 1870-1882

Teepee City ●

● Denison

Gainesville ● Sherman

Mooar Brothers 1875-1876

Ft. Richardson

Ft. Belknap

Rath City ●

Ft. Griffin ●

Dallas

Hidetown (Snyder) ● Robber's Roost
Snyder's Trading Post

Ft. Worth

● Buffalo Gap

Mooar's Deep Creek — Mule Creek Camp — 1876-77-78

Wayne Gard, "The Mooar Brothers, Buffalo Hunters," *Southwestern Historical Quarterly*, LXIII.
Wayne Gard, *The Great Buffalo Hunt* (New York, 1959).

William C. Holden, *Alkali Trails* (Dallas, 1930).
Vernon Lynch, "A Year at Fort Griffin on the Texas Frontier," West Texas Historical Association *Yearbook*, 1965.

# THE CATTLE KINGDOM

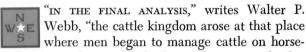 "IN THE FINAL ANALYSIS," writes Walter P. Webb, "the cattle kingdom arose at that place where men began to manage cattle on horseback. It was the use of the horse that primarily distinguished ranching in the West from stock-farming in the East." The place where men began to manage cattle on horseback was the southern tip of Texas, a region bounded by the waters of the Gulf on the east, by the Rio Grande on the southwest, by a line running from Laredo to San Antonio on the northwest, and by a line running from San Antonio to Old Indianola on the northeast. In this diamond-shaped area— a region of excellent grass, mild climate, sufficient water, and open country shaded by mottes of oak— the Anglo-American cowboys of the Austin and DeWitt colonies met the Mexican vaquero and the Mexican Longhorn cattle. The vaquero taught the cowboy all of the skills and tricks of the trade.

While the cattle kingdom originated in South Texas in the decades before the Civil War, the drives to eastern markets prior to 1860 were both irregular and inconsequential. When, however, Texans discovered that a range cow worth three to four dollars in Texas would bring thirty to forty dollars on the northern market, they made desperate efforts to get Texas cattle to northern buyers and the expansion of the cattle kingdom began.

It is estimated that 260,000 head of cattle crossed the Red River in 1866 bound for Baxter Springs and Sedalia. By 1867 Joseph G. McCoy had induced the railroad to build out onto the Kansas prairie at Abilene and the "golden age" of the trail drive began. Several major trails led out of Texas.

1. Largely prior to the Civil War, cattle were driven from Texas to Louisiana over the Opelousas Trail. Because of the nature of the terrain in the bayou country, this was not a profitable way to get cattle to market.

2. The Shawnee Trail (also known as the Kansas Trail and the Texas Road) was established in the 1850's and continued to be the only trail leading north until the opening of the Chisholm Trail in 1867. Beginning south of the Nueces, the Shawnee Trail ran by way of Austin, Waco, and Dallas to cross into the Indian Territory at Red Bluff Crossing near Preston. From the Red River, the trail continued northeasterly to Boggy Depot, Fort Gibson, Baxter Springs, Sedalia, and Kansas City.

3. The Chisholm Trail, established by Jesse Chisholm in 1866, originally ran only from present Wichita, Kansas, to Council Grove, a site near present Yukon, Oklahoma. In common usage, however, the name was later applied both to the northern and southern extensions of the trail. The Texas extension of the trail was formed by the juncture of a number of South Texas trails east of San Antonio; the trail then passed through

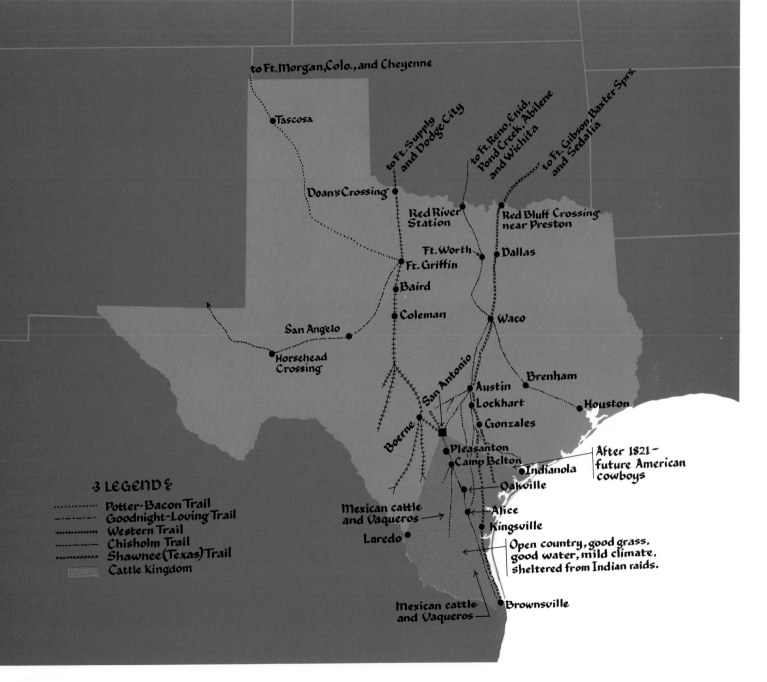

to Ft. Morgan, Colo., and Cheyenne

Tascosa

to Ft. Supply and Dodge City

to Ft. Reno, Enid, Pond Creek, Abilene, and Wichita

to Ft. Gibson, Baxter Sprs. and Sedalia

Doan's Crossing

Red River Station

Red Bluff Crossing near Preston

Ft. Worth

Dallas

Ft. Griffin

Baird

Coleman

Waco

San Angelo

Horsehead Crossing

San Antonio

Austin

Brenham

Lockhart

Houston

Gonzales

Boerne

Pleasanton

Camp Belton

Indianola

After 1821 – future American cowboys

Oakville

Mexican cattle and Vaqueros

Alice

Kingsville

Laredo

Open country, good grass, good water, mild climate, sheltered from Indian raids.

Mexican cattle and Vaqueros

Brownsville

### ঃ LEGEND ঃ
```
············· Potter-Bacon Trail
–·–·–·– Goodnight-Loving Trail
++++++++ Western Trail
–··–··– Chisholm Trail
×××××××× Shawnee (Texas) Trail
▨▨▨ Cattle Kingdom
```

Guadalupe, Hays, Travis, Williamson, Bell, McLennan, Bosque, Hill, Johnson, Tarrant, Wise, and Montague counties. Variations from the direct route are many but fixed points were the Colorado River crossing in present east Austin, Brushy Creek at Round Rock, Kimball Bend on the Brazos, and Trinity ford crossing (below the confluence of the West and Clear forks) in present Fort Worth. The Red River was crossed at Sevell's Bend or Red River Station. From there the trail continued northward through Yukon and El Reno, Enid, and Pond Creek, Oklahoma, to Caldwell and Wichita, Kansas.

4. The Western Trail (also known as the Dodge City Trail) became the standard route for all cattle herds moving north after 1876. Formed by a number of "feeder trails," the main trail passed through Bandera, Bexar, Kendall, Gillespie, Mason, McCulloch, Coleman, Callahan, and Shackelford counties to Fort Griffin. From Fort Griffin, the trail ran due north to cross the Red River at Doan's Crossing, and then

through present Woodward, Oklahoma, to Dodge City.

In 1883 A. J. (Jack) Potter pioneered the Potter-Bacon Trail from Hebronville, Texas, to Cheyenne, Wyoming. Potter followed established trails out of the Rio Grande-Nueces country to join the Western Trail to Albany. From Albany, the trail ran northwest by way of Rice's Spring (Haskell), Teepee City, Quitaque Creek, the Goodnight ranch, and present Channing to exit from Texas in present Dallam County. The Goodnight-Loving Trail, established in 1886 by Charles Goodnight and Oliver Loving, ran from Young County, Texas, to the Pecos River (along the Butterfield stage route) and up the Pecos into New Mexico.

Wayne Gard, *The Chisholm Trail* (Norman, 1954).
Wayne Gard, "The Shawnee Trail," *Southwestern Historical Quarterly*, LVI.
Wayne Gard, "The Impact of the Cattle Trails," *Southwestern Historical Quarterly*, LXXI.
Walter P. Webb, *The Great Plains* (Boston and New York, 1931).

# NORTHWEST TEXAS RANCHES, 1876-1895

 WITHIN a few brief years after the Palo Duro defeat of the Comanches and Kiowas, the vast army of buffalo hunters had cleared the West Texas ranges, and great herds of cattle and cattlemen sought new locations on the ancient hunting ground of the Indian. The early settlement of the Texas Panhandle and the northwestern plains is largely the story of the cattle kingdom. Charles Goodnight started the great migration in 1876. Many others followed, and, within a few years the range cattle industry saw its

"golden era" dawn and then pass with the coming of barbed wire and the big pasture. Some of the early northwest cattle ranches include the following:

1. The J. A. Ranch (**A**), was established in 1876 by Charles Goodnight in partnership with John Adair; the ranch, located in the Palo Duro Canyon, covered sections of Armstrong, Briscoe, Hall, Randall, Donley, and Swisher counties.

2. The Young Ranch (**YG, ╤**), established in 1878 by W. C. Young who employed Ben Galbraith as ranch

manager, was located first in Shackelford County but was later moved to Garza, Scurry, and Borden counties; in 1880 the Llano Cattle Company was organized by Young and the brand was changed to the curry comb (≢).

3. The Bar BAD (B̄A̅D̅) was established by Mrs. E. C. Milligan in Scurry County in 1876.

4. The Quarter Circle J Ranch (℮) was located on Bugbee Creek and the Canadian River in 1877 by Thomas G. Bugbee; in 1882 he sold his cattle to the Hansford Cattle Company.

5. The LIT Ranch (LIT) was established in 1877 on the Canadian River by George W. Littlefield.

6. The LX Ranch (✗), founded by Deacon Bates and David T. Beal in 1877, was located on the Canadian River in present Potter, Sherman, Hansford, and Moore counties.

7. The Anchor T Ranch (⊥) was established on the upper Palo Duro west of the JA by Leigh Dyer in 1877.

8. The Criswell Ranch (C̄C̄) was established on the Canadian River in present Wheeler County by H. W. (Hank) Criswell in 1878.

9. The Diamond Tail Ranch (♦), located in present Collingsworth, Childress, and Hall counties, was founded by Bill Curtiss and T. J. Atkinson in 1878.

10. The Shoe Bar Ranch (Ɔ—) was established by Leigh Dyer and L. G. Coleman in Donley and Hall counties in 1878.

11. The XIT Ranch (XIT) was established by the Capitol Syndicate of Chicago, Illinois, along the Texas-New Mexico boundary in 1879; the XIT properties extended from Dallam County on the north to Hockley and Cochran counties on the south (note map).

12. The LS Ranch (LS) was established in 1879 near Tascosa in Oldham County by W. M. D. Lee and Lucian Scott.

13. The Turkey Track Ranch (ᴨ) was established

by R. L. McNulty in 1879 in Hutchinson and Hansford counties.

14. The OX Ranch (OX), located in Childress, Hardeman, and Cottle counties, was established by A. and J. Forsyth in 1880.

15. The Rocking Chair Ranch (ⅆ) was established in Collingsworth and Wheeler counties by John and Wiley Dickerson in 1880.

16. The Three D Ranch (ᗡ𝖽) was established along the Pease River basin in 1880 by Daniel Waggoner.

17. The Pitchfork Ranch (Ɛ), in King and Dickens counties, was established by D. B. Gardner and J. S. Godwin in 1881 and sold to the Pitchfork Land and Cattle Company.

18. The U Lazy S Ranch (Uᔕ), founded by John and William Slaughter, was located in Crosby, Scurry, Kent, Howard, and Garza counties.

19. The Frying Pan Ranch (—O) was established in 1882 by J. F. Glidden and H. B. Sanborn in Potter, Randall, and Oldham counties.

20. The Francklyn Ranch (◇F) was established in Hutchinson, Gray, and Carson counties by the Francklyn Land and Cattle Company in 1882.

21. The Matador Ranch (ᴦ) was established in Motley, Dickens, Cottle, and Floyd counties by the Matador Land and Cattle Company in 1882.

22. The Spur Ranch ( ⋀ ), located in Garza, Dickens, Kent, and Crosby counties, was established in 1883 by the Espuela Land and Cattle Company of Fort Worth.

In addition to those listed, early ranches in this area also included the Square Compass (⤫X), the Two Buckle (2Ꝋ), the Ten A (IOᐱA), the Spade (ᗡ⌐), the Four Sixes (6666), and the Weed Hoe (△). Further south, the Hashknife (ᴦ) in Taylor County, the SMS ranches (ƧMƧ) in Jones, Haskell, Throckmorton, and Stonewall counties, C. C. (Lum) Slaugh-

ter's Lazy S () on the headwaters of the Colorado, and Oliver Loving's OL Ranch in Young County were all in operation before 1885. On the Brazos River in Palo Pinto County, John Hittson (HIT) and C. C. (Lum) Slaughter (ROS) pioneered ranching prior to the Civil War.

C. L. Douglas, *Cattle Kings of the Southwest* (Dallas, 1939).
Gus L. Ford, *Texas Cattle Brands* (Dallas, 1936).
J. Evetts Haley, *The XIT Ranch of Texas and the Early Days of the Llano Estacado* (Norman, 1953).
Laura V. Hamner, *Short Grass and Long Horns* (Norman, 1943).
W. C. Holden, *Rollie Burns* (Dallas, 1932).
W. C. Holden, *The Spur Ranch* (Boston, 1934).
Curtis S. Manley, "Early Background and Break-Up of the Matador Ranch," West Texas Historical Association *Yearbook*, XXXVIII.
L. S. Sheffy, *The Francklyn Land and Cattle Company* (Austin, 1963).

# GULF COAST RANCHES, 1850-1875

THE CATTLE INDUSTRY along the Gulf Coast of Texas began with the first Spanish-Mexican settlers in the region north of the Rio Grande. The Anglo-American pioneers moved into the area in the 1830's and 40's, and, in the years preceeding the Civil War, they originated the range cattle industry. The major early ranches of what is commonly known as the Coastal Bend include the following:

1. The historic King Ranch () in Nueces, Kenedy, Kleberg, Willacy, Brooks, Hidalgo, and Jim Wells counties began in 1852 when Captain Richard King purchased a Spanish land grant of 75,000 acres on Santa Gertrudis Creek in Nueces County. In 1860 he sold half of his grant to Mifflin Kenedy; this sale marks the origin of the King and Kenedy ranch empires in South Texas. When King died in April, 1885, Robert J. Kleberg, Sr., became manager of the King ranch properties. In 1935 the ranch came under the control of the King Ranch, Incorporated, with Robert J. Kleberg, Jr., as manager and the King-Kleberg descendants as stockholders.

2. The Kenedy ranches—Laureles and La Parra—began with the Richard King-Mifflin Kenedy land sale of 1860; when the partnership was dissolved in 1868, Kenedy bought the Laureles Ranch, located twenty-two miles from Corpus Christi. He organized the La Parra Ranch in 1882, the same year that he sold Laureles to a Scottish syndicate. In 1901 Mrs. Richard King purchased the Laureles Ranch from the Scottish firm.

3. The Bonnie View Ranch, extending from Copano Bay to Woodsboro, was established in 1839 by John H. Wood; the enterprise prospered for many years before D. T. Wood sold the ranch properties to real estate developers in 1906.

4. The Taft Ranch, or the Coleman-Fulton Pasture Company, grew out of a partnership between George Ware Fulton, T. H. Mathis, and Tom M. Coleman in 1872. In the years that followed, the company prospered and acquired land in San Patricio and Refugio counties; in 1900 the primary interest of Coleman and Fulton turned from cattle to land development; the

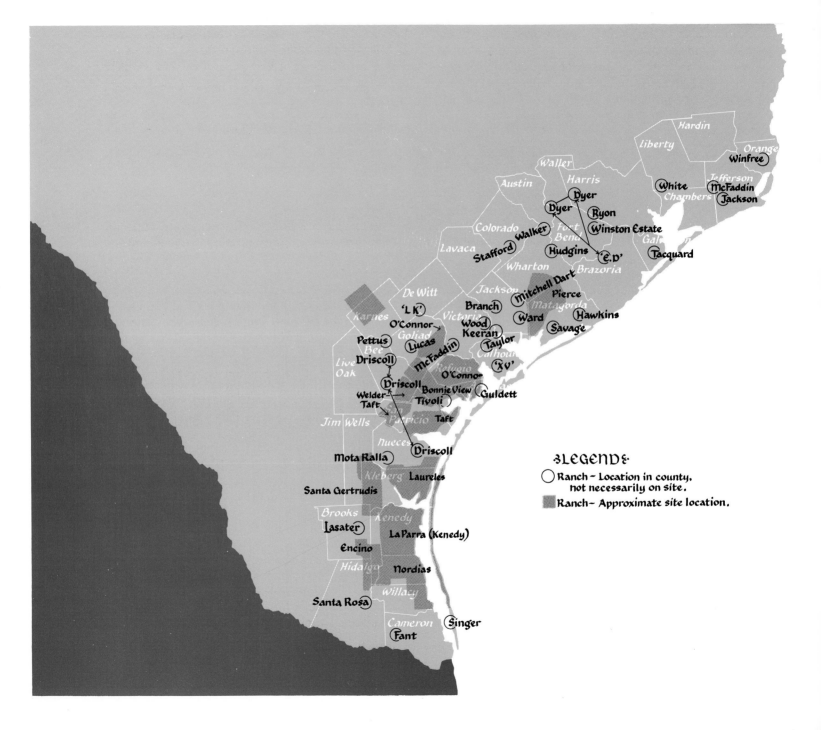

ranch was divided into farm tracts around the towns of Taft and Gregory.

5. The O'Conner ranches were founded before the Civil War by Thomas O'Conner; in the years following the Civil War, O'Conner kept buying land until he had accumulated more than 500,000 acres in Goliad, Victoria, La Salle, McMullen, San Patricio, and Webb counties.

6. The Welder ranches began when John Welder and his two sons, John and Thomas, entered the cattle business in the 1840's. Within a few years they owned large tracts of land in Refugio, San Patricio, and Bee counties.

7. The Carvajal(El Rincón) Ranch was established between the San Antonio River and Cibolo Creek in present Karnes County by José Luis Carvajal in 1830; it was founded on an old Spanish land grant to Don Andres Hernandez and Luis Menchaca in 1758, and Carvajal built his ranch headquarters on Cibolo Creek where La Bahía Road crossed the stream; he abandoned his ranch after 1836.

8. Rancho Grande, located in Wharton and Matagorda counties, was established shortly before and immediately after the Civil War by the colorful A. H. (Shanghai) Pierce; by 1871 the Pierce holdings included 250,000 acres of land (Pierce was president of a partnership known as the Pierce-Sullivan Pasture Company).

Other 19th century ranches along the Gulf Coast include the McFaddin, Winfree, Jackson, and White ranches in Orange, Jefferson, and Jackson counties; the "E D," Ryon, Dyer, Walker, Hudgins, Winston, Hawkins, and Savage ranches in the Brazos-Colorado river country; the Mitchell, Ward, Branch, Wood, and McFaddin ranches along the lower Guadalupe River; and the Lucas, LK, Driscoll, Pettus, Tivoli, and Gullett ranches between the San Antonio and Nueces rivers.

Chris Emmett, *Shanghai Pierce: A Likeness* (Norman, 1953).
Hobart Huson, *Refugio* (2 vols., Woodsboro, 1955).
Tom Lea, *The King Ranch* (2 vols., Boston, 1957).
A. Ray Stephens, *The Taft Ranch* (Austin, 1964).
Junann J. Stieghorst, *Bay City and Matagorda County:* A History (Austin, 1965).
Robert H. Thonhoff, "The First Ranch in Texas," West Texas Historical Association *Yearbook*, 1957.

# THE TEXAS-OKLAHOMA INDIAN FRONTIER, 1860-1896

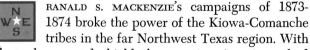 RANALD S. MACKENZIE's campaigns of 1873-1874 broke the power of the Kiowa-Comanche tribes in the far Northwest Texas region. With bow, horse, and shield these native Americans had been lords of the plains for more than two centuries.

In summarizing the last three and a half decades of activity along the Red River frontier, one finds that three primary items stand out: (1) the Texas Indian reservations on the Brazos River, (2) the location of the Kiowa-Comanche-Apache reservation in the Indian

Territory, and (3) the Greer County boundary dispute.

In the summer of 1854 General Randolph B. Marcy, under orders from the War and Interior departments and in accord with an act of the Texas legislature, located two Indian reservations on the upper Brazos River: (1) The Brazos Reservation, consisting of four leagues of land, was located twelve miles south of Fort Belknap on a series of bends in the river; the Brazos Reservation, known as the "lower" reservation to the frontiersmen, eventually became the temporary home of approximately two thousand Caddo, Anadarko, Waco, and Tonkawa Indians. (2) The Comanche Indian Reservation (for the Texas or Penateka Comanches) was located adjacent to Camp Cooper on the Clear Fork of the Brazos. Primarily because of strife between the Indians and Texas frontier residents (much of it provoked by the frontiersmen), the Brazos Reservation was abandoned in 1859 on the orders of R. S. Neighbors, and the Indians moved to the Wichita Indian lands in the Washita River valley of present Oklahoma. At the same time, the Comanche reservation was also abandoned and the residents moved into the Indian Territory.

After the Mackenzie campaigns of 1873-1875, the Comanche and Kiowa Indians were settled on lands immediately north of the Red River, a section of the Indian Territory bordered on the west by the North Fork of Red River, on the south by the Red River proper, on the east by a line paralleling the Chisholm Trail (separating the Comanches and Kiowas from the Chickasaw nation), and on the north by a line intersecting the 100° meridian at a point north of the North Fork of the Red. These lands had been set aside for the Indians by the Treaty of Medicine Lodge in October, 1867. Surrounding present Lawton and Fort Sill (established January 7, 1869), the Comanche-Kiowa-Apache reserve included that part of present Oklahoma west of Rush Springs, Duncan, Comanche, and Marlow—the land drained by the watershed of Cache Creek.

The boundary dispute between Texas and the Indian Territory over Greer County arose when the Commissioner of Indian Affairs discovered, as the result of a survey by A. H. Jones and H. M. Brown, that the Melish Map of the United States (1818) had erroneously placed the 100° meridian more than one hundred miles too far east. Between the Melish line and the Jones-Brown line, the North Fork and South Fork (Prairie Dog Town Fork) of the Red River converged. If Texas accepted the true 100° meridian as its boundary, which branch of the Red River would be considered as the boundary?

Eager to take advantage of the confusion, the Texas legislature passed an act on February 8, 1860, creating Greer County, Texas, between the forks of the Red River and the 100° meridian—a considerable region now encompassing Harmon, Jackson, Greer, and a part of Beckham counties of Oklahoma. By the year 1885 Texas had patented 144,000 acres of the region to the Day Land and Cattle Company (this organization had an additional 203,000 acres under lease) and, in all, some ten families and 60,000 head of cattle belonging to seven or eight Texas firms occupied the lands of Greer County. The boundary dispute between Texas and the United States became more significant in 1890 when President Benjamin Harrison approved an act creating the Territory of Oklahoma and providing for the prosecution of a suit against Texas for a final settlement of the ownership of Greer County. After great legal argument, the United States Supreme Court, on March 16, 1896, decided (1) the true 100° meridian was meant to be the boundary, and (2) the South Fork of the Red River was meant to be the northern boundary of Texas. Thus, Texas lost her case to claim the Greer County territory.

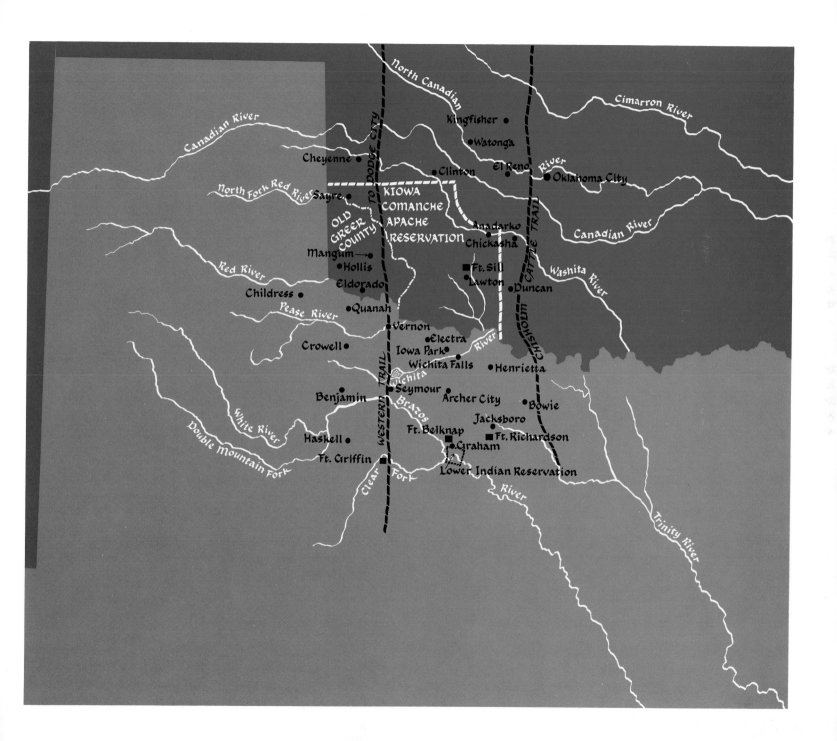

WHEN THE CIVIL WAR and Reconstruction arrested the western advance of settlement, the North Texas frontier line roughly paralleled the Western Cross Timbers from a point near Red River Station in Montague County to the headwaters of the Bosque and Leon rivers in present Erath and Eastland counties. The first settlement in Montague County was a place called Head of Elm (Saint Jo), established in 1856 when the first settlers located along the headwaters of Elm Fork of the Trinity. Montague, named for Daniel Montague, was founded in 1858 when a log courthouse was erected there for the new county of the same name. On a journey across North Texas as a member of an expedition searching for copper ore in 1872, M. K. Kellogg described the Head of Elm as a "hamlet of 5 or 6 log houses—principally grog shops—called 'Saloons' "; Montague as "a miserable hamlet only a little better than 'The Elms' though one or two respectable private houses are in the vicinity and some corn fields"; and the Queens' Peak settlement to the west as "5 or 6 log cabins some protected by stockades." Later on, camped between Montague and Jacksboro, Kellogg recorded, "This is truly a wilderness—no signs of human beings in any direction—it is indeed the limit line of civilization."

Even as the Kellogg expedition worked its way toward the famous Double Mountains, activity was on the increase in the mesquite and oak-covered rolling plains of the divide between the Red and Brazos rivers. Jack County had been organized since 1856 with Jacksboro (initially called Mesquiteville) as the county seat; Decatur, in central Wise County (1856), developed from a settlement known as Bishops Hill (Absolom Bishop); and Weatherford, in Parker County (1856), had been a thriving frontier village since 1857-58. With the solution of the Indian problem in the mid-1870's, restless settlers were ready to move further west in search of land for farms and ranches. "Like a dam beginning to break," writes Billy M. Jones, "small penetrations into the prairies west of the Cross Timbers country before 1870 had signaled the coming flood."

During the decade from 1870 to 1880, a majority of the new settlers pointed their wagons toward the rolling prairies west of Fort Worth and north of Abilene. Moving west from the vicinity of Montague and Jacksboro, the following early sites and communities are of significance:

In Montague County (organized 1858), besides the villages of Montague and Queens' Peak previously mentioned, old Red River Station became an important landmark on the Chisholm Trail in the mid-1860's; Bowie, its location settled earlier by D. M. Cunningham and W. R. Lamb, was surveyed as a townsite in 1882; Nocona, headquarters for the ranch of William Broaddus and D. C. Jordan in the early 1870's, reached the status of a town in 1881-1882; Ringgold was settled in 1872 by A. B. Boren and in 1878 by Will Johnson; and Illinois Bend on the Red River was settled in 1862 by immigrant families from Illinois. To the west in Clay County, where the Census of 1870 gave no figures at all, Cambridge was established as the county seat of the reorganized county in 1873; when the railroad built through in 1882, most of the settlers at Cambridge moved to Henrietta and the latter community became the county seat. In 1867 Buffalo Springs was selected as a site for a frontier fort but was soon abandoned because of a lack of wood and water.

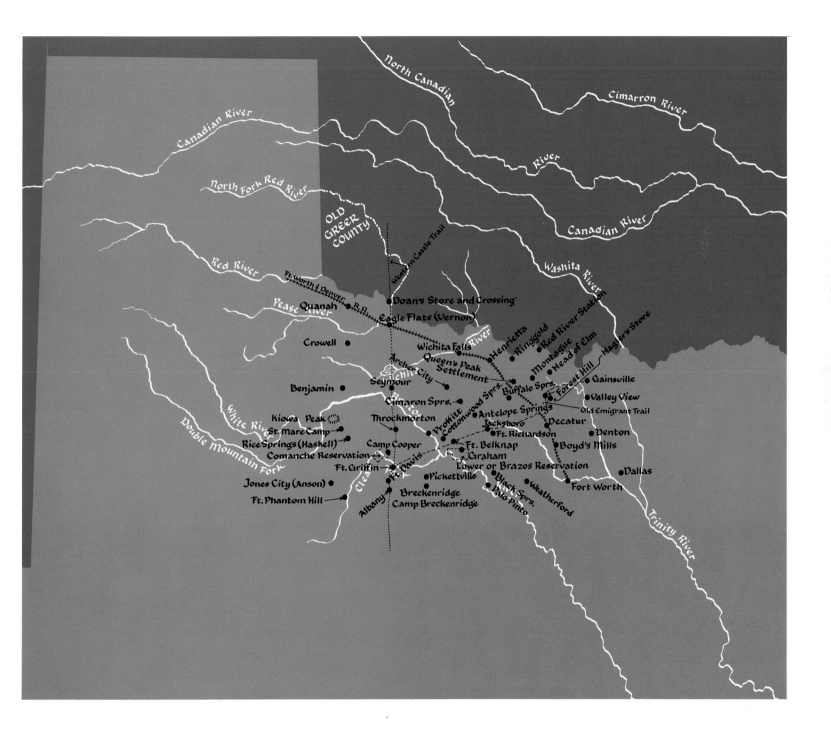

North Canadian

Cimarron River

Canadian River

River

Canadian River

North Fork Red River

Washita River

OLD GREER COUNTY

Red River

Western Cattle Trail

Ft. Worth & Denver R.R.

Pease River

Quanah

Doan's Store and Crossing

Eagle Flats (Vernon)

Crowell

Wichita Falls

Henrietta

Ringgold

Red River Station

Queen's Peak Settlement

Montague

Head of Elm

Hagler's Store

Archer City

River

Gainsville

Seymour

Benjamin

Cimaron Sprs.

Buffalo Sprs.

Forest Hill

Valley View

Old Emigrant Trail

Brazos

Cottonwood Sprs.

Antelope Springs

Decatur

Denton

Kiowa Peak

Throckmorton

Proffitt

Jacksboro

Ft. Richardson

St. Mare Camp

White River

Rice Springs (Haskell)

Camp Cooper

Ft. Belknap

Boyd's Mills

Comanche Reservation

Graham

Lower or Brazos Reservation

Double Mountain Fork

Ft. Griffin

Ft. Davis

Dallas

Pickettville

Fort Worth

Jones City (Anson)

Clear

Breckenridge

Black Sprs.

Weatherford

Ft. Phantom Hill

Albany

Camp Breckenridge

Palo Pinto

Trinity River

Wichita Falls was established at a falls in the Wichita River in the summer of 1875 near the site of an old log cabin built by Tom Buntin, a buffalo hide freighter. To the south of Wichita Falls, Archer City, an older unorganized settlement and ranch center, was established as a town and Archer County was organized in 1880. West of Wichita Falls, Doan's Store marked the site of the first settlement in Wilbarger County. Eagle Flats, or Vernon, was surveyed on the Pease River in 1877. South of Wilbarger, Seymour was established as a village on the Western Cattle Trail in 1878, and to the west of the Pease River the town of Quanah was built immediately after the Fort Worth and Denver Railroad made its survey in 1886.

Further south, along the upper Brazos, the military establishments at Fort Richardson, Fort Belknap, and Fort Griffin afforded protection to the advancing frontier. Young County was created and organized in 1856, with John and Will Pevler among the first settlers and Belknap as the county seat; Graham, founded in 1872, became the county seat in 1874. The small community of Proffitt was established in 1879 by John Proffitt, Billy Boyles, and W. C. Wilkinson. Throckmorton, both the town and county, date from 1879 when the first settlers arrived around Camp Cooper. In Shackelford County the first settlements were along Hubbard Creek, where J. C. Lynch established his ranch headquarters in 1858. After the Civil War, Fort Griffin became the center of activity. John R. Baylor's log cabin on the Clear Fork of the Brazos near present Crystal Falls in 1857 pioneered the settlement of Stephens County (first named Buchanan). When the county was organized in 1876, Breckenridge was named as the county seat. Other early settlements in Stephens County include Crystal Falls (1870), Necessity (1870), and Eolian (1860). To the west of Shackelford, Jones County was organized in 1881 with Jones City (Anson) as the county seat. Between the Pease River and Double Mountain Fork of the Brazos, Haskell County (with Rice Springs, later known as Haskell, as the county seat) was organized in 1885, and Knox County was organized in 1891.

In the meantime, similar expansion was taking place south of the Callahan Divide in the Concho-Colorado river country, and this will be our next area of study.

# THE COLORADO-CONCHO COUNTRY,

# 1870-1890

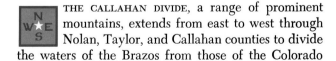 THE CALLAHAN DIVIDE, a range of prominent mountains, extends from east to west through Nolan, Taylor, and Callahan counties to divide the waters of the Brazos from those of the Colorado River. The Concho River system, draining the vast region southwest and west of present San Angelo, empties into the Colorado in northwestern Concho County.

Along the eastern fringe of the Colorado-Concho country, Eastland, Comanche, and Brown counties were the first settled. Prior to the Civil War, Welcome Chandler, Sam Coggins, T. H. Fowler, Ambrose Bull, and John and William Williams (1856-1857) settled in Brown County. Comanche County's first settlers were James Mercer, J. B. Hornsby, Frank Collier, and Dr. Ransom Tuggle; these men came into the area in 1854 to settle between the Comanche and Cora communities. The town of Comanche was established in 1858 by Ransom Tuggle, John Duncan, and T. J. Nabors. Frank Sanchez, who herded cattle near Ranger, was Eastland County's first settler; the families of William Monsker, Charles Blair, and James Ellison followed. While the county was created in 1858, settlement was slow until the 1870's.

The 1860's saw an influx of numerous cattlemen into the region between the Callahan Divide and the Concho rivers: John Hittson established a ranch east of Putnam in 1866; in 1863-1864 Rich Coffee and W. K. Wylie established ranches north of the Colorado River in southern Coleman County; in 1862 John Chisum founded a "Jinglebob" Ranch on the Concho River in northeast Concho County, and Trickham in southeast Coleman County became the trade center for the area. William Guest, the first settler in Runnels County, established his ranch in the northeastern part of the county in 1862. The grass and water of the Middle and South Concho rivers (Tom Green County) attracted the interests of R. F. Tankersley and G. W. DeLong in 1864-65. North of the Colorado, T. L. Odem had established his Wagontire Flat Ranch as early as the late 1850's (he was not a permanent resident until the 1870's) near Fort Chadbourne in the northwest part of present Runnels County. These were the first to enter the region.

The farmers began moving into the Callahan-Colorado-Concho country in the 1870's; towns, communities, and counties were established and organized. Coleman was established in 1876 by J. F. Gordon and R. S. Bowen, and Coleman County was organized in the same year; Santa Anna, established as a town in 1879, grew out of a settlement pioneered by Duke Jackson in the 1860's; Ballinger (known as Hutchins City) was surveyed by the Santa Fe Railroad in 1886; in McCulloch County, Brady (named for Peter Brady) was surveyed in 1876; Paint Rock (1879) and Eden (named for Fred Eden in 1879) were the two early communities; San Angelo (1867-68) grew up around Fort Concho; Ben Ficklin, south of San Angelo, was a well-known community in the early 1870's; Sherwood was founded by Thomas Stonehouse in 1883, and Irion County was created in 1889; and to the west, Rankin was established as Antonia in 1879.

To the north, pioneer settlements along the Callahan Divide included Belle Plain, founded in 1876, and Baird, surveyed as a railroad town in 1880, in Callahan County; Abilene, also a railroad survey, was established in 1881 and replaced Buffalo Gap, a small community since the heyday of the Western Trail, as the county seat of Taylor County (1878); to the west of Abilene, Bitter Creek (1880) and Sweetwater (1877) were the early communities in Nolan County; Colorado City, established in 1880 on the Colorado River, was the oldest settlement between Weatherford and El Paso on the Texas and Pacific Railroad. To the north, Scurry County was organized in 1884 and Fisher County in 1886. In this region, Snyder, a town growing out of Pete Snyder's buffalo supply camp, and Roby, founded in 1885, were the earliest settlements. Fort Chadbourne protected the early settlers in Coke County from Indian raids and the community of the same name had a population of twenty-five in 1880; Coke County was created and organized in 1889 with Hayrick (1877 population of 25) as the county seat. Along the headwaters of the North Concho, Sterling

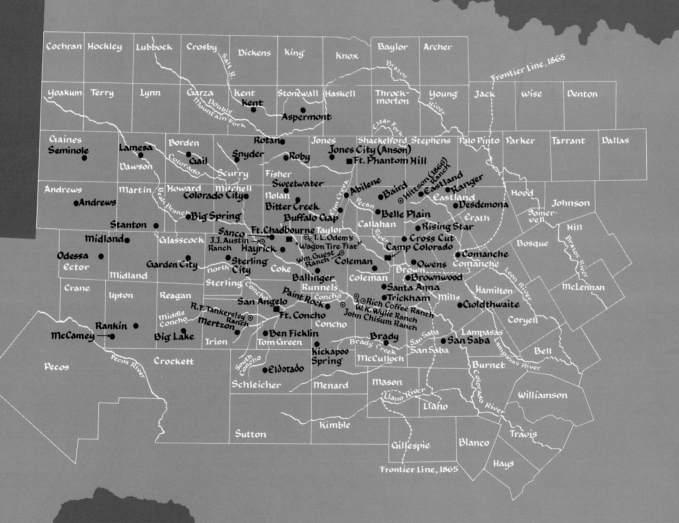

City (named for W. S. Sterling's buffalo camp) was established in 1891, and Garden City was founded in 1893. On the eastern edge of the plains proper, Kent County was created in 1892, and Stonewall County was organized in 1888.

This region of West Texas benefitted greatly from the construction of the Texas and Pacific and the Gulf, Colorado, and Santa Fe railroads. A Jay Gould enterprise, the Texas and Pacific began construction between Fort Worth and El Paso in 1880, "through twelve counties inhabited principally by Indians, prairie dogs, and coyotes." The Santa Fe, building west from Temple, also crisscrossed the region in the 1880's.

T. R. Havins, "The Frontier Era in Brown County," West Texas Historical Association *Yearbook*, XIII.

W. C. Holden, *Alkali Trails, or Social and Economic Movements of the Texas Frontier, 1846-1900* (Dallas, 1930).

Charles Kenner, "John Hittson: Cattle King of West Texas," West Texas Historical Association *Yearbook*, XXXIV.

Joseph Carroll McConnell, *The West Texas Frontier* (Jacksboro, 1933).

"Notes on Coleman County History," West Texas Historical Association *Yearbook*, XXXIV.

Jimmy Skaggs, "The Route of the Great Western Cattle Trail," West Texas Historical Association *Yearbook*, XLI.

Lewis Clyde Smith, *Frontier's Generation* (Brownwood, 1931).

J. W. Williams, "The Butterfield Overland Mail Road Across Texas," *Southwestern Historical Quarterly*, LXI.

# THE SOUTH TEXAS BRUSH COUNTRY,
# 1865-1890

 THE STORY of the early years of settlement in brush country of South Texas is primarily the story of the cattle industry. The western cattle industry originated in this region (as we have seen) and dominated the economic and social order of the land from 1865 until 1880. Since the turn of the century, the cow people have continued to exert a major influence in the development of this region.

Towns and communities of great significance in the early years of the western American cattle kingdom were Goliad, Beeville, Oakville, Tilden (Dog Town until 1876), and Fort Ewell, which was little more than a post office for the surrounding area. Other towns were established as the need arose. For many years Cotulla, Frio Town, Cometa, and Callaghan were no more than ranch headquarters with a store (or stores) that stocked supplies needed on the range.

Among the earliest settlers in the brush country were José Antonio Navarro, who settled in Atascosa County in 1845; Joseph Cotulla, who settled in La Salle County in 1868; M. Woodward, who settled in Zavala County in the late 1860's and fenced his range with timber; and Ben and W. J. Slaughter and William A. A. (Bigfoot) Wallace, who settled in Frio County in the 1860's. In 1870 the Bates brothers, who settled in Zavala County, received a two-section grant of land from the state in order to initiate the first irrigation project in the area.

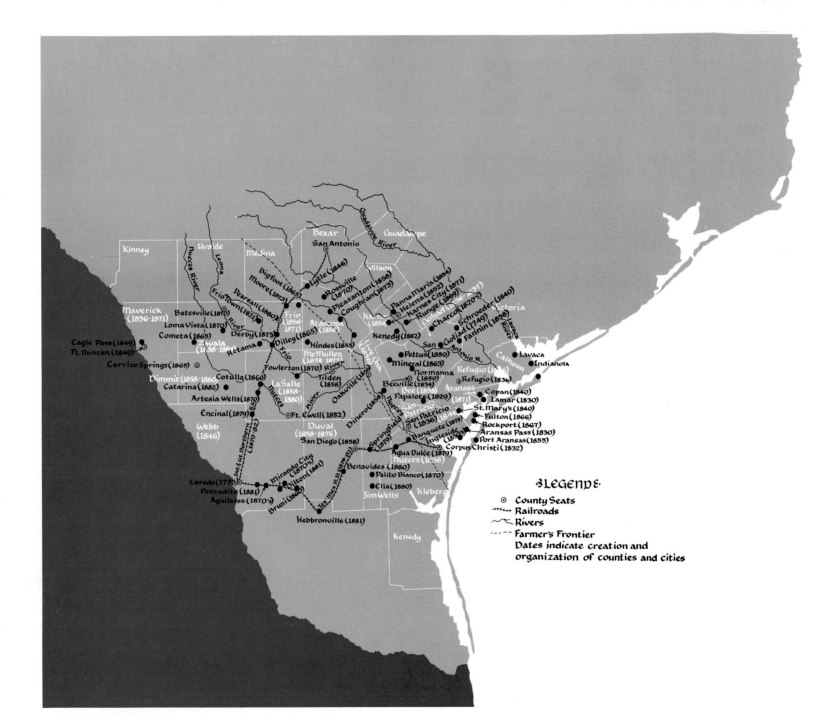

Kinney

Uvalde

Medina

Bexar

San Antonio

Guadalupe

Guadalupe River

Wilson

Bigfoot (1865)

Lytle (1846)

Rossville (1870)

Pleasanton (1858)

Coughran (1873)

Panna Maria (1854)

Helena (1852)

Karnes City (1871)

Runge (1889)

Karnes (1854)

Charco (1820's)

Goliad (1836-1897)

Schroeder (1840)

Goliad (1749)

Fannin (1858)

Victoria

Lavaca River

Maverick
(1856-1871)

Moore (1973)

Frio Town (1871)

Pearsall (1880's)

Batesville (1870)

Loma Vista (1870)

Cometa (1865)

Derby (1875)

Frio (1858-1871)

Atascosa (1858)

Dilley (1865)

Hindes (1855)

Kenedy (1882)

San Antonio R.

Lavaca

Indianola

Calhoun

Eagle Pass (1849)

Ft. Duncan (1849)

Carrizo Springs (1865)

Zavala (1858-1884)

Retama

McMullen (1858-1877)

Frio River

Pettus (1850)

Mineral (1863)

Normanna (1850)

Refugio (1834)

Refugio (1836)

Dimmit (1858-1860)

Catarina (1882)

Cotulla (1860)

Artesia Wells (1870)

Fowlerton (1870)

Tilden (1858)

LaSalle (1858-1880)

Oakville (1856)

Beeville (1834)

Bee (1858)

Papalote (1829)

Aransas (1871)

Copano (1840)

Lamar (1830)

St. Mary's (1840)

Encinal (1879)

Nueces River

Ft. Ewell (1852)

Dinero (1876)

Duval
(1858-1876)

San Diego (1858)

San Patricio (1836)

Springfield (1879)

San Patricio (1846)

Webb
(1846)

Fulton (1866)

Rockport (1867)

Aransas Pass (1830)

Port Aransas (1855)

Ingleside (1859)

Banquete (1879)

Corpus Christi (1832)

Agua Dulce (1879)

Nueces (1846)

Mirando City (1870's)

Laredo (1755)

Pescadito (1881)

Aguilares (1870's)

Oilton (1881)

Bruni (1860)

Benavides (1880)

Palito Blanco (1870)

Ella (1880)

Jim Wells

Kleberg

Hebbronville (1881)

Kenedy

## ᘔLEGEND᙭

⊙ County Seats

⟋⊢⟍ Railroads

⌇⌇ Rivers

- - - Farmer's Frontier
Dates indicate creation and
organization of counties and cities

On the roads leading from San Antonio to Laredo and Eagle Pass, Lytle Station (now known as Lytle), was named for William Lytle, who established a cattle ranch on the Medina River in 1846; Frio Town, located where the old Presidio Road crossed the Frio River, was established in 1871 as the county seat of newly-organized Frio County; southeast of Frio Town, Pearsall was surveyed when the I. and G. N. Railroad built through the area in 1881; to the southwest, Carrizo Springs was founded in 1865 with cattle raising as the only industry, and in 1907 Colonel Ike T. Pryor established La Pryor on part of his Seven D Ranch; Dilley, known as Darlington until named for a railroad official in 1881, was founded in 1865; Cotulla, named for Joe Cotulla, grew into a community after 1868; and Callahan (an official misspelling of Callaghan) and Encinal, in La Salle and Webb counties respectively, were established in 1881 as shipping points for the Callaghan Ranch. On the Rio Grande, Laredo (1755) dates from the days of the hacienda of Tomás Sánchez, and San Ygnacio, downstream, from the hacienda de Dolores of José Vásquez Borrego.

In the late decades of the 19th century, the principal towns of the Nueces, Frio, and Atascosa river country were Tilden, established in a bend of the Frio River in 1877; George West, named for its founder, a retail and shipping point after 1900; and Beeville, founded as a townsite in 1860 (later a significant shipping point for the ranchers of the region). Alice, founded as a depot on the San Antonio and Aransas Pass Railroad in 1888, was first known as Bandana and, later, Kleberg; the name was changed to Alice (Alice King Kleberg) in 1904. Kingsville, located in the heart of the King Ranch, was established on the St. Louis, Brownsville, and Mexican Railroad in 1904.

The other towns of South Texas, including those in the lower Rio Grande valley, trace their origins to more recent decades and feature economic orders based either on the citrus fruit and vegetable industry or petroleum.

# THE PANHANDLE & SOUTH PLAINS, 1870-1900

 THE MAP on the opposite page shows the earliest communities and towns that came into being in the 1870's and 1880's in that section of Texas to the west and immediately to the east of the Cap Rock escarpment. All of the population clusters shown, however, were related (most of them directly) to the cattle industry. The farmers' frontier had not, at this time, advanced very far beyond the 1865 line; therefore, many familiar names of towns will be missing from the map and from this description.

In order (more or less) from north to south, the ranchers' frontier of the Texas Panhandle included the following settlements in the 1870's and 80's; Buffalo

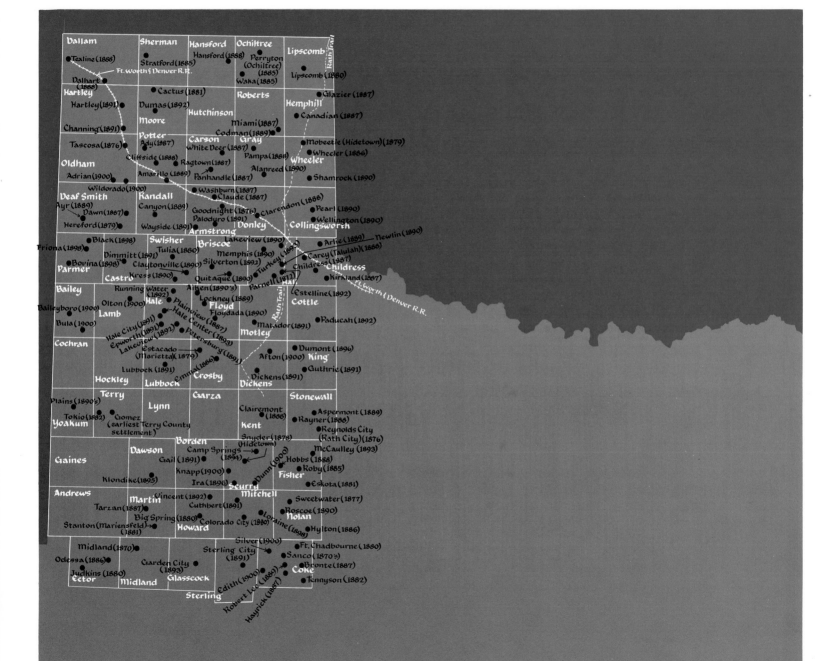

Springs, a cow camp near Agua Fria Creek in the northern part of present Dallam County, was the first headquarters of the XIT Ranch; Coldwater, located on Coldwater Creek in the eastern part of Sherman County, was established as a cowboy camp in the 1870's and was populated by "some fifteen cowboys of the William B. Slaughter ranch" when Sherman County was organized in 1890; Timms' City was established in the 1880's as a cow camp by George Timms in present Lipscomb County; with a few stores and saloons, Timms' City was a favorite overnight stop for cowboys trailing cattle into the Indian Territory; Old Mobeetie, in the northwestern part of present Wheeler County, was established in 1875 as a trading post for Fort Elliott; Tascosa, on the Canadian River northwest of present Amarillo, was settled in the early 1870's by Mexican colonists and developed into a significant shipping point and trade center for the nearby ranches; Amarillo, known as Ragtown when the Fort Worth and Denver Railroad construction crews reached the site, was surveyed as a town in 1887; and Aberdeen, located in northeastern Collingsworth County, was established in 1880 as the headquarters of the Rocking Chair Ranch.

South of present Amarillo, Ayr, named for Ayr, Scotland, was founded in 1890 by survey crews of the Fort Worth and Denver Railroad; Bovina in present Parmer County, originated in the late 1880's as the Hay Hook line camp of the XIT Ranch; Parmerton, a small village in Parmer County, was designated as the county seat when the county was created in 1876 (the town never developed); Old Happy, located near the northern boundary of Swisher County, was a cow camp;

Hale City, in present Hale County, was surveyed in 1891 but failed to develop; Della Plain was established in present Floyd County in 1887; Teepee City was founded in 1879 near the South Pease River as a supply station for wagon trains, freighters, and ranchers; Estacado was established in present Crosby County in 1879 by a group of Quakers under the leadership of Paris Cox; Dockum's Ranch, located in present Dickens County, consisted of W. C. Dockum's store and dugout in 1877; Lubbock, presently the most significant city of the South Plains, was established in 1890; and, southeast of Lubbock, Post City was founded a few miles east of the Cap Rock (in present Garza County) by Charles Williams Post as an experiment in colonization. Far to the south, Lamesa was founded in 1905. Two other present-day towns, Childress and Clarendon, developed with the coming of the railroad in 1887-1888, although Clarendon had been established by Henry Carhart in 1879 some six miles north of its present location. Canyon, selected as the headquarters of the T Anchor Ranch by Jot Gunter and William B. Munson in 1878, became a village in 1889 when L. G. Connor settled there. Plainview, located where the MacKenzie Trail crossed Runningwater Draw, was founded in 1887 by Z. T. Maxwell and E. L. Lowe.

To the southeast, Cottle County remained unsettled for twenty years after its creation in 1876. The Census of 1880 showed 24 people in the county. Between 1880 and 1890, J. J. McAdams settled at present Paducah, and J. H. Cansler settled in a dugout on Buck Creek. Neighboring King County was organized in 1891 with Guthrie as the county seat.

# THE EDWARDS PLATEAU
# & THE PERMIAN BASIN, 1870-1910

IT WAS SHOWN on an earlier map that the westward advance was stalled by the fear of Indian tribes and by the coming of the Civil War on a line running (for this particular area) from San Saba County on the Colorado River to Fredericksburg on the Pedernales, to Kerrville on the Guadalupe, and to Eagle Pass on the Rio Grande. Only a few courageous individuals had ventured west of this line before the war years, 1861-1865. The westward advance into the Edwards Plateau, the western subdivision of the Hill Country, came during the 1870's and 1880's. Beyond the plateau to the northwest, the communities of the Permian Basin began with the construction of the Texas and Pacific Railroad.

Looking at this phase of the occupation from east to west, one sees the first settlers moving into the Edwards County territory in 1876 when Lafayette M. Pullen bought the first block of school land sold in the county and built a house on Cedar Creek; the site was later named Barksdale. Rocksprings was established by Roberts Sweeten in 1890, and the county was organized in 1891. In Real County, Anglo-American settlement began in 1857 when John Leakey built a home in the Frio Canyon near the site of present Leakey. In 1883 Leakey was made the county seat of Edwards County and became the county seat of Real when the county was established in 1913.

In Val Verde County, Del Rio, first called San Felipe del Rio, had a population of 50 in 1880; Val Verde County was created in 1885 and organized the same year. To the north, Sonora developed in 1879 when E. M. Kirkland established a sheep ranch on the open range nearby. Other ranchers settled in the region, and in 1890 Sonora, still a small village, became the county seat of Sutton County. To the east, the first settlers arrived in Kimble County in 1858, but the county was not organized until 1876 with Junction City as the county seat. In Schleicher County, sheepmen began to drift slowly into the area by 1882; the use of the windmill was instrumental in solving the water problem, and the county was created in 1887 and organized in 1901 when ranchers rushed into the region to take advantage of a sale of school lands by the state (Eldorado was founded in 1895).

Crockett County, a vast territory east of the Pecos, was created by the legislature in 1875 but organization had to wait until the summer of 1891. North of the Pecos drainage basin, Big Lake began to develop as a community in 1911; Crane (where the population of Crane County was listed as fourteen in 1918) had to wait for the discovery of oil in 1925 for its first substantial growth. McCamey (Upton County) was another boomtown, coming into existence in 1920 (marked by only a boxcar on the railroad). This overall study of West Texas establishes the fact that the Texas legislature had the bad habit of creating counties totally without population.

In the Permian Basin, settlement in Midland County began in the early 1880's along Johnson's Draw in the southern part of the county and Mustang Creek in the northeastern corner. The town of Midland had a population of 300 in 1890. Odessa (1886) and Big Spring

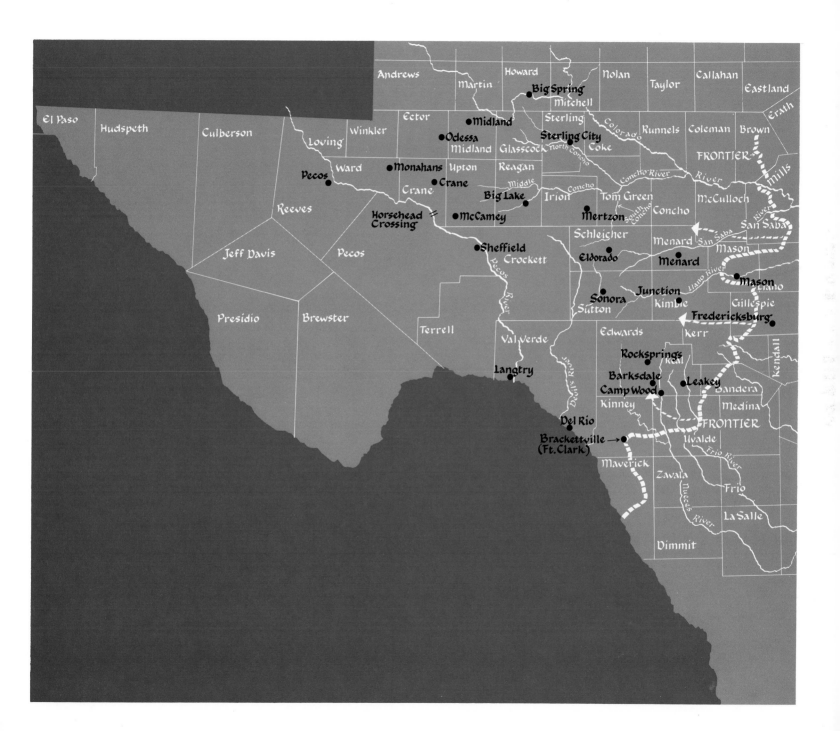

(1882) were railroad towns along the Texas and Pacific; however, it is of significance that when Big Spring became the county seat of Howard County in 1882 it was a "settlement of hide huts of buffalo hunters, a few tents, a wagon yard, a hotel, and eight saloons." To the north, Andrews County (1890 population—24) was organized in 1910 with the town of Andrews as the county seat, and Gaines County (with Seminole as the county seat) was established in 1905. The arid plains of the region where the 103° meridian intersects the 32° parallel were largely unpopulated at the turn of the century—as they are now.

# TRANS-PECOS TEXAS

 PRIOR TO THE CIVIL WAR, Trans-Pecos Texas was a vast uninhabited wasteland of desert vegetation, sand and salt, grass and sky. After 1849, the maps of this bleak but beautiful region were crisscrossed by the trails of such explorers as Marcy, Michler, Bryan, Johnston, Emory, Smith, Whiting, and Pope. In addition, water holes and mountain ranges were marked as were such geographical place names as White Sand Hills, Ojo de San Martín, Salt Lagoons, Sierra Blanca, Van Horn's Wells, Dead Man's Hole, Head of Limpia, Kings Spring, the Comanche Trail, Wild Rose Pass, Delaware Creek, Castle Mountain, Horsehead Crossing, Agua Delgada, Ojo del Berrendo, Sierra de la Cola de Aguila, Hot Spring, Apache Spring, Hueco Pass, Comanche Springs, Eagle Springs, Guadalupe Pass, Emigrant Trail, Toyah Creek, Sierra Diablo, and Rattlesnake Springs—all a part of the earlier chronicle of this western landscape that forms the southeastern corner of the deserts of the American West.

It is of significance, however, that early settlements were made west of the Pecos at present El Paso and at Presidio on the north bank of the Big Bend of the Rio Grande. While the early Spanish explorers passed through the "Pass of the North," it remained for Juan María Ponce de León to establish the De León Ranch near the present city in 1827; later on, Franklin Coons lived in the region long enough to name the outpost Franklin; and Hugh Stevenson, James W. Magoffin, and Anson Mills all arrived in the area during the 1850's. Fort Bliss was established in 1854 and became a permanent army post in 1877. Downstream from El Paso, Ysleta grew out of the early settlement of Corpus Christi de la Ysleta in 1682 (listed as the oldest permanent settlement in Texas); Socorro, a Spanish mission settlement was also established in 1682; and San Elizario was founded in 1772 when the Spanish moved the San Elizario Presidio to a site nearby. Many miles down the river, Ben Leaton, a former Mexican War soldier, acquired a small trading post that had been built in 1846; Leaton reconstructed and enlarged the building and named it Fort Leaton. The present town of Presidio, located a short distance downstream from the confluence of the Rio Grande and Rio Conchos (opposite La Junta or Presidio del Norte), was established by Ben Leaton, John W. Spencer, and John D. Burgess in 1850. A few years later, Fort Stockton (near Comanche Springs), Fort Davis, and Fort Quitman

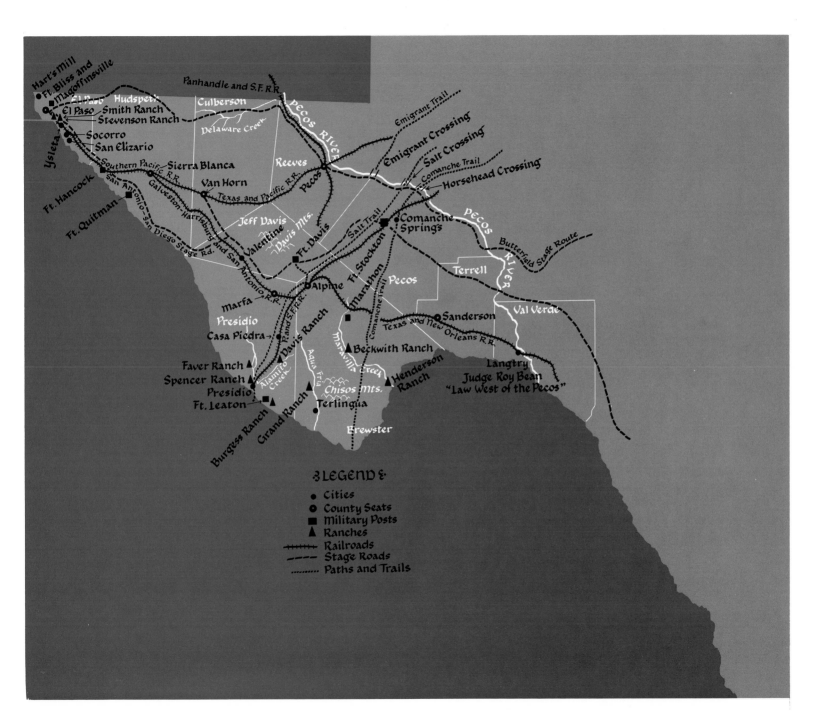

(1858) completed the pre-Civil War efforts to settle Trans-Pecos Texas.

A decade and a half after the close of the Civil War, community settlement came to the Trans-Pecos region with the building of the railroads. In the south, Langtry was founded west of the Pecos in Val Verde County in 1881 with the completion of the Texas and New Orleans Railroad; Marathon was founded in 1882 on the Circle Dot Ranch of Meyer Halff; Fort Stockton grew up in the 1870's around the military post by the same name; Alpine, known as Osborne and Murphyville for awhile, originated in 1882 as a water tank on the Texas and New Orleans; Marfa, established in 1881, was another water-tank town on the Texas and New Orleans; Valentine was named by the railroad construction crew at the site of their job on St. Valentine's Day, 1882; Van Horn (1881) was established as a water stop on the Texas and Pacific Railroad; Sierra Blanca, also founded in 1881, served as the junction

of the Texas and New Orleans and Texas and Pacific railroads; Pecos, located near the west bank of the Pecos River, began as a water-tank town on the Texas and Pacific; Toyah, situated on San Martin Draw in Reeves County, originated as a shipping point for ranchers of the immediate region; Balmorhea, on Toyah Creek in Reeves County, was an exception to the rule in that the community was founded in 1906 by a firm of land promoters.

Early cattle ranches in this region of far West Texas included the Meyer Halff Circle Dot Ranch south of Pinta; Colorado Springs near Marathon; the "02" Ranch, established south of Marathon in 1878 by John Beckwith; and the A. H. Gage (1882) and the H. L. Kokernot (1897) ranches, both located near Alpine.

Map of Texas and Parts of New Mexico, 1857, Bureau of Topographical Engineers, Washington, D. C.

# GOAT & SHEEP RANCHING, 1850-1968

 IN CONTRAST to the cattle industry, the history of goat and sheep ranching in Texas has been completely neglected by the historian. Nevertheless, since the 1920's, Texas has produced about 85 percent of the mohair clipped in the United States, and for several decades Texas has been the leading sheep-raising state of the nation. The wool and mohair industries of the state are (and have been) concentrated in the counties of the Edwards Plateau and Texas Hill Country.

Goats were brought into Texas during the Spanish colonial period but were used for home consumption of milk and meat. The first Angoras were brought to Texas by Colonel W. W. Haupt of Hays County, who, in 1857, acquired some stock from Dr. James B. Davis of South Carolina. The Angora goat of today has resulted from years of crossbreeding with the slick-haired Mexican goat; by the time the Turkish government prohibited the further exportation of Angoras in 1895, the improved American stock exceeded that of its Asiatic ancestors. The goat ranching industry, more highly concentrated than sheep ranching, forms the

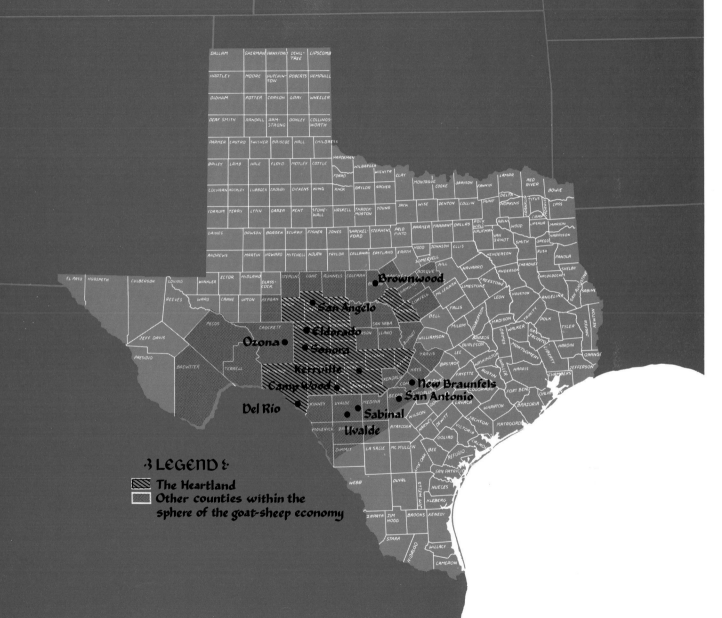

DALLAM | SHERMAN | HANSFORD | OCHIL-TREE | LIPSCOMB
HARTLEY | MOORE | HUTCHIN-SON | ROBERTS | HEMPHILL
OLDHAM | POTTER | CARSON | GRAY | WHEELER
DEAF SMITH | RANDALL | ARM-STRONG | DONLEY | COLLINGS-WORTH
PARMER | CASTRO | SWISHER | BRISCOE | HALL | CHILDRESS
BAILEY | LAMB | HALE | FLOYD | MOTLEY | COTTLE | HARDEMAN
COCHRAN | HOCKLEY | LUBBOCK | CROSBY | DICKENS | KING | KNOX
YOAKUM | TERRY | LYNN | GARZA | KENT | STONE-WALL | HASKELL
GAINES | DAWSON | BORDEN | SCURRY | FISHER | JONES | SHACKEL-FORD
ANDREWS | MARTIN | HOWARD | MITCHELL | NOLAN | TAYLOR | CALLAHAN

● **Brownwood**

● **San Angelo**

● **Eldorado**

**Ozona** ● ●**Sonora**

**Kerrville** ●

**Camp Wood** ●

**Del Rio** ● **New Braunfels**

**San Antonio**

● **Sabinal**

**Uvalde**

## ·3 LEGEND ୫·

▨ **The Heartland**

▦ **Other counties within the sphere of the goat-sheep economy**

primary basis of the economy of the Texas counties located between the Balcones Escarpment and the Pecos River; as time has passed, the industry has spread into the Trans-Pecos region, the upper Rio Grande Plain, and into the counties of the Western Cross Timbers and the Grand Prairie regions. San Antonio, San Angelo, and Kerrville are the most important mohair markets; other local markets include Rocksprings, Uvalde, Camp Wood, Sabinal, and Utopia. In the 1960 census report, the leading counties with the number of goats reported were the following: Edwards, 207,990; Uvalde, 150,590; Sutton, 125,937; Mason, 110,316; Kimble, 108,488; Val Verde, 103,521; Mills, 93,860; Real, 88,780; Kerr, 82,274; and Gillespie, 81,566. In 1964 mohair brought $27,428,000 into the Texas economy.

The first sheep were brought into Texas by the Franciscan fathers who founded the Spanish missions in the late 17th and early 18th centuries, but it was not until the years following annexation that much attention was given to sheep-raising. In 1857 George Wilkins Kendall, journalist and founder of the New Orleans *Picayune*, bought a ranch in present Kendall County and began raising sheep. During the years that followed, Kendall interested many of his friends and neighbors in the sheep and wool industry. After the Civil War, sheep-raising spread over much of South and Southwest Texas in spite of the fact that it was unpopular in areas where cattlemen were already established. Over the years there has been much advancement in the sheep-raising business, aided by the Texas Agricultural Experiment Station at Sonora—an institution specializing in range problems and scientific breeding. The primary sheep and wool markets are located at Sonora, Del Rio, Kerrville, and San Angelo. Textile mills are located at Brownwood, Eldorado, and New Braunfels. In 1964 wool brought $21,473,000 to the Texas economy.

# THE LATIN-AMERICAN IN TEXAS

THE LATIN-AMERICAN, also known as Spanish-American and Mexican-American, people of Texas have a history that can be traced back to the Spanish conquest and the three-century Spanish rule of the lands of the American Southwest. While their culture and traditions extend back to 1519, the rapid growth of the Latin-American population of Texas is relatively recent.

As the map on the opposite page shows, the great majority of Latin-Americans reside in the counties of South and Southwest Texas, an area extending along the Rio Grande from its mouth to El Paso and bordered on the north by a line running from Corpus Christi through the Lockhart-San Marcos-San Antonio region, and then northwest across the Edwards Plateau to the Pecos River in present Reeves County. Counties in the section of the state having the largest concentration of Latin-American people include Cameron, Hidalgo, Starr, Webb, Nueces, San Patricio, Bexar, Val Verde, Maverick, and El Paso. Beyond the South Texas-Edwards Plateau-Trans-Pecos territory, Harris County, Dallas County, Tarrant County, and Tom

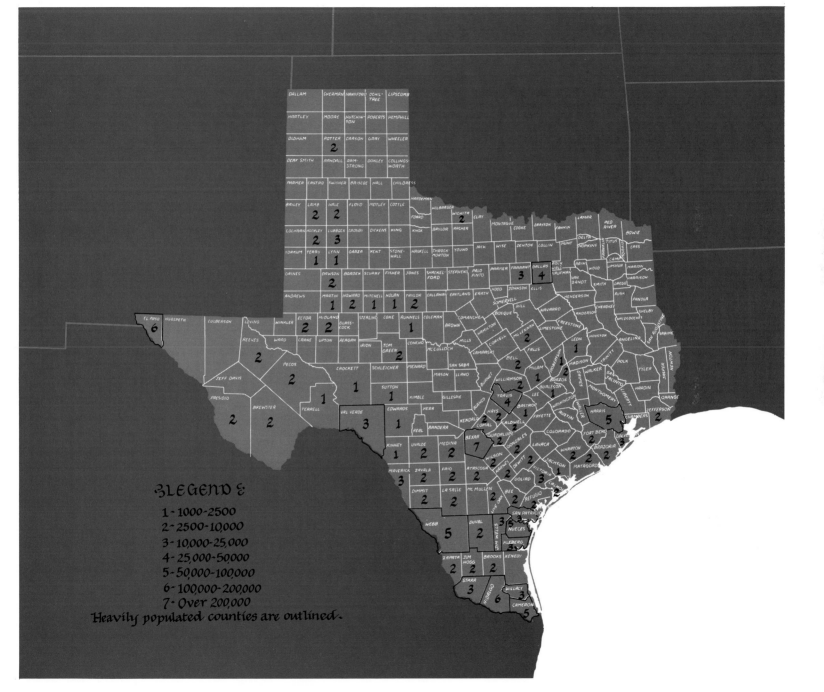

ЗLEGEND Ɛ
1 - 1000-2500
2 - 2500-10,000
3 - 10,000-25,000
4 - 25,000-50000
5 - 50,000-100,000
6 - 100,000-200,000
7 - Over 200,000
Heavily populated counties are outlined.

Green County are areas of significant Latin-American communities.

These people have played an important role in the past history of Texas, and, it would seem, their role in the future will be even more important.

Stanley A. Arbingast, *et al.*, *Atlas of Texas* (Austin, 1967).

# THE NEGRO IN TEXAS, 1860-1960

THE AMERICAN NEGRO was brought to Texas in slavery by those migrating to Stephen F. Austin's colony. The overwhelming majority of the colonists of Texas emigrated largely from slave states. In spite of the opposition of the Mexican government, Austin obtained permission for the 300 families of his first colony to bring in their slaves, and when the constitution of Coahuila and Texas prohibited slavery in 1827, he persuaded the legislature to pass a law recognizing labor contracts with indentured servants. The result was a continuation of slave importation. The census of the Austin colony, taken in 1825, showed 443 slaves. In 1836 the Constitution of the Republic of Texas recognized slavery, and in 1845 Texas was annexed as a slave state.

The first United States Census for Texas, that of 1850, showed 58,161 slaves and 397 free Negroes. At least one of the free Negroes, William Goyens (or Goings), achieved prominence in the vicinity of Nacogdoches. Born in North Carolina in 1794, Goyens came to Texas in 1820 (before the "old three hundred") and lived in Nacogdoches the remainder of his life. He was a blacksmith and a wagon manufacturer and engaged in freighting between Nacogdoches and Natchitoches. On a trip to Louisiana in 1826, Goyens was seized by

William English, who attempted to sell him into slavery. Goyens, in return for freedom, was forced to sign a note agreeing to peonage (to English) for himself; an obligation which was annulled after his return to Nacogdoches. Goyens was prominent as a legal counsel in the settlement of a number of suits arising under Spanish law. He operated an inn in Nacogdoches for a number of years. Prior to his death in 1856, he had accumulated a considerable estate centering around his two-story house, sawmill, and gristmill.

For nearly a century after the close of the Civil War, the Negroes of Texas lived mainly on the small farms of East Texas, where they constituted most of the sharecropper, farm-tenant classification. As a result of the depression of the 1930's and the policies of the New Deal's agricultural program, the Negroes began to move to the cities and the industrial areas of the state where they found employment. As the map shows, the greatest concentration of Negro population in the 1880's was found in the Coastal Plains region along the lower Brazos and Colorado river valleys (as well as in the counties of deep East Texas). In the 1960's this area of concentration had shrunk to include only the East Texas counties from Cass and Morris

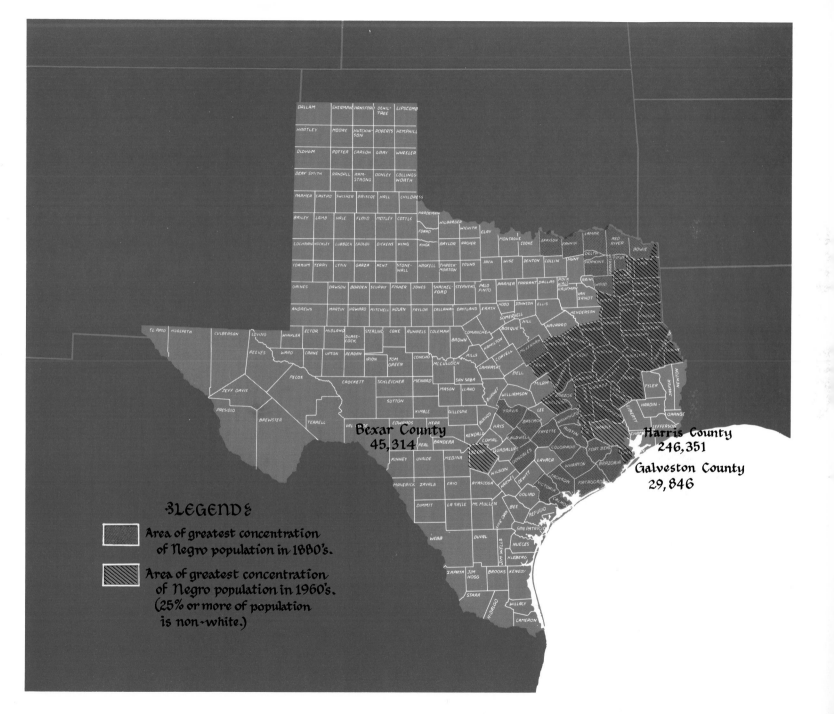

Bexar County
45,314

Harris County
246,351

Galveston County
29,846

ℨLEGENDℰ

Area of greatest concentration
of Negro population in 1880's.

Area of greatest concentration
of Negro population in 1960's.
(25% or more of population
is non-white.)

on the north to Waller and Montgomery on the south. It would seem, however, that these statistics are somewhat deceiving in that they show only percentages. The Gulf Coast region still combines with East Texas to provide a home for a great majority of the state's Negro population, but because of the significant shift in the Anglo-Saxon population (as tens of thousands left the small farms and ranches of the interior for the employment advantages of the building trades, shipyards, petrochemical plants, and aircraft and related manufacturers of the Coastal Bend industrial complex), the percentage of Negroes in this region is smaller in relation to the total population.

# GERMAN SETTLEMENTS IN TEXAS, 1836-1900

 THE GREAT GERMAN MIGRATION to the prairies of Texas began in 1838 when Friedrich Ernst founded a German settlement at Industry in Austin County. As noted previously, large-scale German immigration began with the founding of the *Adelsverein*, also known as the *Mainzer Verein*, in April, 1842, at Biebrich-on-the-Rhine for the purpose of purchasing land in Texas and encouraging emigrants to move to the American Southwest. The *Adelsverein*, through the efforts of Prince Carl of Solms-Braunfels, established New Braunfels at the site of Comal Springs in present Comal County in 1845 and, under the leadership of John O. Meusebach, Fredericksburg in the spring of 1846. The thousands of German immigrants that arrived in the years immediately following tended to settle on land in the Texas Hill Country or along the Colorado River in the vicinity of Industry, Cat Springs, and La Grange.

As the years passed and the German migration became more extensive, the later arrivals tended to settle on the fertile lands of the Coastal Prairies, the Blackland Prairie, and the Grand Prairie. As a result, a map of the German settlements in 1900 shows a wide belt of settlement running almost the length of Texas from the Red River on the north to the Nueces River on the south. While the activities of the *Adelsverein* had placed German settlers principally in the present counties of Comal, Gillespie, Llano, Guadalupe, Kerr, Mason, Kendall, Bexar, and Blanco, the later immigrants settled in Galveston, Harris, Austin, Washington, De Witt, Lavaca, Fayette, Lee, Travis, Williamson, McLennan, and Dallas counties. While the above-named areas represent the area of greatest concentration in 1900 for the German-American Texans, these people had also settled in considerable number in Coke, Grayson, Clay, Lamar, Denton, Tarrant, Johnson, Ellis, Bosque, Hamilton, Coryell, Bell, Falls, Robertson, Milam, Burleson, Grimes, Brazos, Waller, Fort Bend, Wharton, Colorado, Jackson, Victoria, Goliad, Karnes, Wilson, Gonzales, Caldwell, Bastrop, Hays, and Medi-

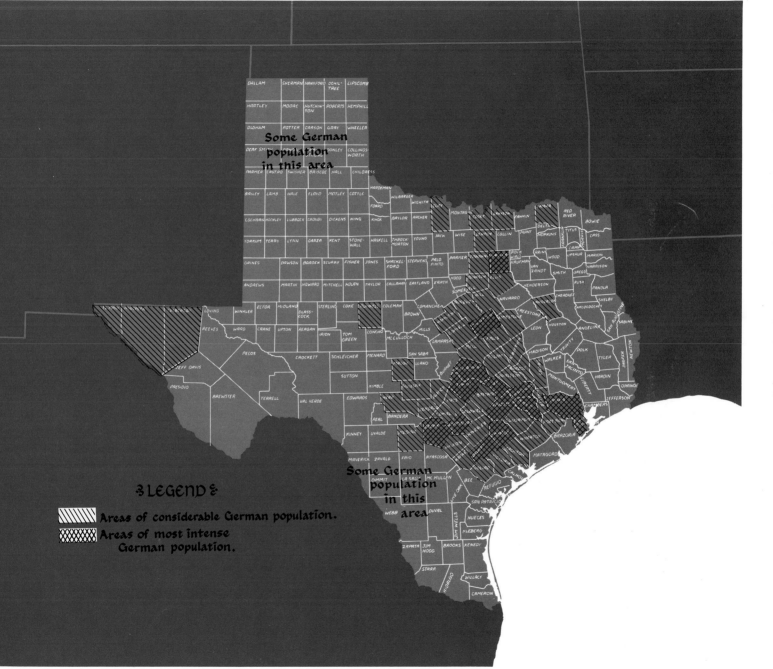

Some German
population
in this area

Some German
population
in this
area

❦ LEGEND ❧

Areas of considerable German population.

Areas of most intense
German population.

na counties—and it is in these primary areas that their descendants remain today.

Rudolph L. Biesele, *The History of the German Settlements in Texas, 1831-1861,* (Austin, 1930).

D. H. Biggers, *German Pioneers in Texas* (Fredericksburg, 1926).

Irene Marschall King, *John O. Meusebach, German Colonizer in Texas* (Austin, 1967).

Louis Reinhardt, "The Communistic Colony of Bettina," *Quarterly of the Texas State Historical Association,* III.

# THE NORWEGIAN & SWEDISH SETTLEMENTS IN TEXAS, 1845-1900

 THE NORWEGIAN MIGRATION to Texas was pioneered by Johannes Nordboe, who settled near present Dallas in 1838 or 1839; Johan Reinert Reierson, who established a Norwegian colony at Normandy (present Brownsboro); and Kleng Peerson, the leader of the move to Bosque County in 1853-54. Johan R. Reierson visited Texas in 1843, conferred with Sam Houston concerning a possible site for a Norwegian colony, and returned to Norway to write a book on the United States. In 1845 Reierson and a small group of colonists set sail for New Orleans, where they arrived in June. From New Orleans, Reierson led his colonists to present Henderson County, Texas, where he established a colony known as Normandy (later as Brownsboro). In 1848, Reierson established a second colony at Four Mile and Prairieville on the Kaufman-Van Zandt county line; between 1848 and 1853 both the Brownsboro and the two Kaufman-Van Zandt colonies grew and prospered.

In 1851-1853 Kleng Peerson explored the region west of the Trinity River and in 1854 Ole Canuteson, Hendric Dahl, and Jens Ringness led the move to newly-organized Bosque County; there, bounded roughly by Bee Creek to the north, the Bosque River to the east, and extending west into central Hamilton County, the three pioneers founded the extensive Norwegian settlement in Bosque and Hamilton counties. Other Norwegian pioneers stopped at Waco, and, later on, many moved to the Dallas area as the small settlements in East Texas declined in importance, but the Bosque-Hamilton county area has remained the primary Norwegian settlement in Texas.

The Swedes were led to Texas by Sir Svante Palm and S. M. Swenson. S. M. Swenson arrived in Houston in 1838; Palm arrived in Galveston in 1844 and joined Swenson in a mercantile establishment at La Grange. Both men moved to Austin in the 1850's to continue their interest in the mercantile business; all the while they were encouraging their fellow countrymen to migrate to Texas—Swenson as an immigration agent, Palm as the Swedish vice-consul to Texas. The Census of 1870 listed 364 Swedes in Texas; by 1890 the num-

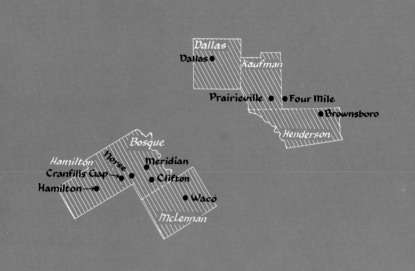

Dallas

Dallas ●

Kaufman

Prairieville ●  ● Four Mile

● Brownsboro

Henderson

Bosque

Hamilton  Norse  Meridian

Cranfills Gap → ●  ● Clifton

Hamilton → ●

● Waco

McLennan

Williamson

● Georgetown

Palm Valley → ●  ● Hutto

Round Rock → ●  ● New Sweden

Austin ●  ● Elgin

Trav  Manor

ber had increased to 2806; and by 1900, to 4388. Some of these early immigrants settled in Houston and Galveston, but the majority found homes in the rural communities of Travis and Williamson counties where they founded, or helped to found, such places as Manor, New Sweden, Elgin, Round Rock, Hutto, Palm Valley, Govalle, Lund, Swedonia, Swensondale, and Georgetown.

Axel Arneson, "The First Norwegian Migration into Texas," *Southwestern Historical Quarterly*, XLV.

C. A. Clausen (ed.), *The Lady with the Pen, Elise Waerenskjold in Texas* (Northfield, 1961).

Darwin Payne, "Early Norwegians in Northeast Texas," *Southwestern Historical Quarterly*, LXV.

Oris E. Pierson, "Norwegian Settlements in Bosque County, Texas" (unpublished M. A. thesis), University of Texas Library, Austin, Texas.

# CZECH SETTLEMENTS

GEORGE FISCHER (Rybar), Frederick Lemsky, and Karl Anton Postel were the leaders in the vanguard of immigrants from Bohemia and Moravia to Texas. In the 1840's many individual Czech families came to Texas. In 1849 Josef Ernst Bergman (whose name had been changed from Horak) landed at Galveston and settled at Cat Springs in Austin County. The first real Czech immigrant group, refugees from the oppression that followed in the wake of the 1848 revolution in Central Europe, landed at Galveston in 1852. The early pioneers in this migration came by way of New Orleans and Galveston; they came with enough money to buy land; they brought their families with them; and none returned to Europe. For eight years the tide of migration increased, slowed for awhile during the Civil War (Czechs, like the Germans, were universal in their opposition to the war), and increased in the decades that followed the war.

Since the early Czech immigrants were from the rural districts of Bohemia and were either farmers or artisans, they settled primarily on the rich lands of the Coastal Prairies and the Blackland Prairie belt from Denton and Grayson counties on the north to Brownsville on the south. The late Dr. Henry R. Maresh points out that the region of heaviest Czech settlement covers thirty-two Texas counties and extends from Denton and Kaufman counties on the north to Calhoun, Karnes, and Atascosa counties on the south. Of these the most densely Czech-populated counties include Fayette, with twenty-two Czech communities; Lavaca, with thirteen; Austin, Burleson, and Williamson with ten each; Wharton, McLennan, and Fort Bend with nine each; and Bell and Victoria with five each. Karnes and Lee counties are other areas that contain a heavy Czech population today.

Estelle Hudson and Henry R. Maresh, *Czech Pioneers of the Southwest* (Dallas, 1934).

Henry R. Maresh, "The Czechs in Texas," *Southwestern Historical Quarterly*, L.

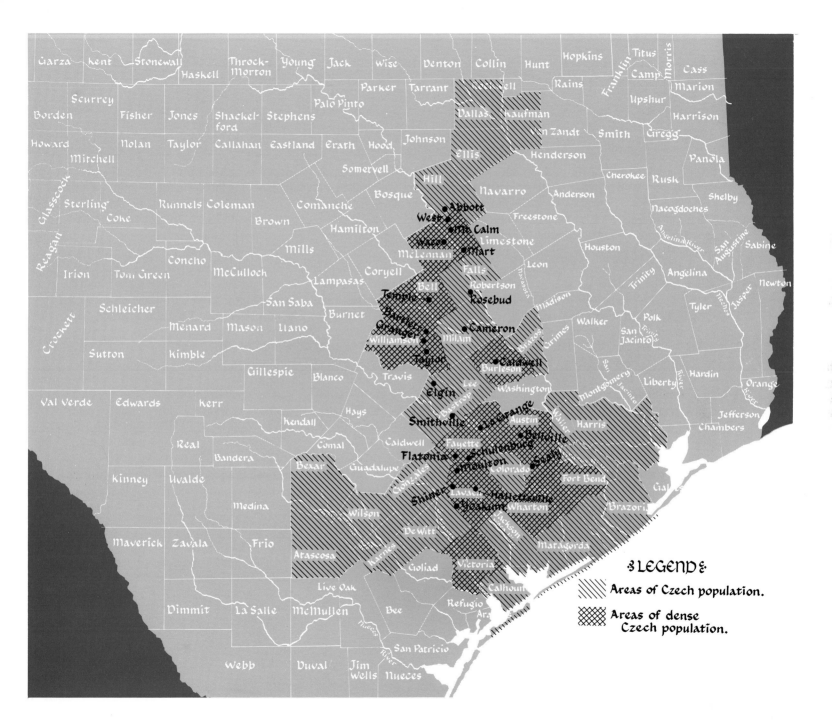

LEGEND

Areas of Czech population.

Areas of dense Czech population.

# THE POLISH SETTLEMENTS

EARLY in the year 1854 Father Leopold Moczygemba, a Franciscan who had worked in the German settlements of New Braunfels and Castroville, joined John Twohig of San Antonio on a horseback trip to inspect and explore the lands near the junction of the San Antonio and Cibolo rivers in present Karnes County. As a result, Moczygemba and Twohig entered into a contract whereby the priest agreed to settle a large number of Polish families near the confluence of the two streams. In October, 1854, one hundred families left their homes in Upper Silesia (then a part of Prussia) for Galveston, Texas. On arriving at Galveston, following a difficult voyage across the Atlantic, the immigrants traveled to their ultimate destination by way of Indianola, Victoria, and Yorktown. In describing the difficulties of the journey, Edward J. Dworaczyk writes: "Gradually, as the procession proceeded, these dreams grew wan and dismal. The sufferings they endured on the sea were nothing to what they were to suffer on land. Few had any money, none of them ever had the proper nourishment and, due to change of climate, their bodies were susceptible to the slightest disorder. Many more died on the way. Even babies were born by the wayside. Some starving and unshod, for even wooden shoes were a luxury, carried small children. Others weary and silent, homesick, and fearful of Indian raids, plodded along the vast wilderness, no longer sensible to the wet wintry days,—feeling only for the crying children that clung to mother's protecting skirt or a frozen hand.

"Discouragement on the part of some, contentment in settling in locations along the wayside that seemed promising, caused many to drop out of the procession. Thus, a few remained in Victoria, others around the German settlement of Yorktown. The bulk of the original one hundred marched on to their destination."

Their destination was a hill near the junction of the San Antonio and Cibolo rivers, where, on December 24, 1854, they established the village of Panna Maria. The first settlers at Panna Maria included Joseph, Anton, August and John Moczygemba; and the families of Philip Przybysz, Constantine Wajass, John Dziuk, Gervas Gabrysch, Frank Manka, John Rzeppa, Joseph Kyrish, Frank and Simon Bronder, Mathew and Anton Urbanczyk, Theodor Kniejski, Casimer Szguda, and Stanislaus Kiolobassa.

Many of the people who arrived at Panna Maria in 1854-1855 eventually moved to new locations where they founded settlements at Meyersville, St. Hedwig, and Bandera. Later arrivals settled at Cestochowa, Falls City, Kosciusko, Yorktown, Los Gallinas, San Marcos, San Antonio, McCook (Hidalgo County), New Waverly, Brenham, Marlin, Bremond, Bryan, Anderson, Chapel Hill, Bellville, Rosenberg, and Richmond. After the Civil War, a group of Polish farmers pushed as far west as White Deer in the Texas Panhandle.

Edward J. Dworaczyk, *The First Polish Colonies of America in Texas* (San Antonio, 1936).

Robert Thonhoff, "A History of Karnes County" (unpublished M. A. thesis), Library, Southwest Texas State College, San Marcos, Texas.

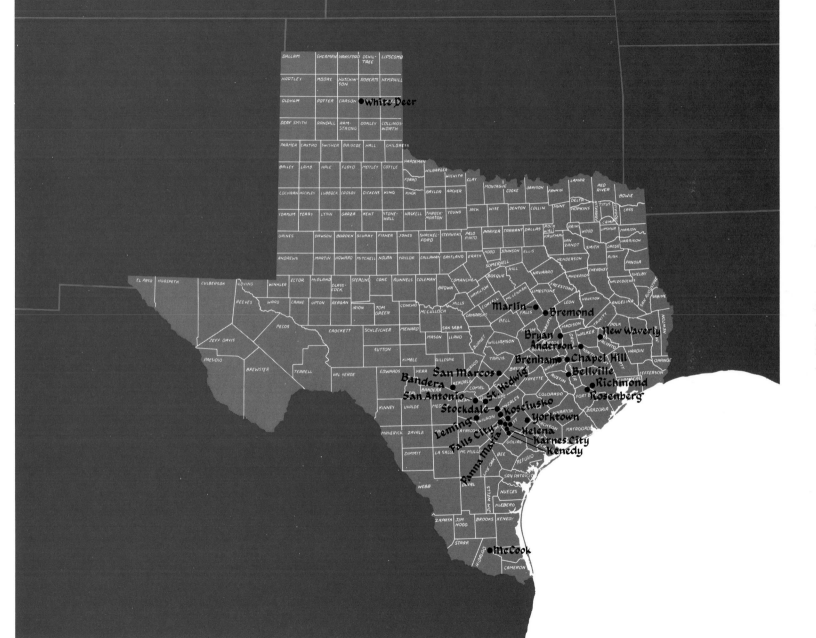

THE POPULIST MOVEMENT and the People's Party in Texas were outgrowths of the agrarian unrest which was characteristic of all of the midwestern states in the late 1880's and the 1890's. In Texas, as elsewhere, the strength of the People's Party was based on the Farmers' Alliances of the state. The agrarian revolt (with the help of the Knights of Labor) began to take shape in 1886, when the discontented farmers in Comanche County, led by Thomas Gaines, nominated a "Farmer's Democratic" or "Peoples" ticket and successfully ousted the Democratic establishment in the summer elections. At the same time, a similar protest movement was successful in Erath County and in Lampasas County. In 1888 Lampasas County voters organized a "non-partisan" party, and Dr. Pat B. Clark of Red River County adopted the name "the People's Party" for his group of dissenters. By 1890 the Populist movement had spread over the entire state.

Basing their program on the Jeffersonian doctrine of equality and endorsing the "Omaha platform of 1892" (the free and unlimited coinage of silver, produce sub-treasuries where farmers could deposit their surplus produce against treasury notes, government ownership of railroads, telephone and telegraph systems, a graduated income tax, an eight-hour day, popular election of Senators), the Populists struck telling blows against the established order. Seventy-five weekly newspapers, including the *Southern Mercury* at Dallas carried the message to thousands of readers. A small corps of gifted stump speakers, including Thomas L. Nugent, Jerome Kearby, T. P. Gore, and James H. (Cyclone) Davis, made their voices heard throughout the state. When the Democratic Party chose the conservative Grover Cleveland, a champion of "sound money," as its presidential candidate in 1892, the People's Party of Texas really came into its own as thousands of small farmers and day laborers joined the protest. From 1892 until 1900 every election in Texas was hotly contested and a bitter political rivalry prevailed.

The geographical strength of the People's Party in Texas lay in the counties of East Texas and in those of the west central part of the state. A list of the local areas carried by the People's Party in two or more of the elections of the decade includes, in the region of the Grand Prairie and Western Cross Timbers, the counties of Jack, Palo Pinto, Erath, Comanche, Bosque, Hamilton, Mills, Lampasas, Burnet, Blanco, and Kimble; and in deep East Texas, the counties of Sabine, San Augustine, Nacogdoches, Polk, Walker, Houston, Grimes, Madison, Leon, Navarro, Van Zandt, Raines, and Titus. In the South Texas region, the strength of the party shows markedly in Lee, Bastrop, Caldwell, Gonzales, Wilson, Karnes, Bandera, Goliad, and Dimmitt counties. In addition, scattered counties throughout the state voted Populist in at least one of the elections of the 1890's.

Aside from the election of many state legislators in all three elections, in the gubernatorial campaign of 1892 the People's Party polled over 100,000 votes and finished third. In 1894 Thomas L. Nugent, the Populist, polled nearly 160,000 for governor and E. L. Dohaney polled almost 200,000 as a candidate for justice of the Court of Criminal Appeals. In 1896 Jerome Kearby, aided by the Republicans, polled 238,-692 votes to Charles Culberson's 298,692 in the governor's contest. The national presidential campaign of 1896 brought about the downfall of the People's Party in Texas as thousands of Populists returned to the

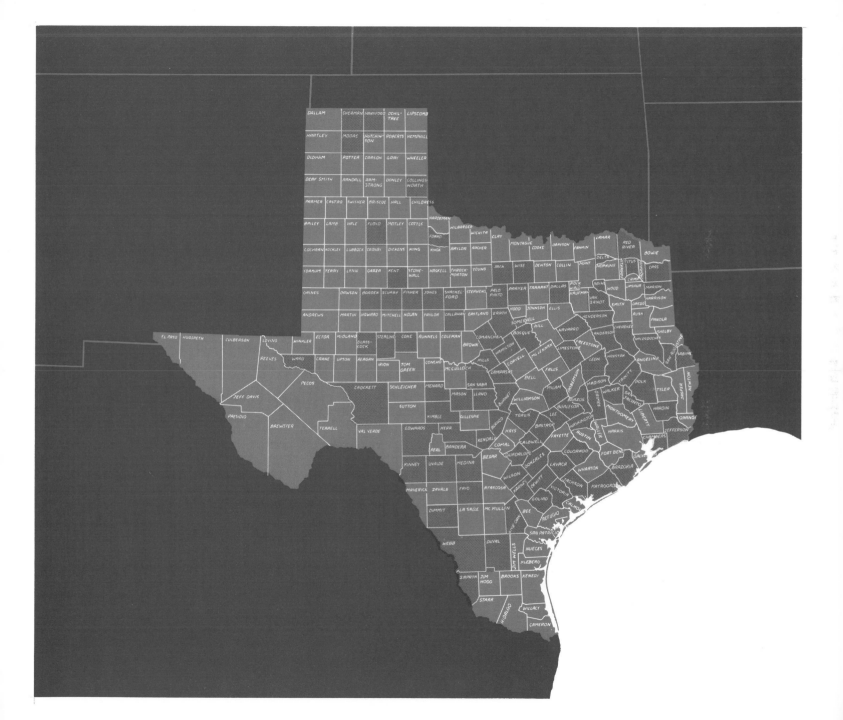

Democratic Party under the banner of William Jennings Bryan to give that organization the seeds of liberalism that later bore fruit in Woodrow Wilson's "New Freedom" and Franklin D. Roosevelt's "New Deal."

Clifton McCleskey, *The Government and Politics of Texas* (Boston and Toronto, 1963).

Roscoe C. Martin, *The People's Party in Texas* (Austin, 1933).

James R. Soukup, Clifton McCleskey, and Harry Holloway, *Party and Factional Division in Texas* (Austin, 1964).

# THE PIONEER OIL FIELDS, 1896-1918

OIL WAS DISCOVERED in Texas in 1543 by Luis de Moscoso, who used seepage from oil springs near Sabine Pass as calking for his hand-built boats. The East Texas Indians, and later the French and Spanish frontiersmen, had known of seepage from similar oil springs in the Nacogdoches area. As time passed, oil seeps were found in other areas of Texas. Jack Graham dug an unsuccessful oil well in Angelina County, and in 1866 Lynis T. Barnett drilled a producing well near Melrose. Barnett's pioneer effort suffered from the fact that there was little or no market for his oil.

Other intermittent efforts were made (by the Petroleum Prospecting Company at Oil Springs in 1886, by Martin Meinsinger near Brownwood in 1878, and by George Bullnig in Bexar County in 1886) to locate and capitalize on producing wells, but the Texas oil boom years began at Corsicana in 1896. The map on the opposite page shows the major petroleum discoveries in Texas between 1896 and 1918; in chronological order, these pioneer oil fields include the following:

1. The Corsicana field began in Navarro County in 1895-1896 and made the town of Corsicana the first boomtown in Texas.

2. The Spindletop field resulted from the famous Lucas gusher in early 1901. This well, located by A. F. Lucas, an authority on salt domes, was drilled by Alfred and James Hamil of Corsicana; the tremendous gusher blew in on the morning of January 10, 1901, and signaled a new era in the economic history of Texas.

3. The Sour Lake field in Hardin County was opened in 1901 in the wake of the great success at Spindletop.

4. The Saratoga field in Hardin County, near the community of Saratoga, was established by the completion of the Hooks No. 1 in 1901.

5. The Batson field, also in Hardin County and also a salt dome area, became the scene of considerable oil activity, 1901-1903.

6. The Humble field in Harris County (another salt dome) was explored by C. E. Barrett; the field was established by a successful strike in 1905.

7. The Henrietta field in Clay County resulted in 1902 when a farmer named Lochridge struck oil while drilling for water.

8. The Petrolia field in Clay County was opened in 1904 principally as a gas field and a shallow-well oil field.

9. The Electra field in Wichita County resulted in 1904 when W. T. Waggoner struck oil while drilling

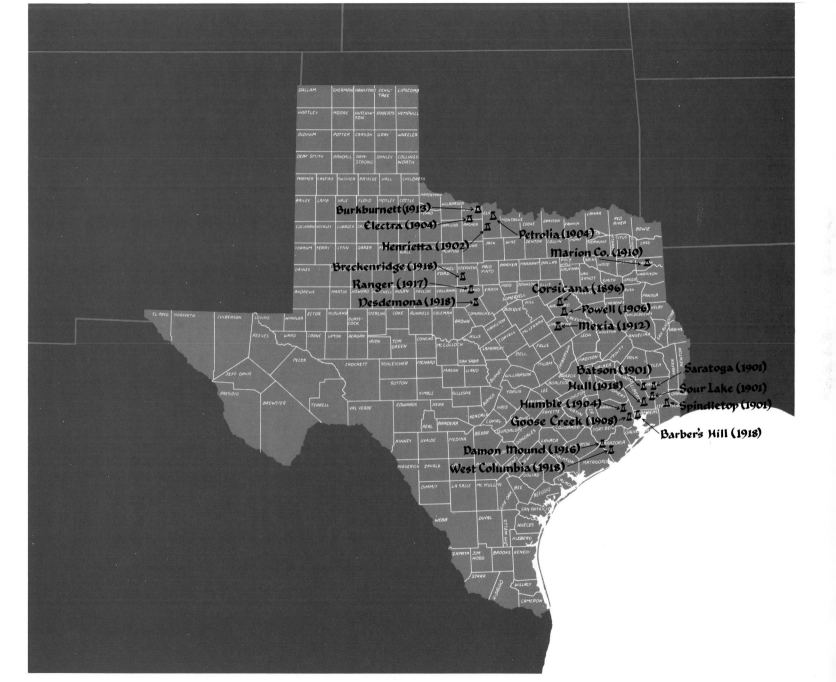

Burkburnett (1913)

Electra (1904)

Petrolia (1904)

Henrietta (1902)

Marion Co. (1910)

Breckenridge (1918)

Ranger (1917)

Corsicana (1896)

Desdemona (1918)

Powell (1906)

Mexia (1912)

Batson (1901)

Saratoga (1901)

Hull (1918)

Sour Lake (1901)

Humble (1904)

Spindletop (1901)

Goose Creek (1908)

Barber's Hill (1918)

Damon Mound (1916)

West Columbia (1918)

for water on the Three D Ranch. In 1911 a gusher in the area signaled the beginning of another boom.

10. The Powell field in Navarro County began with the early explorations of 1900 but the production of shallow wells reached a peak in 1906.

11. The Goose Creek field in eastern Harris County was established in 1908 and became a major oil field shortly thereafter.

12. The Mexia field in Limestone County was first noted for its gas production; established in 1912 as a shallow field, it became a major producing area with the completion of A. E. Humphrey's No. 1 in 1920.

13. The Ranger field was established in 1917 in Eastland County as the result of W. K. Gordon's deep test well.

14. The Desdemona field, also in Eastland County, resulted from the discovery of a 2000-barrel well in 1918.

15. The Breckenridge field in Stephens County was opened in 1918 following the completion of the Chaney Number 1 well.

16. The Barbers Hill field in Chambers County was discovered in September, 1918.

In addition to the above, the Marion County field, discovered in 1910, became a significant producing field at a later date.

Boyce House, *Oil Boom* (Caldwell, Idaho, 1941).
*Important Facts about Texas Oil, 1919-1944* (The Texas Mid-Continent Oil and Gas Association, 1944).
Carl Coke Rister, *Oil! Titan of the Southwest* (Norman, 1949).
*Texas Oil and Gas* (The Texas Mid-Continent Oil and Gas Association, 1952).

# PETROLEUM DISCOVERIES, 1918-1960

 NOW that the pioneer oil fields have been pointed out specifically, we will look at the developments within the petroleum industry with emphasis on the period since the First World War. This tremendous growth is illustrated by the fact that in the mid-1920's Texas supplied slightly more than 15 percent of the world's petroleum. In the early 1930's, on the other hand, Texas produced about 40 percent of the national total and about 25 percent of the world's supply. By 1930 Texas produced 25 percent of the total United States refinery products and was the nation's leading state in this industry. Over 70 percent of the state's refining capacity was concentrated along the Texas Gulf Coast, largely in the Houston-Beaumont-Port Arthur area. Houston, as a focal point for pipe lines and oil shipments, became the center of the Texas petroleum-refining industry.

Between 1920 and 1960 new oil discoveries (in addition to the earlier fields shown again) touched a vast majority of Texas counties as scientific deep-well exploration made possible the development of producing areas in the Panhandle, in West Texas, on the southern interior prairies near and south of San Antonio, and in deep East Texas. At the present time, only a few counties west of the Pecos, along the west of the Balcones Escarpment, and in the Panhandle are classified as non-producing areas.

Too numerous to survey in detail, the discoveries of

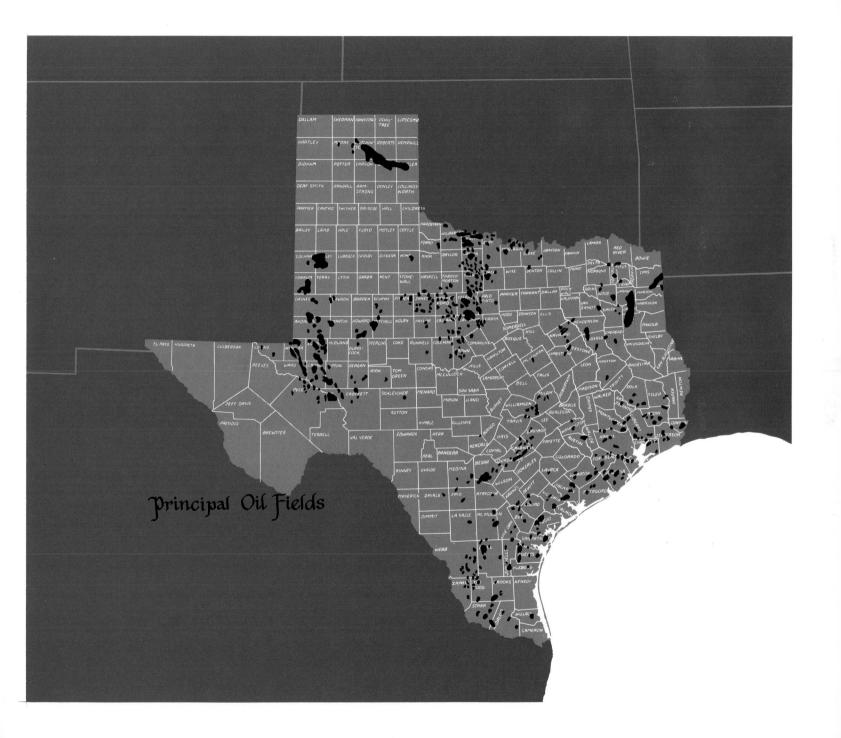

Principal Oil Fields

the past four decades include new discoveries near Mexia in 1920, the Luling field in 1922, the Powell field in Navarro County in 1923, the Big Lake field in Reagan County in 1923, the Hendricks field in Winkler County in 1926, the Yates field in Pecos County in 1926, the fabulous East Texas field in 1930-31, the Conroe field in 1931, the Panhandle field in 1929, and the Penn and Camden fields near Odessa in 1929 and 1930. In more recent times additional oil deposits have been discovered in Andrews, Gaines, Hockley, Culber-son, Oldham, Ochiltree, Lipscomb, Hemphill, Floyd, Motley, Cottle, Dickens, and Lynn counties.

It would be difficult to exaggerate the significance of oil to the economy of Texas.

*Annual Report of the Oil and Gas Division*, The Railroad Commission of Texas (Austin, 1964).
*Report* of the U. S. Study Commission—Texas, II (March, 1962).
Carl Coke Rister, *Oil! Titan of the Southwest* (Norman, 1949).

# RAILROAD TRANSPORTATION, 1870-1944

 IN 1870 Texas had only 583 miles of railroad track within the state, all constructed prior to the Civil War in Southeast Texas—in fact, all of these first railroads radiated out from Houston. The Houston and Texas Central track to Millican was the only pre-war attempt to link the coast with the interior counties. When Texas returned to the Union in 1870, railroad construction began again and, with the help of state land grants, increased rapidly during the decades of the 1870's and 1880's.

In 1871 the Houston and Texas Central constructed its line from Millican to Corsicana; the following year (1872), the road was completed to Dallas, and in January, 1873, the H. and T. C. reached Denison. The Missouri-Kansas-and-Texas crossed the Red River in 1872, where construction stopped for a ten-year period. The International and Great Northern completed its track from Shreveport, Louisiana, to Longview in 1872, then to Austin in 1876, and, in the months that followed, to San Antonio and Laredo. The Gulf, Colo-rado, and Santa Fe, incorporated in Galveston in May, 1873, reached Richmond in 1878 and Fort Worth in 1881; in the meantime, a branch line had been completed from Temple to Brownwood. The Texas and New Orleans, backed by Collis P. Huntington, completed a line from Houston to San Antonio in 1877 and from San Antonio to El Paso, 1877-1881. Under the management of Jay Gould with Grenville Dodge as the construction engineer, the Texas and Pacific spanned West Texas from Fort Worth to El Paso, 1876-1880. The Fort Worth and Denver City completed its railroad from Fort Worth to Wichita Falls in 1882 and, between 1883 and 1887, crossed the Texas Panhandle to Texline. Thus, the pioneer railroad systems of Texas, with many "feeder" lines, had been completed by the year 1890.

By the time of World War II the Texas railroads, with the exception of a few independent organizations, had been consolidated into seven major systems: (1) the Burlington system (including the Rock Island

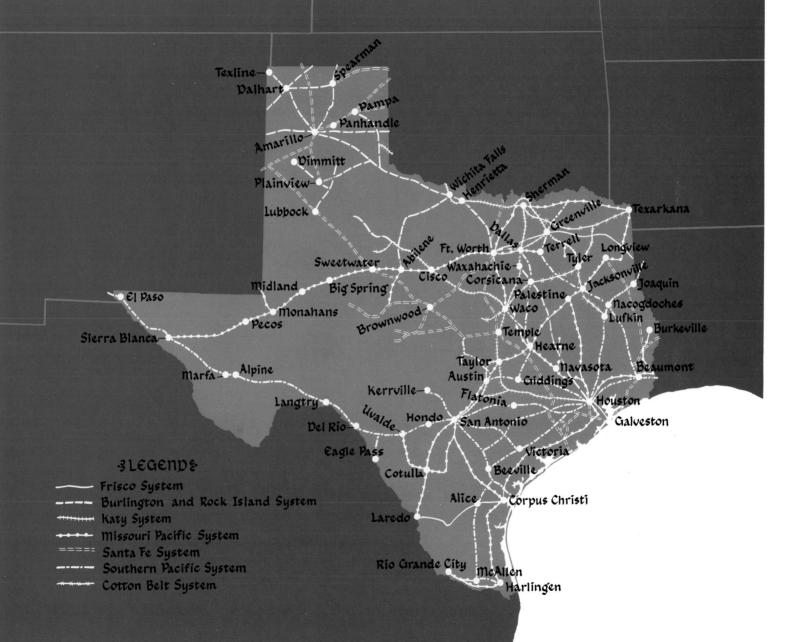

Texline—
Dalhart—
Spearman
Pampa
Panhandle
Amarillo—
Dimmitt
Plainview—
Lubbock
Wichita Falls
Henrietta
Sherman
Texarkana
Greenville
Sweetwater
Abilene
Ft. Worth
Dallas
Terrell
Longview
Waxahachie—
Cisco
Corsicana—
Tyler
Jacksonville
Joaquin
Midland
Big Spring
Palestine
Nacogdoches
El Paso
Waco
Lufkin
Monahans
Brownwood—
Temple
Burkeville
Pecos
Hearne
Sierra Blanca—
Navasota
Beaumont
Marfa
Alpine
Taylor
Austin
Giddings
Kerrville—
Flatonia
Houston
Langtry
Hondo
Del Rio—
Uvalde—
San Antonio
Galveston
Eagle Pass
Victoria
Cotulla
Beeville
Alice
Corpus Christi
Laredo

Rio Grande City
McAllen
Harlingen

·³LEGEND³·
——————— Frisco System
— — — — Burlington and Rock Island System
—+—+—+— Katy System
—•—•—•— Missouri Pacific System
===== Santa Fe System
—·—·—·— Southern Pacific System
—×—×—×— Cotton Belt System

railroad properties); (2) the Frisco system; (3) the M-K-T (Katy) system; (4) the Missouri-Pacific system and the Texas Pacific system (Missouri Pacific owns 74.6 percent of the stock of the latter); (5) the Santa Fe system; (6) the Southern Pacific system; and (7) the Cotton Belt system.

In addition to the above-named systems, the following companies maintained an independent status: the Angelina and Neches River; the Aransas Harbor Terminal; the Bois d'Arc and Southern; the Eastland, Wichita Falls, and Gulf; the Hamlin and Northwestern; the Kansas, Oklahoma, and Gulf of Texas; the Moscow, Camden, and San Augustine; the Nacogdoches and Southeastern; the Paris and Mount Pleas- ant; the Rio Grande and Eagle Pass; the Rockdale, Sandow, and Southern; the Roscoe, Snyder, and Pacif- ic; the Sabine and Neches Valley; the Texas Mexican; the Texas Southeastern; the Waco, Beaumont, Trinity, and Sabine; and the Wichita Falls and Southern.

The Railroads of the State of Texas, a map prepared by the Railroad Commission of Texas, Austin, October, 1944.
V. V. Masterson, *The Katy Railroad and the Last Frontier* (Norman, 1952).
Richard Overton, *Gulf to the Rockies, the Heritage of the Fort Worth and Denver and the Colorado and Southern Railways, 1861-1898* (Austin, 1953).
S. G. Reed, *A History of Texas Railroads* (Houston, 1941).

# COLLEGES & UNIVERSITIES

 EDUCATION IN TEXAS can be traced to the early mission schools of the Spanish colonial period and to the "old field schools" and academies of the American settlements. T. J. Pilgrim founded an academy in the Austin colony in 1828 and Miss Frances Trask established a boarding school at Cole's settlement as early as 1834. It is of significance, however, that for many years after independence private schools and academies dominated the Texas educational scene; San Augustine University (1837), Rutersville College (1840), Galveston University (1841), Marshall University (1845), Baylor University (1845), McKensie College (1848), and Soule University (1855) were representative institutions of the antebellum years. In spite of legislative acts declaring good intentions, public education lagged behind the private schools (with selective enrollments) until after the Reconstruction Era.

In 1876 the Agricultural and Mechanical College of Texas—the first public-supported college—opened its doors to students at College Station near Bryan. Three years later (1879), both Sam Houston Normal School at Huntsville and Prairie View A and M College at Prairie View were opened. The University of Texas, established in 1881, opened at Austin in 1883 (the Medical School at Galveston began its teaching service in 1891). In 1899 Southwest Texas State Normal at San Marcos and North Texas State Normal at Denton began operations. These schools were in the vanguard of the development of a state-supported system of higher education. In the meanwhile, private and denominational institutions continued to play an im-

Bishop College (1881)
Baylor University College of Dentistry (1905)
Southern Methodist University (1912)
University of Texas Southwestern Medical School (1943)
University of Dallas (1956)
University of Texas at Dallas (1969) (Plano)

•Canyon
West Texas State University (1910)

Wayland Baptist College (1908)
•Plainview
Midwestern University (1922)
Wichita Falls
Texas Tech University (1923)
•Sherman
Austin College (1849)
•Lubbock
East Texas State University (1917)
Lubbock Christian College (1950)
•Commerce
North Texas State University (1901)—(1901?)
Jarvis Christian College (1912)
Texas Woman's University (1901)—(1901?)
•Denton
Hawkins
East Texas Baptist College (1912)
Texas Christian University (1873)
Fort Worth
•Dallas
•Marshall
Wiley College (1873)
Texas Wesleyan College (1891)
Arlington
Longview
•Abilene
UT at Arlington (1923)
LeTourneau College (1946)
Hardin-Simmons University (1891)
•Stephenville
Abilene Christian College (1906)
McMurry College (1923)
Tarleton State College (1917)
•Nacogdoches
•el Paso
Odessa
UT at Permian Basin
•Brownwood
Waco
Stephen F. Austin State University (1923)
UT at El Paso (1913)
San Angelo
Mary Hardin-Baylor College (1845)
Angelo State University (1928)
Howard Payne College (1889)
Baylor University (1845)
•Belton
•Huntsville
Sam Houston State U. (1879)
Paul Quinn College (1872)
Georgetown
College Station
Southwestern University (1840)
A&M University (1876)
•Alpine
UT at Austin (1883)
•Austin
Prairie View
•Beaumont
Huston-Tillotson College (1952)
St. Edward's University (1885)
•San Marcos
Sul Ross State University (1920)
Southwest Texas State U. (1903)
Lamar University (1923)
Texas Lutheran College (1891)
Seguin
Houston
St. Mary's University (1852)
San Antonio
Galveston
University of Texas Medical Branch (1911)
Trinity University (1869)
Incarnate Word College (1881)
Our Lady of the Lake College (1911)
UT Medical School at San Antonio (1959)
Prairie View A&M College (1876)

University of Texas Dental Branch (1905)
Baylor University College of Medicine (1909)
Rice University (1912)
Texas Southern University (1926)
University of Houston (1927)
Sacred Heart Dominican College (1946)
University of St. Thomas (1947)
Houston Baptist College (1963)

Texas A&I at Corpus Christi
Corpus Christi
•Laredo
•Kingsville
Texas A&I at Laredo
Texas A&I at Kingsville (1917)
Pan American University (1927)
Edinburg

portant role in the education of the youth of Texas. The current institutions, too numerous to discuss individually, are shown on the map.

Frederick Eby, *The Development of Education in Texas* (New York, 1925).

C. E. Evans, *The Story of Texas Schools* (Austin, 1955).

# TEXAS COUNTIES: A SUMMARY

 IN CONCLUSION, it would be well, perhaps, to look at the map of Texas with the dates of the organization of the counties marked. Beginning in 1836, the original counties were Nacogdoches, San Augustine, Jasper, Liberty, Washington, Harrisburg, Austin, Brazoria, Matagorda, Gonzales, Mina (Bastrop), and Milam. All of the above had been municipalities under the Mexican government. In addition, Victoria, Goliad, San Patricio, and Refugio participated in the General Council of 1835, and the provisional government created Jackson, Colorado, Sabine, Shelby, Red River, and (after a fashion) Jefferson.

As has been shown by the several regional maps of this study, the first expansion of population came during the years of the Republic and early statehood. During this era—roughly the years between 1837 and 1860—the area of Northeast Texas between the Red and Trinity rivers and the Coastal Plains of Southeast Texas were the two primary regions of settlement. During the years just before the Civil War, the line of settlements reached the upper Trinity and mid-Brazos country on the north and the eastern section of the Edwards Plateau on the south. Perhaps half of the present state had been settled by at least a few hardy pioneers.

The greatest geographical expansion in the history of Texas came during the quarter of a century following the close of Reconstruction. As has been pointed out, however, many counties were created by the state legislature long before a significant number of people settled within their border. In 1931 Loving County became the 254th Texas county. The cycle of the creation and organization of local county governments had finally been completed.

168

# INDEX TO TEXT

171

# INDEX TO MAPS

186